SCREENWRITING
WITH
BRASS
KNUCKLES

SCOTT W. SMITH

ISBN: 978-0-578-75001-9
ISBN: 978-0-692-06291-3 (ebook)

Book Cover Design
Predrag Capo
(CsapoDesign at 99designs.com)

DEDICATION

For Annye Refoe, Ph.D.
—who pointed the way beyond the eighty-yard run

CONTENTS

ACKNOWLEDGMENTS

A small tribe of people helped this book become a reality:

Edd Blott, Amy Bosley, Casey Frechette, Terry Groner, Cindy Gustafson, Kelsey Holm, Steve Holm, Calvin Johannsen, Gary Kelley, Joel Laneville, Adam Lewis and the gang at Spinutech, Michael Maguire, Josh McCabe, Trish Miceli, Curt Moore, Lisa Oharek, Matthew Porter, Sally Preston, Marc Reifenrath (who first encouraged me to blog), Julie Smith, Janet Selitto, Ken Steele, Kevin A. Thomas, Jon Van Allen, and readers of the blog *Screenwriting from Iowa . . . and Other Unlikely Places*

Editor
Scott Draper

Note: Scott Beck and Bryan Woods wrote the screenwriting equivalent of brass knuckles with their screenplay *A Quiet Place*. They had humble beginnings starting in a middle school in Iowa where they met—less than 30 miles from Dyersville, Iowa where *Field of Dreams* was shot and the words "If you build it, he will come" were first spoken on film.—SWS

FOREWORD

Growing up as cinephiles in Iowa, we were inundated with the often-misquoted mantra "If you build it, they will come." We heard that phrase so often, that it was easy to overlook the metaphorical meaning beneath the surface; the idea that the only way to achieve an impossible dream is to put imagination into action. So as aspiring filmmakers, we realized we couldn't wait for permission to write or direct. It didn't matter that we were 1,600 miles away from Hollywood, or that our backlot consisted of the Mississippi River, or that our budgets were hundreds of dollars instead of millions. We were going to make movies hell or high water.

Your greatest ability as a writer and filmmaker is to create your own opportunities. That may mean many different things: picking up a camera, jotting down story ideas in a journal, producing a local play, or reading this book for advice and inspiration. Every career begins with a small step.

Our career started as teenagers, the day we decided to make our own films in our backyard. We would hold casting calls throughout Iowa, curate "test screenings" at the community college, and premiere our movies at the local IMAX theater. Then we'd do it again and again, learning from each of our mistakes.

If your journey is anything like ours, at some point you'll hit a wall. Festivals will reject your screenplay. Agencies will pass on representing you. Executives are going to tell you no. Then maybe one day, someone will say yes to your script. A financier will come on board. Your movie is greenlit and your screenplay gets produced. A major distributor buys the film. You've conquered Hollywood!

Then the third act twist happens: no one sees your film. You're back to the basics.

Now you have to fight for the next job harder than everyone else. Whether it's luck or tenacity, you get another script set up at a huge studio. Maybe you'll spend a year of your life developing the screenplay until your producers are happy. That's when you realize the studio will only make the movie if Hollywood's hottest A-list actor will come onboard. He won't, and the studio cans the project.

You realize films are hard to get made, but television is a gold rush. You take one of your discarded feature ideas and adapt it into a series pitch. A producer is interested and sets up meetings with a dozen studios. All of them pass but one. They want to pay you to write the script, but only if they can get a network on board to co-finance. The studio arranges over 30 meetings with different networks. In every room, you have to perform your 25-minute pitch. You come incredibly close to selling the show, but after several weeks… everyone passes.

When you get to this point in your career, you might want to quit. Don't. You can't succeed until you fail. And you can't fail until you create.

Our breakthrough came after two decades of creating. We had encountered countless setbacks and hurdles when we dusted off an idea that had been long gestating, called *A Quiet Place*. The concept was something we had loved forever, and knew if no one in Hollywood wanted to produce the film, we could go back to Iowa and make it ourselves. We finished the script in a few months, knowing that failure and success aren't factors in determining our journey. All that mattered is that we would create something ourselves.

Your fate is in your hands. The good news is, you've already taken the initiative by reading this book. It doesn't matter if you're from Iowa or Iceland. You don't need an agent or a manager. You don't need to place first in a screenplay competition. You don't need to wait for permission. All you need, is to start.

If you build it, they will come.

Scott Beck & Bryan Woods

September 2020

PREFACE

"I wasn't born knowing how to write a play."
—Sam Shepard, Pulitzer Prize winning playwright

"Whatever success I've got has come after like eight years of nothing working out trying to get a job in films."
—Quentin Tarantino, Oscar winner in a 1994 interview

In the more than 12 years of writing the blog *Screenwriting from Iowa . . . and Other Unlikely Places*, I've found advice and insight on the creative process from more than 700 gifted screenwriters, filmmakers, and teachers. I realized that I could consolidate and curate the most powerful of that material as a book, revising and reorganizing it in ways that I thought would be most helpful to people's creative journeys. I want these ideas to function like brass knuckles in an old-school professional wrestling match.

I don't know if Aristotle ever used brass knuckles, but they are said to have been around since the ancient Greeks. Abraham Lincoln's secret service men carried brass knuckles. And legend has it that brass knuckles were Al Capone's favorite weapon.

The term "loaded fist" in Japanese martial arts refers to a martial arts version of brass knuckles that can turn a punch into a sledgehammer. As a troubled youth in Hong Kong, Bruce Lee carried brass knuckles, giving a twist of meaning to his trademark movie *Fist of Fury*.

Today brass knuckles are brandished in popular video games and music videos. Spike Lee even wore promotional brass knuckles to the 2019 Academy Awards.

My introduction to brass knuckles was watching professional wrestling on TV as a kid. This was not the high-dollar spectacle of today but the low-budget version, usually taped in a TV studio in Tampa, Florida.

Actor Dwayne "The Rock" Johnson's father, Rocky Johnson, was a wrestler in the pre-WWE era when professional wrestling was a regional sport and the bag of tricks and storylines more limited. (Rocky Johnson was actually the 1976 NWA Brass Knuckles Champion.)

This was at a time in my youth when I didn't know if professional wrestling was real or not. What I did know was that professional wrestling had a cast of characters with colorful names like Abdullah the Butcher, André the Giant, and Dusty "The American Dream" Rhodes and it was flat out entertaining. (Rhodes was the main influence Hulk Hogan used as Hulkamania helped transform pro wrestling into a global phenomenon.)

Inevitably, back then when one wrestler was getting beat up and close to losing a match, brass knuckles would magically appear (usually emerging from someone's wrestling trunks).

The announcer Gordon Solie would say something like, *Wait a minute, what's he have in his right hand? It looks like a foreign object. Oh no, it looks like a pair of brass knuckles!*

At the last minute, this would give the almost beaten wrestler an upper hand in the match. It would result in not only a victory for the trickster but also in a fake bloody mess. For a ten-year-old boy this was as good as a vampire movie.

My goal with this book is not to create a bloody mess, but to offer the equivalent of brass knuckles for writers — screenwriters in particular. Ideas found in this book can serve as powerful resources in urgent moments of desperation—or to avoid those moments altogether.

By *screenwriting* I mean any screen: the big screen, TV, computers, tablets, mobile devices, virtual reality, video games, and even some non-screen dramatic writing such as theater and podcasts.

This is one of the reasons why I break from transitional conventions of making a differentiation between a screenwriter and a TV writer. What do we call someone who writes for Netflix? A streaming writer? So I just call anyone who writes for something to be viewed on a screen (big screen, little screen, TV, computer, iPad, mobile phone)—I call them a screenwriter.

This book will not substitute for a good writing teacher or mentor, but it can give you some valuable ideas to hang on to, "foreign objects" thrown into the ring to help as you struggle to craft and tell your own stories.

INTRODUCTION

"You can't learn bull riding, except by getting on the bull."
—David Mamet

"How did I learn screenwriting? It was a matter of years of trying to develop my writing in the same way that some people spend years learning to play the violin."
—Screenwriter Frank Darabont (*The Shawshank Redemption*)

Can screenwriting be taught?

That's ridiculous. Of course it can.

When it comes to most things in life, we expect that we must be taught how to do them properly. We are taught how to ride a bike, swim, recite our A-B-C's, drive a car, practice medicine, or fix engines. Talent and drive will play a part in how well we do something, but Tiger Woods' dad taught him how to hit a golf ball and Archie Manning taught his boys (Peyton and Eli, both Super Bowl MVPs) how to throw a football.

Watch the 2021 movie *King Richard* to see how Venus and Serena Williams emerged from an unlikely place to become dominant pro tennis players.

For some reason when it comes to the arts, many yield to the old saying that it is a talent we are simply born with. I took photography classes in high school and college and learned about lighting, composition, exposures, etc. I took bad and mediocre photos and teachers told me what I did wrong. I read photography books and magazines and studied great photographers. I learned how to be a photographer. While I don't claim to be the next Ansel Adams, that skill has paid a few bills over the years.

Here's what the famed Iowa Writers' Workshop states on their website:

"Though we agree in part with the popular insistence that writing cannot be taught, we exist and proceed on the assumption that talent can be developed. If one can 'learn' to play the violin or to paint, one can 'learn' to write, though no processes of externally induced training can ensure that one will do it well."

Okay, so maybe they had a lawyer look over that document, but it essentially says writing can't be taught but is something you can learn. Fine. I'm in their camp on this matter. If they don't want to use the word "taught" that's their prerogative. With their track record they can call what goes on there whatever they want. (But I do think we're dealing with a degree of semantics between educating, training, honing skills, inspiring, developing, encouraging, and teaching.)

"I didn't know how to write a screenplay. But my whole thing was I was learning how to do it and trying to replicate the experience that I felt when I was [in Iraq]."
—Oscar-winning screenwriter Mark Boal (*The Hurt Locker*)

Often when people talk about being self-taught, they mean they weren't taught in the formal sense of going to school and taking classes. But make no mistake, they were taught. One can learn in a variety of ways outside a classroom, but having a mentor is one of the best ways to learn a trade. That is how the Renaissance painters learned. Mentorship is in fact a tradition in a wide variety of trades, whether a blacksmith, glass blower, or carpenter. There are many ways to learn.

Screenwriter and playwright Moss Hart grew up in relative poverty with immigrant parents in New York City and didn't have the benefit of higher education. But he did have enough drive and raw talent to work his way up to being a social director each summer at camps and resorts in Vermont, Pennsylvania, and upstate New York. He oversaw nightly entertainment six nights a week for crowds up to 1,500 people.

In the Catskill Mountains, these summer resorts were known as the Borsch Belt or Jewish Alps. For decades starting in the early 20th century, they served as great training grounds for many entertainers: Woody Allen, George Burns, Mel Brooks, Rodney Dangerfield, Phyllis Diller, Danny Kaye, Jerry Lewis, Carl Reiner, Joan Rivers, and Jerry Seinfeld.

Movies and TV shows that capture this era are *Dirty Dancing, A Walk on the Moon,* and *The Marvelous Mrs. Maisel* (episodes 4, 5, and 6 in season two). However, this tradition died out in the '60s and '70s as anti-Semitism diminished, air travel became more frequent, and Jewish people found other places to vacation.)

By directing and acting in several different plays a week Hart learned what worked and didn't work before a live audience. (And those places were also known for appreciating rapid-fire humor.) Those experiences and a play he'd written led to an opportunity to work with the established Broadway playwright George S. Kaufman.

"It is one thing to have a flair for play-writing or even a ready wit with dialogue. It is quite another to apply these gifts in the strict and demanding terms of a fully articulated play so that they emerge with explicitness, precision and form. All of this and a great deal more I learned from George Kaufman."
—Moss Hart
Act One: An Autobiography

But before Hart learned from Kaufman, and before he got the job at the summer camps he had a passion for theater. He worked in a fur warehouse for over two years until he got an office job with a theater manager. One of the perks of the job was he was able to get free tickets to see Broadway plays nightly. This was in an era before television when there were over 70 theaters on during peak season in New York City. Moss said he learned from bad plays as well as the good ones.

"I simply read the plays themselves, I read the published version of plays that I had seen and then plays that I had never seen, sitting there day after day like a bacteriologist trying to isolate a strange germ under the beam of a new more powerful microscope."
—Moss Hart

All of those experiences led to Hart's first Broadway hit (*Once in a Lifetime*) at age 26. A decade later Kaufman and Hart won the Pulitzer Prize for their depression era play *You Can't Take it with You*. As a screenwriter, Hart earned two Oscar nominations and wrote the 1934 version of *A Star is Born* starring Judy Garland.

You'll see a stories like that sprinkled throughout this book. But how would someone today go about teaching themselves how to write, or how would they find a mentor if they lived in the middle of nowhere?

With the internet, for a relatively low cost, one has tremendous access to movies and television programs. Once upon a time I used to pay $15 for a single screenplay. Today you can find thousands of feature screenplays and TV scripts online for free. So where do you begin?

"I think it's absolutely essential to pick a [TV] show that you think is good and dissect the crap out of it."
—Producer/writer Shonda Rhimes (*Grey's Anatomy*)
(*West Wing* by Aaron Sorkin was the show she dissected.)

Screenwriter Joe Eszterhas writes, "Inhale a writer you admire. Knowing nothing about writing a play, Paddy Chayefsky (*Network*) taught himself playwriting by sitting down at the typewriter and copying Lillian Hellman's *The Children's Hour* word for word. He said, 'I studied every line of it and kept asking myself, 'Why did she write this particular line?'" That's a passion for learning.

Before Judd Apatow wrote his first TV pilot, he read 60 scripts of *Taxi and* the first season of *The Simpsons* outlining their structure. He said, "Without taking a class, I just cracked the code of how they were telling stories."

Many writers today are college educated. But it's not a requirement. At one time Neil Simon had four plays running simultaneously on Broadway and a string of hit films. Where did he learn how to write? He credits his older brother Danny.

Academy Award winning writer Quentin Tarantino (*Pulp Fiction*) said, "When people ask me if I went to film school I tell them, no, I went to films." That was his education. He not only didn't go to college, he didn't even finish high school. But he did study acting for several years and that's where he was encouraged to write. He learned writing by writing.

"Education isn't about filling a pail, but igniting a fire."
—Poet W.B. Yeats

Some writers first studied law (John Grisham), some medicine (Michael Crichton), some philosophy (Wes Anderson), and others music (Lulu Wang). Writers come from everywhere and have all sorts of backgrounds. But the one thing writers have in common is they write.

Screenwriters who get produced are relentless. Geoff Rodkey said after his screenplay *Daddy Day Care* was released as a movie, "I've written something like eighteen screenplays, and this is the only one that's ever been made."

And what do writers do before that breakthrough? They keep writing.

"I felt the years go by without accomplishment. Occasionally I wrote a short story that no one bought. I called myself a writer though I had no true subject matter. Yet from time to time I sat at a table and wrote, although it took years for my work to impress me."
—Bernard Malamud (*The Natural* and Pulitzer Prize winner *The Fixer*)

"Learning to write is not a linear process. There is no logical A-B-C way to become a good writer."
—Natalie Goldberg

There may not be a logical way to being a good writer, but having a good mentor or teacher is probably the most common factor found in successful writers. You're fortunate if you can find one in your life. A mentor or teacher guides you through the ups and downs of your learning process. They invest in you as a writer and as a person. They nurture your writing. John Steinbeck went as far as saying "teaching might even be the greatest of the arts since the medium is the human mind and spirit."

I had one teacher at Lake Howell High School in Orlando who took an interest in developing in me a skill in writing that I really did know I had. I signed up for Ms. Refoe's creative writing class because it looked like an easy elective. But she was fresh out of Fisk University and ready to teach.

"A teacher who can arouse a feeling for one single good action, for one single good poem, accomplishes more than he who fills our memory with rows and rows of natural objects, classified with name and form."
—Novelist and poet Johann Wolfgang von Goethe

To combine thoughts by David Mamet and Neil Simon, what I've tried to do here is get closer to a mysterious process. One takeaway from this book is that there isn't just one way of writing. Some writers start with a situation, some with characters, some with a theme, and some with just a photograph that sparks an idea. Some writers are verbal, some are visual.

Some talk about the rules of dramatic writing, and other say there are no rules. Some substitute the words principles, laws, and tools for the word rules. But let's try to agree that there are some things that in general have helped storytellers for thousands of years.

"There is a tendency to think that art is finally the place where there are no rules, where you have complete freedom. *I'm going to sit down at the keyboard and it's just going to flow out of me onto the paper, and it's going to be pure art.* **No. What you're describing is finger painting. Rules are what makes art beautiful."**
—Playwright and screenwriter Aaron Sorkin
MasterClass, "Rules of Story"

Both Sorkin and Mamet point to rules in sports as analogous to the arts, and say the rules can be found in Aristotle's *Poetics* written more than 2,000 years ago. Not everyone agrees with each other on the creative process. Some are even cavalier in their answers. Bill Bryson once said, "What inspires me to write? Bills."

Screenwriter John Milius (*Apocalypse Now*) said he could teach all you need to know about screenwriting in 15 minutes. Oscar winning screenwriter Christopher McQuarrie (*The Usual Suspects*) only needed 15 seconds when he said, "Here's how you become a screenwriter: Get yourself a pencil and a piece of paper—you don't need a computer, you don't need Final Draft—and write interior (INT), and then choose any location you want. And decide whether it's night or day. You're a screenwriter."

It took me longer here because I'm not Milius or McQuarrie. And I was attempting to curate and organize essential insights from a diverse group of writers throughout the history of dramatic storytelling.

Several years ago, I went to a workshop with an Oscar, Tony, and Pulitzer Prize winning writer who said he wasn't sure why they asked him to speak since he didn't think there were any rules for dramatic writing, or if there were he didn't know what they were. When I raised my hand and asked, "What about conflict?" he said, "Yeah, you need conflict."

Conflict is a great place to start when talking about screenwriting.

1 CONFLICT

"Screenwriting's one unbreakable rule: Don't be boring."
—Richard Walter

"We all know that it's conflict that makes drama happen."
—Mira Nair *(Salaam Bombay)*

"There are no rules in filmmaking. Only sins. And the cardinal sin is dullness."
—Frank Capra *(It's a Wonderful Life)*

"What is drama, after all, but life with the dull bits cut out."
—Alfred Hitchcock, director *(Psycho)*

"Get that f—ing walk-on off the field" was how my short-lived college football career ended at the University of Miami back in the '80s. I'd dislocated my shoulder during the previous play in practice and was hunched over frozen-like and favoring my twisted left arm. Dr. Kalbac popped my shoulder back in place. I had surgery, put down my helmet for good, and picked up a camera.

One thing football and screenwriting have in common is they are both full of conflict. Screenwriting's mantra should be "Conflict—Conflict—Conflict." It's why I chose to start this book with conflict rather than structure, character, or plot. Major conflict often happens early in a movie:

E.T. misses his space ride.

Juno discovers she's pregnant.

Rocky loses his boxing gym locker.

A barracuda kills Nemo's mother and siblings.

What are your favorite movie scenes? There's a good chance they're full of meaningful conflict. Famous lines across all genres are steeped in conflict:

"Houston, we have a problem."
(*Apollo 13*)

"I'm melting."
(*The Wizard of Oz*)

"We are at war."
(*The King's Speech*)

"I have this problem with my apartment."
(*The Apartment*)

"Yeah . . . I'm gonna need you to come in on Saturday."
(*Office Space*)

"I'm gonna make him an offer he can't refuse."
(*The Godfather*)

"I'm as mad as hell, and I'm not going to take this anymore!"
(*Network*)

"I am the one who knocks."
(*Breaking Bad*)

"Say hello to my little friend."
(*Scarface*)

"Are you going to be something else I have to survive?"
(*Erin Brockovich*)

"I coulda been somebody. I coulda been a contender."
(*On the Waterfront*)

"You come at the king, you better not miss."
(*The Wire*)

"Come not between a dragon and his wrath."
(*King Lear*)

"I will have my vengeance, in this life or the next."
(*Gladiator*)

"Of all the gin joints in all the towns in all the world, she has to walk into mine."
(*Casablanca*)

"You're breaking up with me?! I thought you were proposing."
(*Legally Blonde*)

"I'm not going to be ignored Dan."
(*Fatal Attraction*)

"Put that coffee down. Coffee's for closers only."
(*Glengarry Glen Ross*)

"Run, Forrest! Run!"
(*Forrest Gump*)

"What's in the box?"
(*Se7en*)

"No 9000 computer has ever made a mistake or distorted information."
(*2001: A Space Odyssey*)

"Hey Sal, how come you ain't got no brothers on the wall here?"
(*Do the Right Thing*)

"Look at me. I'm the captain now."
(*Captain Phillips*)

"I'm your number one fan. There's nothing to worry about."
(*Misery*)

"There's trouble in the air—you can smell it."
(*Hamilton*)

Conflict-Conflict-Conflict.

Sometimes movies start out with a measure of balance in the world yet give a hint of conflict to come like this line from *Tangled*: "And for that one moment, everything was perfect. And then that moment ended." Conflict is powerful because it brings change to the status quo.

"Baboom! Something comes in and turns your character's life upside down. The thing that was their grand passion gets taken away from them. Woody gets displaced by Buzz."
—Writer/director Michael Arndt discussing *Toy Story*

A shark attacks the young woman in opening scene of *Jaws*. A young boy in *Citizen Kane* is forced to leave his mother and father. A banker goes to prison in *The Shawshank Redemption*. The sound from a child's toy endangers an entire family in *A Quiet Place*. These are all examples of life-altering conflict.

But conflict is also scalable. It can be small. *Seinfeld* is not a TV show about nothing, but a show about a thousand tiny conflicts. It's Jerry's pirate shirt, Kramer's jockey shorts, George's thick wallet, and Elaine's awkward dance. It's the Penske file, the close-talker, shrinkage. *Seinfeld* = conflict.

"Plays are about conflict. Plays are about people not getting along."
—Playwright Edward Albee

In Neil Simon's play *Broadway Bound*, two brothers struggle to make it as writers and one of them says, "The ingredient in every good sketch we've ever seen—is conflict!" It can be as simple as somebody wanting something bad— "money, a girl, to get to Philadelphia"— and somebody trying to stop them from getting what they want.

"Generally in a lot of my plays, two people are in major confrontation with each other, like in *The Odd Couple* or *Barefoot in the Park* or *The Sunshine Boys*."
—Playwright and screenwriter Neil Simon

"Never put two people in a room who agree on anything."
—Screenwriter and professor Lew Hunter
Lew Hunter's Screenwriting 434 (Based on a UCLA class he taught.)

One of the easiest ways to have conflict between two people is to have them fight over the same thing. In *Raiders of the Lost Ark,* Indiana Jones risks his life to capture an idol, only to have it taken away by Belloq—"So once again, Jones, what was briefly yours is now mine."

The formula is 2 dogs + 1 bone = Conflict.

"To catch a character in trouble and to tell about it is the basis for almost any story."
—Novelist and screenwriter Jesse Hill Ford

I love the simplicity of "a character in trouble." This is true of Luke Skywalker, Dorothy, Juno, Rocky, Ripley, Maximus, Tom Joad, Butch Cassidy (and the Sundance Kid), James Bond, Clarice Starling, Nemo, Princess Leia, Snow White, and kidnapped Chris Washington in *Get Out.*

Character in trouble = Conflict

The word protagonist flows from the Greek word agōn, and basically means struggle (The word agony also has roots in agōn.). Thinking of your main character as the one who struggles — and the antagonist as the one struggling against your main character—conjurers up powerful imagery. Think of Olympic wrestlers as symbolic of screenwriting.

Struggle = Conflict

The struggle can be as grand as saving the world (*Deep Impact*), but it can also be as simple as cooking a turkey dinner. In fact, Peter Hedges' micro-budget film *Pieces of April* is a good example of having a character struggling on many levels. April (Katie Holmes) struggles to find a place to cook a Thanksgiving dinner after her oven breaks, she struggles with her neighbors, her boyfriend, her family, society, herself, and even her salt and pepper shakers.

In Pixar's *Inside Out*, the emotion Joy reflects a girl's life with great friends and a great home life; "Things couldn't be better. After all Riley's 11 now. What could happen?" A second later a "SOLD" sign plops in front of Riley's house and sending her perfect life into a downward spiral.

"A story without a struggle can never be a dramatic story. . . . There are millions of different kinds of struggles, but in all this variety the

dramatic struggle has its definite requirements. It is a struggle to eliminate the disturbance."
—Eugene Vale
The Technique of Screenplay Writing

Disturbance = Conflict

"Screenwriting is a craft based on logic. It consists of the assiduous application of several basic questions: What does the hero want? What hinders him from getting it? What happens if he does not get it?"
—David Mamet
On Directing Film

Mamet's thought boils down to one word: conflict.

"Character comes to a fork in the road and a choice must be made. Take the high road (the healthy responsible choice) or the low road (unhealthy, irresponsible choice). If the character chooses the right thing you really don't have a story."
—Screenwriter Michael Arndt *(Toy Story 3)*

Bad choices = Conflict

Daily, news reports are filled with people making unhealthy and irresponsible choices. In the 1996 movie *Up Close & Personal*, Robert Redford's character gives well-known journalistic advice, "If it bleeds, it leads."

Blood = Conflict

"In order to create viable art that will hold someone's attention, you must have dramatic tension. Which, in screenwriting, is created by a line of action and opposing forces. Tension = Attention."
—William Froug
Screenwriting Tricks of the Trade

Dramatic Tension = Conflict

"I believe characters boil down to pretty much one clear dilemma. A

dilemma is a choice between two equally good things or two equally bad things."
—Filmmaker/consultant Jim Mercurio
Jim Mercurio's Complete Screenwriting: From A to Z to A-List, DVD

In Alan J. Pakula's script for *Sophie's Choice* (based on a novel by William Styron) a mother in a Nazi concentration camp is forced to choose which of her children will she keep with her and which child will be sent away to a children's labor camp (hard labor), or worse, a gas chamber (death).

One clear dilemma = Conflict

"I have to stick — really closely, like it's a life raft — to intention and obstacles. Just the basics of somebody wants something, something is standing in their way of getting it."
—Aaron Sorkin

Creative Screenwriting podcast interview with Jeff Goldsmith

Intention and obstacles = Conflict

"A good character always has a crisis lurking inside them like a ticking time bomb."
—Screenwriter Michael Arndt (*Little Miss Sunshine*)
MovieMaker interview with Jennifer M. Wood

Crisis = Conflict

"I think the greatest scare in horror is turning the corner in *The Shining* and finding the girls at the end of the hallway."
—Writer/director Jordan Peele (*Get Out*)

Scary = Conflict

"All character, all structure, all drama is built on the war between opposites."
—John Yorke
Into the Woods: A Five Act Journey Into Story

War between opposites = Conflict

Yorke points out "war of opposites" examples of Antigone and Creon, Macbeth and Lady Macbeth, and Captain Kirk and Spock, which succinctly covers the time from ancient Greece to the future Final Frontier in space.

And just to drive this point home …

"One of literature's few unbreakable rules is simply this: Without conflict, there is no drama."
—Director Edward Dmytryk (*The Caine Mutiny*)
On Screen Writing

Shakespeare, Chaplin, Hitchcock — Conflict, Conflict, Conflict

Spielberg, Scorsese, Tarantino — Conflict, Conflict, Conflict

I Love Lucy, The Sopranos, Chernobyl — Conflict, Conflict, Conflict

The fairy tale *Little Red Riding Hood,* the documentary *Hoop Dreams,* and the podcast *Dr. Death* — Conflict, Conflict, Conflict.

"Airplanes that land safely do not make the news. And nobody goes to the theater, or switches on the tube, to view a movie entitled *The Village of the Happy Nice People*."
—Richard Walter
Essentials of Screenwriting

The "Miracle on the Hudson" emergency plane landing did land safely and make the news, and even became the movie *Sully*. But that's an exception to the rule. And it's still a story rooted in conflict.

MEANINGFUL CONFLICT

All conflict is not created equally. But in every scene you write there should be some level of conflict. It could be rising conflict (the calm before the storm) or resolution afterwards. But conflict is at the core of every great story. Conflict with self, conflict with society, conflict with friends and family, conflict with nature — have conflict with something.

Meaningful conflict usually takes place on at least two levels. In *Jaws*, the town has conflict with a shark that is eating people, and an economic conflict if tourists are kept away which leads to conflict in society, which leads to conflict within Chief Brody's family. To top it off, Brody has his own internal conflicts because he's a city cop in a seaside community and he's also afraid of the water. *Jaws* is not just a run-of-the-mill special effects movie. In fact, the special effects aren't all that special because the filmmakers had conflict with a mechanical shark that didn't always work as designed.

The reason conflict is such a powerful component of filmmaking is because we can relate to it in our own lives. Boxing champion Mike Tyson said, "Everyone has a plan, until they are punched in the mouth." Country musician legend Hank Williams recorded the 1949 hit song *I'm So Lonesome I Could Cry*—a song Elvis said was "probably the saddest song I've ever heard."

We can relate to life's disappointments and conflicts. Every day we deal with conflict on many levels. Pick any genre of music and you will find many favorite songs laced with conflict: from The Rolling Stones (*I Can't Get No) Satisfaction* to Whitney Houston's *Where Do Broken Hearts Go.*

IS THERE A BODY COUNT?

I once pitched a story to an executive and was asked, "Is there a body count?" A body count is conflict where the stakes are life and death. It gets our attention as it did in the opening scene of *Sunset Boulevard.*

"You see, the body of a young man was found floating in the pool of her mansion, with two shots in his back and one in his stomach. Nobody important, really. Just a movie writer with a couple of "B" pictures to his credit. The poor dope. He always wanted a pool. Well, in the end he got himself a pool – only the price turned out to be a little high."
Joe Gillis (William Holden)
Written by Charles Brackett & Billy Wilder & D.M Marshman, Jr.

As important as conflict is to your story, it's not your story. Next, we'll look at the role of concept as you develop your screenplay ideas.

2 CONCEPT

"Most aspiring screenwriters simply don't spend enough time choosing their concept. It's by far the most common mistake I see in spec scripts."
—Screenwriter Terry Rossio (*Shrek, Pirates of the Caribbean*)
Wordplay website, "A Foot in the Door"

"One lesson I've learned in Hollywood is that right out of the gate a screenplay will be judged solely on its concept or premise."
—Chandus King
Now Write! Screenwriting

How do you test your story concept? What filter system do you have in place that tells you, "This concept is worth a major investment of my time and talent"? The best time to test your concept is before you write your screenplay. Many writers ignore warning signs and fail to discover their concept's shortcomings until after their script is completed.

If the concept is weak, all that's left is "polishing brass on a sinking ship."

"This may shock you, but most beginners fail at the concept. It's the single most common problem I've found with scripts. Concept is the core of the script."
—Karl Iglesias
Writing for Emotional Impact

"Trying to be that 1 in a trillion screenwriter who breaks through on a 'nothing' premise is a suicide mission. The number 1 reason a script doesn't sell is because the concept is weak/non-existent. . . .

Be smart and choose a concept that has a chance of selling."

—Carson Reeves

Scriptshadow blog, "Your 2012 Screenwriting New Year's Resolution"

STORIES THAT WILL ALWAYS SELL

"[Rod Serling's] optimism about the human condition led to stories that made one feel good about the race and its chances for emotional triumph. That, well told, will always sell."

—Producer Buck Houghton (*The Twilight Zone*)

The Academy Awards are one key place we can look for the highest quality movies produced every year. Each year, since 1929, the best films of the year are voted on by Academy members to win an Oscar.

Look at past Best Picture Oscar nominations and see how many end with an "emotional triumph." They don't all end well, but it's an interesting gauge. Human beings seem to yearn for stories that have an uptick. And even in movies ending with death there can be an emotional triumph: *Gladiator, Titanic, Braveheart.*

Italian-born writer/director Frank Capra entertained audiences through the rough periods of 1930s and '40s with The Great Depression and World War II. He was nominated for three best directing Oscars (*Mr. Smith Goes to Washington, Lady for a Day, It's a Wonderful Life*) and won three Oscars (*You Can't Take It with You, It Happened One Night, Mr. Deeds Goes to Town*).

"From *Mr. Deeds* on my films were pretty much alike. I mean the same things kept cropping up. But they were not just escapist films. Love thy neighbor is a very deep-seated quality in the human race. It's something that unless we can get more of that into our everyday lives we're just going to go down the rat hole."

—Frank Capra

You can argue that Capra's positivity for humanity was a product of his times. That he was overcompensating for world at war and one experiencing economic hardships during The Great Depression. When I was in film school it was popular to dismiss Capra's upbeat films by calling them Capricorn. But he tapped into something timeless and universal.

And if you revisit *It's a Wonderful Life*, you'll realize—as filmmaker Edward Burns points out—that George Baily (Jimmy Stewart) goes "through some really tough, dark stuff."

You may be surprised to learn that the writer/director of *The Shawshank Redemption*, Frank Darabont, had this to say about his beloved movie, "*Shawshank* is basically *It's a Wonderful Life* in a prison."

The 2014 film *Birdman* won four Oscars including Best Picture and Best Writing, Original Screenplay and is a gritty story that seemed headed for despair until the very last shot when Sam (Emma Stone) looks up instead of down. It's a subtlety that marks the difference between hope and nihilism.

Stories of emotional triumph come from a deep well, and as long as human beings face hardships in life, there will always be a desire to drink from that well.

WHAT ARE PRODUCERS AND DIRECTORS LOOKING FOR?

If you like simplicity in screenwriting advice, then you'll like this exchange from *MovieMaker* magazine.

Jennifer M. Wood: As producer, what are three things you look for in a script?

Chris Columbus: Conflict, great characters, and a gripping storyline.

Simple, right?

But what does Columbus mean by a "gripping storyline"? One could write a whole book on those two words. The gripping storyline is the concept. It's the element that gets producers and directors interesting in making the film, the studios interested in financing the film, the actors interested in signing on to do the film, and the audiences interested in watching the film.

One tool some writers use to crystalize their concept is to use a logline. A brief (usually a one or two sentence) description of their dramatic story that helps people see the movie in their mind, and even envision what the movie poster would be.

"[Before writing the script] I try to see the trailer in my head. . . . And then I work and try to create that."
—Writer/director Shane Black (*Lethal Weapon, Iron Man 3*)

This shorthand tool of a logline line is helpful before writing your story, as well as pitching your story to others.

That usually only leaves room for three to five elements:

1. Main character (his or her flaw is a bonus)
2. Main goal
3. Main opposition
4. Stakes
5. Irony (definitely a bonus)

Christopher Lockhart, WME story editor (and founder of the Facebook group The Inside Pitch), has an excellent 54-page PDF called *I WROTE A 120 PAGE SCRIPT BUT CAN'T WRITE A LOGLINE: THE CONSTRUCTION OF A LOGLINE*. It's the best thing I've read on loglines and you can track it down online.

Lockhart offers this logline example from *The Wizard of Oz*:

After a twister transports a lonely Kansas farm girl to a magical land, she sets out on a dangerous journey to find a wizard with the power to send her home.

Like any tool, not everyone uses loglines, but they are common. A version of loglines is also used in the radio/podcasting world.

Alex Blumberg, former NPR radio producer and current CEO of Gimlet Media uses what he calls The Story Formula:

I'm doing a story about X
And it's interesting because of Y

Others use the term The Focus Sentence.

"A successful focus sentence is the most basic, bare-bones version of your narrative arc."
—Jessica Abel
Out on a Wire

Abel learned about the focus sentence from Rob Rosenthal at The Transom Workshop, who learned it from Tod Maffin's book *From Idea to Air: Getting Paid for Your Writing on Public Radio.*

Someone
does something,
because...
but... Embedded in that is a main character/protagonist doing something because they have a goal, but something or someone stands in their way. The outcome is unknown. Ideally, resolving that conflict will lead to a conclusion.

But remember, you're just giving a thumbnail version of the concept. Later in chapter five we'll look at ways writers flesh out and structure the overall story.

THE GREAT SCRIPT VS. THE RIGHT SCRIPT

Lockhart has read over 50,000 scripts and works for one of the largest and most established talented companies in the world. During a Q&A with him a few years ago, he told me about his concept for "The right script."

SCOTT W. SMITH: It's been said that most screenplays range from bad to not very good, and that a great script will not go unnoticed. Do great scripts always open doors in Hollywood?

CHRISTOPHER LOCKHART: Always? Of course not. A writer must have access to the business. What good is a "great" script if the right people don't get the opportunity to read it? Having a "great" script is only a percentage of what a writer must accomplish to evolve a career.

Teachers and purveyors of HOW TO books use "great" every chance they get. What else can someone say? "Great" makes everyone look smart. Writers are writing great scripts, and Hollywood is selling/buying great scripts.

And, in such a tough, puzzling business, "great" allows the writer to actively strive for something specific (so he thinks). He enthusiastically tells himself, "All I have to do is write a great script and Hollywood's doors will open for me!"

But anyone who works in the business knows this is not entirely true.

I suggest writers write the "right" script.

When I started talking about the "right" script rather than the "great" script, I was criticized and lambasted. But I still believe that lots of factors play a role in getting writers to the professional level. For instance, "timing."

What makes a script a "right" script?:
1) CONCEPT
2) EXECUTION
3) MARKETING

CONCEPT is king in the Hollywood spec market – especially for new writers. I hear lots of concepts from new scribes and rarely do any resonate with the sound of a "Hollywood movie."

Part of being successful in this business is having a good head for concepts. I still believe that a new writer needs to develop a "movie" concept. Most writers develop concepts that are neither dramatic nor cinematic. They'd make great poems — but not great movies.

So, a "right" script has to be great but it also includes other factors that some "great" scripts often lack.

IS IT A MOVIE?

"When you are reading a script, only one thing truly matters: Is it a movie? Not is it a good idea, or is it well written, or is there some big star attached. Is. It. A. Movie?"
—Producer Rick Schwartz (*The Departed*)

"I like to feel with absolute certainty that the fundamental idea for the film is, without a doubt, an exceptional premise, one that implies that a film must be made from it, without question."
—Screenwriter Terry Rossio (*Shrek*)
Make Your Story A Movie interview with John Robert Marlow

When I heard NPR's *Morning Edition* broadcast "Inmate With Stock Tip Wants To Be San Quentin's Warren Buffett," I instantly thought, "That's a movie." In fact, I imagined Hollywood executives were on the phone with the show's producers, Davia Nelson and Nikki Silva (The Kitchen Sisters), before the broadcast ended.

The arc of the story is all there: a young black man grows up on the streets of Oakland where he ends up in a gang, committing crimes that land him in prison. He doesn't learn to read and write until he's in prison. He's never even heard of the stock market until a fellow inmate tells him, "This is where white people keep their money." BAM! There's your inciting incident. Let the transformation begin.

From there he throws himself into learning everything about the stock market, sometimes staying up all night and reading as many as 500 articles in a single day, and eventually becoming very savvy in predicting the rise and fall of stocks. Inmates, prison workers, and even outside traders take notice and he earns the nickname Wall Street. We could give it the working title *Inside Trading* or *Insider Trader.*

But the real question is: Is it a movie? It's not hard to see a great role there for Denzel Washington, Samuel L. Jackson, or Michael B. Jordan. Perhaps a comedy with Jamie Foxx, Eddie Murphy, or Kevin Hart. But is it something that would inspire producers to spend years trying to produce? Is it something that studios would spend millions of dollars to produce and then millions more to market? Is it something that would attract name actors that would help attract a large audience? I'm not writing the checks, but from my perspective the answer is yes.

There are a few precedents that can help with the decision. There are movies like *The Pursuit of Happyness* (about a homeless man turned stockbroker, starring Will Smith) and *The Shawshank Redemption* (where education/redemption are key themes). There's also Matt Damon as the in-trouble-with-the-law janitor who turns out to be a math genius in *Good Will Hunting,* finding a second chance in life and paying back his debts to society.

There's also the fact that San Quentin is one of the most recognizable prisons in the country, open since 1863 and now the oldest prison in California. Here's just a short list of films, TV shows, and pop culture references connected with San Quentin: *Escape From San Quentin* (1957), *Dark Passage* (Humphrey Bogart), the Johnny Cash album *At San Quentin, The Lincoln Lawyer* (Matthew McConaughey), *Beyond Scared Straight, Lock Up, Fruitvale Station,* and *Ant-Man.*

So, yeah, San Quentin is a part of Hollywood, and it's deeply embedded in the American psyche. Also, again, *Inside Trader* is a prison reform story, similar to and yet also distinguishable from what's been produced before. An initial examination of the concept suggests that it holds promise.

One of the strengths of the *Scriptnotes* podcast is that screenwriters John August and Craig Mazin look at the business side of Hollywood screenwriting and filmmaking. In *Episode 201* ("How would this be a movie?") they have a fascinating exchange speculating whether a story that's ripped from news headlines could be a movie.

While they come at it partly from the perspective of "if I were running a studio," Their insights translate well for the indie filmmaker or just about anybody who wants to tell a story and attract an audience but does not know yet whether the investment would be worth it.

Does a news story or other source have enough potential to justify the investors' time and money? It can be an intriguing story, but is it a movie?

One of the news stories considered by August and Mazin was an athletic scandal involving corruption on an international level. They discussed what kind of movie it could be. Comedy? Political thriller? Straight drama? What is the tone of the movie? Is it like *Cool Runnings, Invictus,* a Coen Brothers comedy, *Erin Brockovich, American Hustle, Moneyball,* or *Traffic?*

Here are some of insights and questions they hit on:

"Whoever we pick as our hero, what is going to be her journey through this movie? And how are we going to find the moments of triumph and failure along the way? How are we going to get to that place where all hope is lost?"
—Screenwriter John August

"Every movie ultimately must be about people. We simply don't watch fictional movies, even dramatizations of real things for the events themselves. That's why we watch documentaries. And even in documentaries, they make it about people. Otherwise, it's a textbook."
—Screenwriter Craig Mazin

So look at the questions of "Is it a movie?" and "How would this be a movie?" as different sides of the same coin. Keep in mind that "Is it a movie?" doesn't have to mean, "Is it a big-budget Hollywood movie?" Otherwise, some great indie, international, or lower-budget studio films would never get made.

"Is it a movie?" is also a scalable question—from the big-budget Hollywood film all the way down to a short film. A short version of *Insider Trader* could absolutely be shot in one day, inside one prison cell (with one cell phone), starring one actor.

You could also do the *Orange Is the New Black* version with Halle Berry, Octavia Spencer, or Taraji P. Henson playing the character named Wall Street. Maybe a Pete Rose-type character inspired by the *USA Today* article "Inside prison baseball with the San Quentin Giants." Or where the main character starts a financial podcast in prison and becomes the next financial wizard.

According to a *CNN Money* article, San Quentin State Prison inmate Curtis "Wall Street" Carroll, also called "The Oracle of San Quentin," co-teaches a class to inmates with Robin Williams' son, Zak Williams (who has an MBA from Columbia). I think that will be a movie someday.

FILM VS. TV VS. STREAMING WRITING (10 DIFFERENCES)

"With film you are closing doors. You're telling a two-hour story, and you're closing doors. With television you're opening as many as you possibly can to leave yourself avenues for five or six years of storytelling."
—Film and TV writer/producer Melissa Rosenberg (*Twilight, Dexter*)

"We don't know what a movie is anymore. We don't know how long it is, we don't know where you see it, we don't know how you monetize it. What if it's a net series? . . . *Mad Men* is a movie. It's a 79-hour movie."
—Writer/director Paul Schrader (*First Reformed*)
Vulture interview with Mark Jacobson

How do you know whether your story is a feature film idea or a TV idea?

Here are ten ways I've gleaned from various books, magazines, podcasts, and interviews that can assist you in knowing if you have an idea that is a better fit for film or TV or something else altogether (like a limited series for streaming on Netflix, Amazon, Hulu, etc.). This is not an exhaustive or definitive list, but it can give you a solid track to run on.

1. Ordinary vs. Extraordinary

Matt Damon getting stuck on Mars in *The Martian* is a movie moment— a once in a lifetime event. If that same character returned to earth safely and opened a bar, that's a more television-friendly slice of life, kind of like Sam (Ted Danson) the ex-baseball player in *Cheers* who opens a bar.

"What is the story of *Cheers*? It's the story of people who show up at a bar where they find camaraderie in a way they don't anywhere else. There's nothing about that that suggests *movie*."
—Emmy winner Craig Mazin (*Chernobyl*)
Scriptnotes podcast, episode 218

Another way to look at it is ordinary vs. extraordinary. Much of broadcast television takes place in ordinary worlds where place is important. Usually that place, that world, is a home or workplace that we return to again and again. It's the bar in *Cheers*, the offices in *Mary Tyler Moore, Mad Men*, and *30 Rock*, or the living rooms in *All in the Family*, *The Jeffersons*, and *Seinfeld*.

Aaron Sorkin, who's excelled in writing both feature films and TV shows, said, "If it's the place you're attracted to [writing about], that's a TV series." That helps explain the success of his shows *The West Wing* (The White House), *Sports Night* (an ESPN-like studio), and *The Newsroom* (a newsroom).

Cable TV and streaming shows are increasingly showing extraordinary worlds and blurring the lines between film and TV. Complex shows *Deadwood, Breaking Bad*, and *Game of Thrones*—and the limited series *Chernobyl*— paved the way for new ways of storytelling that are sort of a film/TV hybrid.

2. Static vs. Transformational

In broadcast TV, static lives are the norm. The focus in movies is life-changing, whereas TV is life-living. Tony Danza's character in *TAXI* wants to be a champion boxer, but in one episode he gets a fluke shot to fight the champ. If he wins that fight, he'll quit his job and make his living boxing. But he loses and goes back to his steady, regular job as a taxi driver. The movie version of that concept is *Rocky*. Rocky likewise doesn't beat the champ in the first movie, but the direction of his life is forever transformed as he goes from being a debt collector for a loan shark to (in sequels) a champion boxer.

"Generally, TV characters don't change. Their relationships with others change, and we learn new things about them. They may change jobs. But they don't change who they are. This is changing as television gets more sophisticated and storytelling gets more linear. But it is still fundamentally true."
—Alex Epstein
Crafty TV Writing

Epstein's book was published in 2006, two years before *Breaking Bad* began airing. Part of what made Walter White in *Breaking Bad* such a dynamic (and unusual) character was that he not only changed, but he changed for the worse. And audiences still cared. They still tuned in.

Epstein was right on both accounts; TV is changing, and it's still fundamentally true that TV characters don't change —especially network programs.

And even when streaming TV characters change, the transformation is usually years in the making. Don Draper (Jon Hamm) in *Mad Men* is a good example of that.

3. Visual vs. Verbal

The opening of *The Social Network* is over five minutes of two characters talking. That's unusual in movies. Movies like *The Revenant* and *A Quiet Place*, by contrast, could be understood with the sound off. Television is more like theater where much more is communicated verbally.

Police procedurals have been popular on TV since the days of *Ironside* and *Columbo* and show no sign of slowing down. The basic question of "Who done it?" has sold many murder mystery novels and so it's not surprising that it's a popular genre on TV well. Police, detectives, and lawyers can stand around and speculate what happened. And the courtroom is always on standby for additional banter.

This is not to say that movies don't also involve procedurals and courtrooms; it's just that these genres are a staple of TV because of its verbal nature. When movies do procedurals well, they are more visual and cinematic in nature, as in *Se7en* and *Silence of the Lambs*.

Movies tend to excel visually when they show large, sweeping vistas. Consider the western landscapes of John Ford's *The Searchers*, the chaos on the Odessa steps in Sergei Eisenstein's *Battleship Potemkin*, or the vastness of space in Alfonso Cuarón and Emmanuel Lubezki's *Gravity*.

4. 2 Hours vs. 100 Hours+

Although some movies have run times over three hours, the majority are around the two-hour mark. Specials and TV movies aside, television programs tend to only have run times of half an hour to an hour per episode, but the total running time is only limited to how many episodes run each year, and how many years the show runs. (That could be one season or more than 30 years like *The Simpsons*.)

5. Big vs. Small

This is covered in many areas: shooting days, budgets, big-name actors, screen sizes, etc. In general, more time and money is spent on feature films. And while the final season of *Games of Thrones* became the first TV show to break the $20 million per episode budget, dozens of movies have been made for over $200 million (and a few over $300 million).

The most I've paid to watch a single movie is close to $20, but I can watch TV 24 hours a day for free with a rabbit ears antenna. So, while the movie-going experience is getting more expensive, online streaming services for a month of movies and TV programs are still less than the price of a single movie at the box office.

6. Many Characters vs. Fewer Characters

Movies tend to focus on a few main characters. TV and streaming shows have more time so they can include more characters.

"When you end up creating a show with seven, eight, nine characters—ask yourself, how can you appropriately dramatize that many characters within the framework of an hour television show? And the answer is that you can't. So you say, O.K., what we have to do is spill over the sides of our form and start telling multi-plot, more serial kinds of stories."
—Steven Bochco (*Hill Street Blues, NYPD Blue* creator)
Writing the TV Drama Series by Pam Douglas

TV shows often revolve around families (*The Brady Bunch, The Cosby Show, Modern Family, Black-ish, The Simpsons*), even if they are slightly dysfunctional.

"[The Evans family, from *Good Times*] in particular affected me, and it affected my family, and it affected other families that didn't look like my family. It really showed that at the core — rich or poor — family is about love and about sticking together. And I think that that is one of those specific universalities that really influenced and informed what my show does."
—*Black-ish* creator Kenya Barris
2016 *Fresh Air* interview with Terry Gross

People at work in TV shows are often surrogate families (*TAXI, The Office, Mad Men, 30 Rock, Scrubs*). Movies often feature orphan characters, men and women with no family. Matt Damon in *The Martian* is a good example of a movie character cut off from the world. In general, you have more family or surrogate families in the TV world than you do the film world.

7. Aspirational vs. Heightened Reality

Traditional network television pays the bills by selling things. It has commercial breaks to sell cars, shampoo, beer, and a better life. And oftentimes TV shows themselves are selling an aspirational version of life.

Fitness gurus consider beer "liquid bread," but in beer commercials beer appears to make you slender, beautiful, and happy. Driving an Audi also apparently makes you slender, beautiful, and happy. In fact, Doritos, Colgate toothpaste, and Nike shoes also make you slender, beautiful, and happy.

"Advertising is based on one thing, happiness. And you know what happiness is? Happiness is the smell of a new car."
Don Draper in *Mad Men*

Network TV shows lean towards an aspirational life where problems are resolved in 30 minutes, crimes are conveniently solved within an hour, and life is just like it is in Lake Wobegon where "all the women are strong, all the men are good looking, and all the children are above average."

Movies (and increasingly cable TV and streaming) reflect a fallen world, or sometimes a dystopia. And when they're not doing that, they are saving the world, playing in the championship game, or some other version of heightened reality.

8. Open-ended vs. Closed-ended

"If the characters metaphorically speaking die at the end of the story— if there's no more story after that, then it's a feature."
—Aaron Sorkin

Being stuck on an island gives us a good example of how film and TV handle open-ended vs. closed-ended stories. On *Gilligan's Island*, seven people are stranded on an island after a boating accident and must learn to live together. Their conflict with each other is more the point of the show than actually getting off the island.

On the other hand, the major dramatic question of *Cast Away* is whether Chuck Nolan (Tom Hanks) will survive being marooned on an island and be rescued. When finally makes his way back home, he finds that everything is different, including himself. The movie moment version of his life is over. The circle is complete. We don't know where Nolan is heading next. but we do know that this chapter of his life is over.

The lines between open-ended and closed-ended stories are now blurred with the streaming services. Some movies have become more episodic with the ongoing storytelling of *Jurassic Park*, *James Bond*, *Rocky*, *Star Wars*, and the *Avengers* movies. Some movies evolved into TV or streaming programs (*The Odd Couple*, *M*A*S*H*, *Friday Night Lights*, *Fargo*, *Westworld*). And sometimes TV shows become movies (*Star Trek*, *Mission: Impossible*, *The Untouchables*, *South Park*, *Miami Vice*).

My filmmaker friend Matthew Porter (while his youngest son was watching *LEGO Jurassic World: The Secret Exhibit*) posted on Facebook, "If you're keeping score, that's a TV show based on a videogame based on a toy inspired by a film. Based on a book."

9. Writing Alone vs. Writing Rooms

Writing for features is often a one- or two-person job. And according to Larry Brody in his book *Television Writing from the Inside Out*, writers have been gathering in writers' rooms since not only the early days of television, but back when Bob Hope and Jack Benny had radio programs. For the most part, that is a tradition that survives to this day.

"A lot of this job is attitude. Be someone that people want to spend 11-12 hours at a stretch with. One of the most important things of a TV writer's room is to just keep the conversation going."
— *Breaking Bad* creator Vince Gilligan

Do you prefer to write with others in a group or with others? That's a simple question that may push you toward pursing film or TV writing.

Another consideration is most TV writing is done in Los Angeles, making that more difficult to do outside of LA. for unestablished writers.

10. Opportunity vs. Opportunity Plus

"I think right now television is the best that it's ever been, and I think that it's the worst that film has ever been—in the 50 years that I've been doing it, it's the worst."
—Dustin Hoffman
Independent interview, 2015

There are many more paid writing gigs in television than in feature films, and when you dump digital/online/corporate/gaming storytelling into the mix there are more opportunities than ever. Short-form social media storytelling is also in growth mode because of consumers' viewing habits. Just in recent years there's been a plethora of changes and viewing options including square videos, vertical videos, 360-degree videos, and virtual reality videos.

Emerging opportunities such as these inevitably add new layers to our understanding of the differences between TV (broadcast, cable, streaming) and feature films. I'll revisit this in Chapter 10.

And lastly, when the Netflix streaming series *Homecoming* starring Julia Roberts is based on a podcast, and when people watch Steven Soderbergh's *High Flying Bird* on their iPhone (that he shot on an iPhone), and when *Bird Box* starting Sandra Bullock reportedly had 45 million Netflix accounts accessing it, then you know the entertainment landscape has already shifted.

But it's worth noting that TV writer/creator Shonda Rhimes (*Gray's Anatomy, Scandal*) explained the appeal of TV writing when she said that in film the director fires the writer, but in TV the writer fires the director.

WHERE DO IDEAS COME FROM?

"The way to have a great idea is to have lots of ideas."
—Linus Pauling
Nobel Prize winning scientist

Where do creative ideas come from? When David Mamet's kids asked him that question he told them that there's this guy from out of town who "drives in on the weekend and sells them off the back of his truck."

Katie Couric once asked Jerry Seinfeld where his funny ideas came from and he said, "That's like asking where trees come from."

I hate to disagree with Seinfeld, but I think ideas come from everywhere.

Here's the formula: A+B = C. There, doesn't that help? This is how Seinfeld connects things: "Now why does moisture ruin leather? I don't get this. Aren't cows outside most of the time?" Basic, funny, and original.

People who are a lot smarter than me call this dialectical logic. You connect two unrelated things. A+B= C is simply the result of something new after we've connected two unrelated things.

When I was a kid there was a commercial for Reese's Peanut Butter Cups where a guy comes around the corner eating peanut butter from a jar (like we all walk around doing) and another guy comes from around the other corner eating chocolate, and they bump into each other. One guy says, "Your chocolate is in my peanut butter" and the other guy says, "Your peanut butter is in my chocolate." But they try the PB/chocolate mix and both decide it's good.

A (peanut butter) + B (chocolate) = C (Reese's Peanut Butter Cup).

Illustrator Gary Kelley says, "Creativity is just connecting influences." If you go into his art studio you'll find a menagerie of torn-out photos from magazines (taped to his easel) and art books all there to inspire him.

Art directors and designers have long used mood boards to gather and inspire all their creative ideas. Some filmmakers find them useful as well.

"I tape photos right into the script, so when we're shooting I have a direct visual reference."
—Oscar-winning writer/director Sophia Coppola (*Lost in Translation*)

Creativity is not something that only a few mystical souls can tap into. Nor is it just limited to the arts.

In the 1960s, a couple of guys became enormously wealthy after they bolted a sail to a door and called it a "windsurfer." Arthur Fry looking for a way to hold bookmarks in his hymnal while singing in his church choir resulted in the invention of Post-it notes. The founder of the zillion-selling *...for Dummies* books purportedly was in a bookstore one time and overheard a guy ask the salesperson, "Do you have a basic book on computers? Like computers for dummies?"

"You can't wait for inspiration. You have to go after it with a club."
—Jack London
(A popular re-phrasing of a quote by London.)

Many of us are guilty of saying something like the following:

"If I could just head to the beach or the mountains and get a little place without all the day-to-day distractions... *then* I could really get some ideas down on paper! No kids, no work issues. No people problems. Just a place of nirvana where my creativity would be free flowing."

We're artists, after all. We like to fantasize.

There was an episode of an old TV show where one of the characters goes to a quiet cabin in the woods with the goal of becoming a writer. He's got a typewriter, paper, and is ready to go. Time to finally write that book. After he tidies up the room a bit. After he washes the dishes. After he makes a cup of coffee. Now it's time for lunch . . . and so on.

It's easy to find reasons not to write.

After I go to this seminar . . .
When I get a new computer . . .
When I get that new software . . .

But how do you go at inspiration with a club?

"In action, there is power, grace and magic."
—Goethe

You simply start writing. It may just be notes on a piece of paper, but it's a start. It may not be any good. It probably won't sell. You don't even have to show it to anyone. But you will learn from it, and it will give you confidence for the next script.

The creative process is hard to explain and hard to show on film. But the movie *Pollack* with Ed Harris has a wonderful scene where we see the spark of creativity that became Jackson Pollack's signature style. He's in the process of painting when he accidentally spills some paint on the canvas, and he does it again and then again. He has an epiphany, and it happens not while he's reading a book on painting, but while he's painting.

Creativity is a messy process. You're going to get paint on your shoes so to speak, but you will make discoveries in the process.

A great example in photography is Ansel Adams. Adams was brilliant, but it took decades of photography before the world embraced his work. He would often go into the mountains with a donkey carrying his large format cameras and camp out to watch what the light would do over an extended period of time.

He's known particularly for his early photographs in Yosemite National Park, but one of his most famous photographs is called *Moonrise Over Hernandez*. He captured that photograph late one afternoon while driving in New Mexico. By the time he pulled over and set up his 8"X10" camera, the light was fading fast and he couldn't find his light meter so he guessed on the exposure. His experience paid off but he was only able to take one shot before the light was gone on the cross that had grabbed his attention. It is one of his most recognizable photographs. He had a firm understanding of his craft so he could recognize an opportunity when he saw it.

Stephen King says that as a writer he's like a paleontologist. He sees something interesting buried in the dirt and goes over and brushes away the dirt. He unearths stories, and then writes them down.

It's important to write down what you find. Comedian Rodney Dangerfield was asked how he came up with so much material and he said that three funny things happen to everybody every day; he just writes them down.

One real estate investor told me that the secret to his success is "Always be looking" for deals. When you need to find a deal on a house over the weekend, it's difficult. But if you're always looking, there's a good chance you'll find a good investment.

You need to cultivate looking for ideas. Sometimes they seemingly out of nowhere. It is all about discovery.

Recently I heard a man on the radio telling an interviewer about what it's like to re-enter society after being in prison for years. He said that when you first get out you're in sensory overload. Colors are more vibrant; you hear sounds more clearly. When he first got out he wanted to run up to people and say, "Do you see those colors?" His senses were alive.

Keeping your senses alive to the world around you heightens your experiences and makes you feel alive. And when our senses are alive, we are more likely to be creative (idea-prone) because we are making new connections.

"An idea is nothing more nor less than a new combination of old elements."
—James Webb Young

Or A + B = C

"An idea is a feat of association."
—Poet Robert Frost

A + B = C

Arthur Koestler wrote a book on the creative process (*The Act of Creation*) and stated, "The Creative act . . . uncovers, selects, reshuffles, combines, synthesizes already existing facts, ideas, faculties, skills."

Stephen King says there is no "idea dump" where you go gather story ideas. Instead, "two previously unrelated ideas come together and make something new under the sun."

A+B=C

This could easily fit under chapter five on construction of a story, but it also fits well in this chapter. The idea for one of Mike Birbiglia's Netflix specials was rooted in his jealousy of his newborn daughter.

Without getting into the weeds of what Friedrich Hegel, Immanuel Kant, or any other 18th or 19th century philosopher taught, the triad of thesis, antitheses, and synthesis has proven helpful to some writers today.

The New One, centers around he and his wife (Jen Stein, who co-wrote the special) having their first a child.

Act 1: "All of the reasons no one should ever want to have a child."
Act 2: "How I had a child and how I was right."
Act 3: "And then in the emotional twist— *how I was wrong.*"

He started out with a point of view (thesis), he tested the opposite view (antitheses), and came up with a third view (synthesis).

A: He and his wife enjoyed being a couple. Kids would just mess that up.

B: After he and his wife had a child, Birbiglia felt like he was the third wheel. His wife and child not only had a special bond, but taking care of the baby's needs was taking a lot of his wife's time and attention. Birbiglia was actually jealous.

C: Eventually they all settled into family life and were one happy family.

Back in the '90s David Mamet wrote in his book *Three Uses of the Knife* that dramatic structure "is an exercise of a naturally occurring need or disposition to structure the world as thesis/antithesis/synthesis."

A (thesis) + B (antithesis) = C (synthesis)

The more you have in your brain to select and reshuffle, the more creative you can be.

"Expose yourself to the best things humans have done and then try to bring those things into what you are doing."
—Steve Jobs

Paul Schrader once thought he could write a screenplay with Bob Dylan but soon realized why it wouldn't work. While most people think in terms of one-two-three, A-B-C, Dylan apparently thinks in terms of one-blue-banana. His unique way of connecting the dots.

Peter Hedges wrote *Pieces of April,* which is a story about a wayward young girl who wants to make amends with her family as her mother is dying of cancer. She simply wants to cook a Thanksgiving dinner for her family at her small New York City apartment.

As her family drives in from the suburbs her oven breaks and her single goal in life is to find a way to get the turkey cooked so it doesn't turn into another family disaster. Her desperation to cook the turkey is a powerful central image. Hedges said he heard a similar true story years ago and connected it with his mother dying of cancer.

When you hear a story or have a thought that strikes your fancy, write it down. Your background and twist on life will give it originality. *Juno* was not the first unplanned pregnancy movie in history or even of 2007. But Diablo Cody's slant gave it originality, and that originality was what earned her an Academy Award.

In some cases, you may not even be able to figure out the origin of your best ideas.

But some have noted that ideas and creativity flow doing repetitive and seemingly mundane tasks like pulling weeds in a garden or taking a shower. Julia Cameron writes about this in *The Artist's Way.* She quotes Einstein as having asked, "Why do I get my best ideas in the shower?"

"I take maybe six or eight showers a day when I'm writing. Not because I'm a germophobe, but it just gives me a little energy shot, and putting on fresh clothes makes me feel, especially if I'm not writing well—that I'm getting a do-over."
—Aaron Sorkin
Time Out London interview with Trevor Johnston

"In the shower, with the hot water coming down, you've left the real world behind, and very frequently things open up for you."
—Four-time Oscar-winning writer/director Woody Allen

"The relaxing, solitary and non-judgmental shower environment may afford creative thinking by allowing the mind to wander freely and causing people to be more open to their inner stream of consciousness and daydreams."
—Scott Barry Kaufman, Ph.D.
Co-author, *Wired to Create: Unraveling the Mysteries of the Creative Mind*

And just maybe it's not the shower, but the water. Screenwriter Dalton Trumbo used to write in the bathtub, and Quentin Tarantino says he takes long swims in his heated pool as part of his creative process. Lakes, rivers, and oceans have stirred people's imaginations throughout time.

Cameron said Steven Spielberg claims some of his best ideas come while driving on freeways. Many writers (like Hemingway) have been regular swimmers and others (Stephen King) have been walkers. Comedian Robin Williams was an avid bicyclist. Musician Jack Johnson hits the waves as he told *Rolling Stone* magazine, "When I get home from a tour, I put away the guitar and surf a lot. After a while, the songs just start comin'."

Whatever the impetus for your story, pull on the threads that are there and see where it leads you.

The movie *Nightcrawler* is a good example of A+B=C. (and also shows that inspiration can come from story components other than character, plot, or theme.)

"The setting came first. I heard about these freelance videographers, who go out in L.A. at nighttime and shoot this footage and sell it. I became really intrigued with it. . . . It had all the elements that I wanted. Nighttime. Movement. Thematic relevance."
—Writer/director Dan Gilroy on *Nightcrawler*
Pop Matters interview with Thomas Britt

"A" was the concept of freelance digital journalists roaming around at night looking for seedy accidents and stories. It was an idea that Gilroy spent years trying to develop. He needed something else to crack the story open. The "B" element for Gilroy came from the rise and popularity of anti-hero characters like Tony Soprano, Ray Donovan, and Walter White, who were on cable TV while he was developing the idea.

Gilroy sprinkled in some reference movies (*Network, Ace in the Hole, The Talented Mr. Ripley, To Die For, King of Comedy*) and the result was "C"—Lou Bloom (Jake Gyllenhaal), a psychopathic Horatio Alger. Gilroy said it was an "unusual equation" and an "unorthodox formula."

Your creativity comes out of the overflow of the people, places, and things you pour into your life. So be curious and connected and try the simple formula A+B=C for a creative jolt.

"The common story is one plus one equals two. But the real genuine stories are about one and one equaling three. That's what I'm interested in."
—Filmmaker Ken Burns (*The Civil War*)

Paul Schrader's version of combining concepts is to start with a problem or personal struggle and find an intriguing metaphor for it. He says he comes up with a plot by driving the problem through the metaphor.

When Schrader was 25 years old and in the hospital with an ulcer, he realized there was "a rip in the moral fabric of society" and hit on the problem of loneliness and the metaphor of a taxicab—"this yellow rectangular coffin floating through the sewers of a metropolis. And inside that coffin is trapped a young man. And the power of that metaphor overwhelmed me. And I knew I had to write that story because I was becoming that young man." The result was the script for *Taxi Driver*.

STEALING, BORROWING, AND PAYING HOMAGE

"The whole *Star Wars* story draws on Kurosawa's 1958 film *The Hidden Fortress*."
—Lawrence Kasdan (*Star Wars, The Empire Strikes Back*)

"All ideas are second-hand, consciously and unconsciously, drawn from a million outside sources."
—Mark Twain

If you listen to interviews of Scorsese, Spielberg, or Tarantino, you quickly begin to grasp how they have deep reserves of film knowledge. Their story senses are shaped by movies throughout film history. That's true to one degree or another for everyone working in the film and television industry.

We're not talking about copyright infringement, but inspiration.

"I have a library of probably 100 scripts that are my favorite scripts and I'm going back and referring to them again and again. How do they do that? How's that written?"
—Screenwriter Stuart Beattie (*Collateral*)
The Dialogue: Learning from the Masters interview with Mike De Luca

"Steal from anywhere that resonates with inspiration or fuels your imagination."
—Filmmaker Jim Jarmusch (*Stranger Than Paradise*)

"Those who do not want to imitate anything, produce nothing."
—Painter Salvador Dalí

"The immature poet imitates, the mature poet plagiarizes."
—T.S. Eliot

"A good composer does not imitate; he steals."
—Composer/pianist Igor Stravinsky

"Oh, I've stolen from the best. I mean I've stolen from Bergman. I've stolen from Groucho. I've stolen from Chaplin. I've stolen from Keaton, from Martha Graham, from Fellini. I mean, I'm a shameless thief."
—Woody Allen

"There's no one working in television or theater today who's not influenced by . . . the fountainhead of this whole thing—which is *Death of a Salesman*.**"**
— *Mad Men* creator Matthew Weiner on Arthur Miller's play

"I steal from every single movie ever made. I love it—if my work has anything it's that I'm taking this from this and that from that and mixing them together. . . . I steal from everything. Great artists steal, they don't do homages."
—Two-time Oscar wining screenwriter Quentin Tarantino
Empire, November 1994

"Arthur Miller's *Death of a Salesman* was like a mirror to the story I had written."
—Iranian filmmaker Asghar Farhadi on his film *The Salesman*

"I think it's fine for young [filmmakers] to out and out rip off people who come before them because you always make it your own."
—Writer/director Francis Ford Coppola (*The Godfather*)

One of the main inspirations for Mickey Mouse was The Tramp. Walt Disney was not secretive about analyzing what made Chaplin's underdog character so mischievous and likable. And so resilient to obstacles that he could beat the odds and come out on top to the audience's delight.

"We wanted something appealing, and we thought of a tiny bit of a mouse that would have something of the wistfulness of Chaplin—a little fellow trying to do the best he could."
—Walt Disney

Christopher Gaze said in a TED Talk that "Shakespeare surrounds us" because the playwright's work is ubiquitous. It's global and timeless.

Shakespeare's work wasn't 100% original, but his plays have endured like no other dramatic writings. Greg Robin Smith, director of The Washington Shakespeare Festival, sees patterns in Shakespeare's work that you may consider stealing to surround your stories.

"These things I call the DOLTS; death, order, love, transformation, sovereignty—these things you'll find in the classics."
— Greg Robin Smith
On the Page podcast interview with Pilar Alessandra

That is death is referred to in his plays, even if it's a comedy. There is a struggle to restore order at the end of his plays (even if people have to die). There is love, or its cousin hate and jealousy. There is transformation. And that transformation isn't always bad to good, but good to bad. And sovereignty comes down to *Who owns me? Who am I?* You'll find Shakespeare story fingerprints everywhere: *The Lion King, House of Cards, Empire, Sons of Anarchy, Ran,* and *West Side Story.*

Here's a great example of how a writer grafts the works of others into something new.

"[For *First Reformed*] I had the character from *Diary of a Country Priest*, I had the premise from *Winter Light*, I had the ending from *Ordet*, I had the levitation from Tarkovsky's *The Mirror*, I had the credits from *Voyage to Italy* — I was stealing all over the place. . . . The secret of stealing is that you have to steal around. You can't go back to the same 7-Eleven every time. They catch you. So you go to the floral shop. Then you go to the gas station. Then you go to that hotdog stand that nobody goes to. And you keep grabbing this stuff and eventually, somebody will think you made it up."
—Writer/Director Paul Schrader (*Taxi Driver*)
The Moment with Brian Koppelman podcast interview

And you don't always have to look for inspiration from established giants. After a TV viewing of the 1957 film *Zero Hour!*, filmmakers David Zucker, Jim Abrahams, and Jerry Zucker gave that movie concept a fresh spin for their 1980 film *Airplane!*—one of the highest-ranked comedies of all time.

"[T]here was a line in Zero Hour that said, 'Stewardess, we have to find somebody who can not only fly this plane but who didn't have fish for dinner.' We just looked at that and we put it directly into *Airplane!*"
—Jim Abrahams, *Airplane!* co-writer/co-director
NPR, "'Airplane!' At 25"

The idea of pulling ideas and elements from other movies has been called everything from "mirror movies," "re-mixing," "cousins," "retelling," "paying homage to," "an interpretation," to "going sideways with an idea."

"Look at *Point Break* starring Patrick Swayze, then look at *Fast and Furious*. Yes, it's the same movie almost beat for beat."
—Blake Snyder

Here's a short list of movies that share at least some DNA:

Antz/A Bug's Life
Armageddon/Deep Impact
Battle Royale/The Hunger Games
Big/13 Going on 30
Chinatown/Who Saved Roger Rabbit?
A Christmas Carol/Scrooged
City on Fire/Reservoir Dogs
The Creature from The Black Lagoon/ Splash/The Shape of Water
Cyrano de Bergerac/Roxanne
Dances with Wolves/The Emerald Forest/Avatar
Doc Hollywood/Cars
Double Indemnity/Body Heat
Emma/Clueless
Fatal Attraction/Unfaithful
Finding Nemo/Shark Tale
Indecent Proposal/Honeymoon in Vegas
Jeremiah Johnson/The Revenant
The Karate Kid/ The King's Speech
Kill Bill/ Kung Fu Panda (according to Tarantino)
The Matrix/ Monsters, Inc.
The Searchers/Hardcore
A Stranger Among Us/Witness
A Streetcar Named Desire/Blue Jasmine
Westworld/Jurassic Park
The Wizard of Oz/Apocalypse Now (according to Michael Arndt)
Yojimbo/A Fistful of Dollars

Sometimes the similarities result from an unconscious decision and other times they are fully conscious. After seeing the movie *Red River*, screenwriter William Bowers told the movie's screenwriter Borden Chase that he'd enjoyed the film. Chase couldn't believe that he'd gotten away with retelling the story of *Mutiny on the Bounty* (1936) without anyone noticing. He'd just changed the adventure at sea into a Western.

Here's how another American Western had roots in a classic Japanese film.

"I wrote the screenplay [for *The Magnificent Seven*]. Johnny Sturges, the director, asked me to make a screenplay out of Kurosawa's [*Seven Samurai*], setting it in the West."
—Walter Brown Newman

When Aaron Sorkin read the 14-page treatment for Ben Mezrich's book *The Accidental Billionaires,* he was not drawn to the modern story of the invention of Facebook, but to a story "as old as storytelling itself. Of friendship, and loyalty, and betrayal, and class, and power"—themes worthy of the Greek tragedies and plays of Shakespeare that Sorkin knew so well.

"How does an artist look at the world? Well, first she asks herself, 'What's worth stealing?' And second, she moves on to the next thing."
—Author Austin Kleon

Here's how a classic TV show had roots in a classic reality TV show. Lloyd Braun, then president of ABC, came up with the idea at a company retreat of taking the *Survivor* concept and turning it into what would become *Lost.*

"[H]is idea was like, 'We should do *Survivor* as a drama series. It would be an incredible pilot for a television show to basically have a plane crash on an island, and then the show would just be about the survivors surviving.'"
—*Lost* co-creator of Damon Lindelof
INSIDER interview with Kim Renfro

When Moss Hart was in his mid-twenties, he attended a performance of *June Moon* on Broadway and it fueled his ambition to write plays. "I started the first act that night on my return from the theatre and three weeks later saw the play finished." That play, *Once in a Lifetime,* launched Hart's career as a playwright and screenwriter. *June Moon* is about a lyricist who journeys to New York to make a name for himself. *Once Upon a Time* is about a vaudevillian team of three from New York City who head to Hollywood to find work.

"My own experience leads me to believe that an original plot is never as essential or, in fact, salable as is fresh and original treatment of a plot that has proved popular."
—Screenwriter Frances Marion

"You need to tell the same story over and over again every generation, so that that generation gets it."
—George Lucas

The Adventure Plot is one of those proven, popular, and timeless movie plots, which explains why *Indiana Jones and the Raiders of the Lost Ark* is "uniquely familiar."

While I can't vouch for its authenticity, the *Raiders of the Lost Ark* story conference transcript that you can find kicking around the internet is a fascinating look at how to develop a concept. It's from a story meeting that occurred over a few days in January 1978 between George Lucas, Steven Spielberg, Lawrence Kasdan, and Philip Kaufman discussing ideas for what would eventually be *Raiders of the Lost Ark.*

There are references to the kind of movie they want to make, which was in line with the Republic Serials of the 1930s (featuring characters like Buck Rogers, Zorro, and Fu Manchu), military movies (*The Guns of Navarone*), Westerns (*The Good, the Bad and the Ugly*), action/adventure *(The Wind and the Lion)*, and James Bond movies. And they drew inspiration from a wide variety of books: *Moby Dick, Lord of the Rings*, and the *Bible.*

As they develop the character of Indiana Jones they talk about the hero mold of John Wayne, Clint Eastwood, and Sean Connery. Other movies and actors that came up included Humphrey Bogart (*Treasure of the Sierra Madre, Casablanca*), Steve McQueen (*The Great Escape, Nevada Smith*), Toshiro Mifune (*Seven Samurai*), and Clark Gable (*Soldier of Fortune*). Perhaps Jones is a gambler like Rhett Butler in *Gone with the Wind.*

When they say they'd like to find a stuntman who can act—someone both goofy and dangerous—Burt Reynolds is mentioned (he was not far removed from starring in *Deliverance* and *Smokey and the Bandit*). They talk about Jones wearing a leather jacket and a felt hat and being "good with a bullwhip. That's really his trademark." They discuss him as an archeologist, an anthropologist, and a "bounty hunter of antiquities" who is also a college professor. Spielberg says, "I like that. The doctor with the bullwhip."

They toss out possible locations to shoot: Bombay, New Delhi, Hong Kong, Rome, South America, Mexico, Berlin, London, Nepal, Paris, the Mediterranean, Japan, and South Africa. They kick around ideas for cliffhangers involving seaplanes, spiders, snakes, a fight in the cab of a truck, camels, monkeys, skeletons, speedboats, Nazis, poisonous darts, and of course, a cave with "a sixty-five-foot boulder" on an incline that Indiana Jones has to outrun. Spielberg says at one point, "What we're just doing here, really, is designing a ride at Disneyland." Mission accomplished.

There is no cookie cutter way to come up with story ideas and concepts, but they seem to appear most often when writers are looking for them. Forming them into a story. Sometimes they start with a character. And that is where our next chapter leads us.

3 CHARACTERS

"Why is Shakespeare the greatest dramatist who ever lived? Because he wrote great characters."
—Actor John Barrymore

"I'm drawn to provocative characters that find themselves in extreme situations. And I think I'm drawn to that consistently."
—Oscar and Emmy winner Kathryn Bigelow (*The Hurt Locker*)

THE END OF THE ROPE CLUB

"I'm not interested in characters who aren't broken."
—John Logan, Oscar-nominated screenwriter (*Gladiator*)

"I was trying to put Glass [Leonardo DiCaprio's character in *The Revenant*] through as many insane things as possible."
—Screenwriter Mark L. Smith

"I would never write about someone who was not at the end of his rope."
—Novelist Stanley Elkin

I've always been fond of the "end of the rope" quote by Elkin and I thought I'd put together a short list of movies from this century with Oscar nominations that are about characters at the end of their ropes:

12 Years a Slave (with a gut-wrenching literal end of the rope scene)
127 Hours
The Artist

A Beautiful Mind
Black Swan
Bridesmaids
Cast Away
Children of Men
Dallas Buyers Club
Erin Brockovich
Flight
The Florida Project
Get Out
Gladiator
Gravity
Halloween
Her
Hotel Rwanda
The Hurt Locker
Ikiru
Into the Wild
Joker
Les Miserables
The Pursuit of Happyness
A Quiet Place
Seabiscuit
Spirited Away
Toy Story 3
Training Day
Winter's Bone
The Wrestler

"Any character who is going to drive the story has to grab and hold the audience's attention at all times. There must be no dead time, no treading water, no padding in the story (and no more metaphors to hammer home the point)."
—John Truby
The Anatomy of Story

"Who is your hero, what does he want, and what stands in his way?"
—Paddy Chayefsky

"Rather than tell the audience who the character is, I like to show the audience what a character wants."
—Aaron Sorkin

"[Wile E. Coyote's] one goal in life is to catch the Road Runner. Nothing will force him to give up."
—David Mamet

Dramatists don't all agree on technique, but when Paddy Chayefsky, Aaron Sorkin, and David Mamet all basically agree on the same approach (a character wanting something), it might be wise to follow their lead.

SCREENWRITING AND IDENTITY

"Thanks in part to the plethora of new books and seminars on screenwriting, a new phenomenon is taking over Hollywood: Major scripts are skillfully, seductively shaped, yet they are soulless. They tend to be shiny but superficial."
—Screenwriter and UCLA screenwriting professor Richard Walter

"Where do we go to solve life's problems? We go to the movies. . . . Stories are the language of the heart."
—Author John Eldredge
Wild at Heart

When we look at characters, let's consider what make movies work, beyond the level of entertainment.

It once seemed like *The Shawshank Redemption* was playing on some TV channel every day. The film trades places with *The Godfather* on IMDB.com as a fan favorite film. It's the highest rated film by *Yahoo! Movies* and by the 2006 readers of *Empire* magazine. *The Shawshank Redemption* resonates with a wide variety of people. Very few of them were once in a prison in Ohio. Rather, we need hope to cope with all of life's danger, toils and snares. We can sympathize with Andy Dufresne and his predicament.

For any writer looking for excuses to not write, don't look to Stephen King. Long before he wrote the novella that would become *The Shawshank Redemption*, he was an unpublished writer with a stack of rejection letters, and teaching high school English in Hampden, Maine.

Once King achieved some success, he had to deal with a drug and alcohol addiction. Later in life, while taking a walk, he was hit by a van while the driver was reaching for "one of those Mars bars." Despite enduring a collapsed lung, a broken leg in nine places, a shattered hip, as well as much physical therapy and pain, King is still cranking out stories.

Stephen King understands hard times.

We understand hard times, too. Hard times are a universal theme.

"Sometimes there just aren't enough rocks."
Forrest in *Forrest Gump* (as Jenny collapses after throwing rocks at her abandoned childhood home where she was abused)

"Are you going to be something else I have to survive?"
Erin (Julia Roberts) in *Erin Brockovich*

"I coulda been somebody."
Terry (Marlon Brando) in *On the Waterfront*

"You don't throw a whole life away just 'cause it's banged up a little."
Tom (Chris Cooper) in *Seabiscuit*

"Sometimes I wish I was dead."
Precious (Gabourey Sidibe) in *Precious*

"Things fall apart; the centre cannot hold."
—Poet William Butler Yeats
The Second Coming

"I wish I could tell you that Andy fought the good fight, and the Sisters let him be. I wish I could tell you that, but prison is no fairy-tale world."
Red (Morgan Freeman) in *The Shawshank Redemption*

I think *Shawshank*'s ongoing popularity is due to its ability to transcend the level of raw entertainment. Director Frank Darabont talks about getting many letters from people thanking him for making that film because it helped them through a difficult time in their life.

It's doubtful that when King wrote the *Shawshank* story or when Darabont wrote the script that either were thinking that this male-dominated prison story would bring comfort to a woman going through a divorce or who had lost a child. But good stories have a way of creeping into our lives in unexpected ways. These are the timeless, evergreen movies.

In workshops I've given, it's amazing to see how the same films pop up when I ask which films people watch over and over again. (Many of these movies are also often discussed on *The Rewatcables* podcast and Facebook group.):

Apollo 13	*It's a Wonderful Life*
Babe	*Jerry Maguire*
Back to the Future	*The Karate Kid*
Braveheart	*Pretty Woman*
Casablanca	*The Princess Bride*
Do the Right Thing	*Raiders of the Lost Ark*
Ferris Bueller's Day Off	*Remember the Titans*
Field of Dreams	*Rain Man*
Fight Club	*Sense and Sensibility*
Forrest Gump	*Star Wars*
Gladiator	*Top Gun*
Good Will Hunting	*Up*
Groundhog Day	*When Harry Met Sally*
Hoosiers	*The Wizard of Oz*

Something resonates in those films with large groups of people. Director Robert Zemeckis (*Forrest Gump, Back to the Future*) once said on a DVD commentary that his films were a mixture of spectacle and humanity. This seems true of most of the films I just listed. They are also films that are strong on theme, a topic I'll address in greater detail in Chapter Eight.

When we write we are writing about ourselves. A great benefit of writing is self-discovery. The odds are good that in the films you see over and over again, you are identifying in a special way with a character or a situation.

This is where we tap into writing beyond the numbers. It's the reason that films that don't fit the typical Hollywood mold find an audience.

Have you ever walked into a show home and been impressed at first, only to determine later that it's well-decorated but impersonal? The house I grew up in had a place in our kitchen where we had a growth chart on a wall. It was up in had a place in our kitchen where we had a growth chart on a wall.

It was fun to look back over the years and see how I had grown. I've never seen a growth chart in a show home. No worn-out carpet, no stacks of paper, no drawings by the kids on the refrigerator. Nothing authentic. No sign of life.

Just as your home should be full of stories and memories—and life—so should your screenplays.

"There should be something in the writing that indicates that it was written by a person."
—William Zinsser
On Writing Well

What sets your writing apart? The answer is the same thing that sets you apart from the crowd: your vision, your life experiences, and your worldview. This is where your voice comes from. It's why first-time writers (like Diablo Cody) sometimes break in with an original story. This insight is a big part of my inspiration behind my blog *Screenwriting from Iowa . . . and Other Unlikely Places*. It's why I think writers from outside L.A., or writers in L.A. who maintain their hometown non-L.A. roots, have a unique opportunity to show audiences something new.

"If you try to write honestly about yourself, you're writing about every single individual in the world."
—Oscar and Emmy nominated screenwriter Walter Brown Newman

"I think it's impossible to be a writer and not draw from your own life. . . . I see shadows all of the time in my work—things from my life."
—Screenwriter Robin Swicord (*The Curious Case of Benjamin Button*)
The Dialogue interview with Jay A. Fernandez

Everyone desires the same basic things: food, shelter, love, purpose, and dignity.

Primal needs.

You don't have to be a salesman to identify with Willy Loman's need for significance in *Death of a Salesman*. In fact, *Salesman* itself was an effort by

Miller to show that you don't have to be a king or a queen to understand the significance of tragedy. Despite what the ancients seemed to assume, even the significance of tragedy. Despite what the ancients seemed to assume, even an average old salesman experiences tragedy, and his drama is equally profound. Great drama connects to universal primal instincts, regardless of the characters' backgrounds.

Sometimes as writers we jump through all kinds of strange hoops trying to guess what will sell. We err on one side by trying to write the sensational story that everyone will love and on the other side by writing the small personal story where nothing really happens.

"It's all one story, really, the story of who we are and how we relate and how we get it wrong."
—Screenwriter Ron Bass (*Rain Man*)

"We spend much of our lives trying to reconcile these two halves of our spirit and soul — call it identity —as we struggle to figure out just what and who we genuinely are…The reason we go to movies is precisely to explore these perpetually unanswerable questions regarding our identity."
—Richard Walter

Think about how these films deal with the theme of identity (Who am I?):

Big	*Office Space*
Elf	*Moneyball*
Fight Club	*Seabiscuit*
Finding Nemo	*Sense and Sensibility*
The Incredibles	*Shrek*
The Lion King	*Toy Story*
The Matrix	*Training Day*

We can identify with not only people, but pigs, fish, horses, and ogres.

Every once in a while, a movie character literally looks in the mirror while they have a brief existential crisis moment. Instead of a man in the mirror moment, Bud Fox (Charlie Sheen) in *Wall Street* looks over New York City at night and says, "Who am I?" (A little on the nose even in 1987.)

Fox is having an identity crisis. Is he moving away from being like his honest father and toward the amoral Gordon Gekko? That battle for identity is played out in movie after movie. From *Babe* to *Bridesmaids*.

Just before Jerry Maguire writes his famous mission statement he says, "I hated my place in this world." Who hasn't identified with that thought at some point in their life? (Writer/director Cameron even sneaks in man in the mirror moment as Maguire has some doubts about his life-changing memo going out.)

When Mulan sees her reflection she sings, "When will my reflection show who I am inside?" The "I want" or "I wish" songs have a long history in musicals of overtly stating what a character wants. From Snow White waiting for her prince charming to Dorothy yearning for a place where "dreams really do come true."

Simba in *The Lion King* can't wait to be "a mighty king," Pocahontas wants to know "What's around the river bend." Rapunzel wants to know "just when will my life begin," Quasimodo wishes he could just be among the people, Ariel in *The Little Mermaid* wishes she was human, Belle in *Beauty and the Beast* wonders "There must be more than this provincial life," the *Fiddler on the Roof* dreams "if I were a rich man...,' and Moana wonders if she had wind in her sail how far she'd go.

Lin-Manuel Miranda (who wrote the *Moana* song) says, "Most of my favorite rap songs are 'I Want' songs in disguise. They are this, 'This is my world and I'm going to get out here.'"

Audiences connect in powerful ways with these characters and their desires. And more importantly they connect with not only what characters say they want or need, but the actions they take to accomplish their goals.

"Each film tells a story in which the central character seeks only to discover his own true identity."
—Richard Walter

"I finally became the man I always wanted to be."
Jerry Maguire's (Tom Cruise) mission statement written by Cameron Crowe

"Storytelling is how we make sense of the world."
—Rick DeMarinis
The Art & Craft of the Short Story

"Stories are equipment for living."
—Kenneth Burke

A writer at a seminar I once gave said movies were cheap therapy. Perhaps you've seen the book *Cinematherapy* which develops that concept. The practice of cinematherapy is widespread. Back when video rental stores were common, I saw a guy pick up *Braveheart* to rent and his girlfriend said, "You've watched that 100 times." He simply responded, "And I'll watch it 100 more times."

We want to be the hero of our own story, and we are inspired to do so by heroes of stories we read and watch. We identify with them. We identify with Luke Skywalker, Erin Brockovich, Cinderella, and even the Will Farrell character in *Elf*.

Not all films have strong identity themes, but those that do tend to not only have a large following, but they tend to do well at award time. Linda Seger points out in her book Advanced Screenwriting, "If we look at some Academy Award winners of the 1980s and 1990s, we can see identity theme shimmering through the philosophical, theological, and/or psychological ideas." That trend continues into the 2020s.

STRONG-WILLED CHARACTERS

"Find a strong-willed character with a nothing-will-stand-in-my-way determination to reach his or her goal confronting strong opposition, add a strong action line, keep throwing obstacles (conflicts) in his or her path, and you're well on your way to a gripping screenplay."
—William Froug

"Strong characters hold our interest in life and on the screen."
—Andrew Horton

We don't have to go very far in theater, literature, or narrative or documentary films to see a pattern of strong willed characters—both saints and sinners to one degree or another (and many of them drawn from the pages of history):

Abraham Lincoln
Alexander the Great
Amelia Earhart
Annie Wilkes
Athena

Blanche DuBois
Bonnie and Clyde

Cain and Abel
Cleopatra
Desdemona
Don Vito Corleone

Darth Vader
Elephant Man
Ellen Ripley
Esther
Francis Farmer
Frankenstein

Gandhi
Genghis Khan

Hamlet

Hannibal Lecter
Harry Potter
Hitler
Indiana Jones
Iron Man
Jesus
Joan of Ark

James Bond
Joseph Stalin
Josephine March
Juliet
Katniss Everdeen

King Lear

King David

Lawrence of Arabia
Mad Max
Margaret Thatcher
Martin Luther
Martin Luther King Jr.
Morpheus

Moses

Nero
Nixon

Norma Rae Webster
Othello
Obi-Wan Kenobi
Queen Elizabeth I
Quasimodo
Patton
Robin Hood
Rocky
Rosa Parks
Rambo
R2-D2
Sacagawea
Scarlet O'Hara
Snow White
Tin Man
Tarzan
Ultraman
Virgil Tibbs
Vincent Vega
Wicked Witch of the West
Wonder Woman
X-Men (Professor X)
Yoda
Zeus
Zorro

It's been said that the History Channel could be called the Hitler Channel because he plays such a key role in many of their programs. Every year it also seems there are at least one or two movies that have something to do with Hitler or World War II.

How memorable are the characters you've created? Do you write characters that are as fascinating to watch as animals at the zoo?

Not every character you write has to be as fascinating as Gordon Gecko in Oliver Stone's *Wall Street,* but your protagonist and antagonist must be somebody we are interested in investing two hours of our lives watching. They could be a shark or a robot, but whatever they are, makes them stand out. You don't even have to shoot the bad guy at the end. Jake LaMotta in *Raging Bull* is despicable, but he's certainly a fascinating case study.

"I'm not interested in having to root for someone; I'm trying to get some sort of understanding as to what makes people tick and what they're about."
—Joe Eszterhas (*Basic Instinct*)

If you do write about an ordinary person, it's best if you put them in an extraordinary situation. Chuck Nolan (Tom Hanks) is a FedEx manager who is involved in a plane crash in *Cast Away,* Roger Thornhill (Cary Grant) in *North by Northwest* is caught-up in a mistaken identity situation and must run for his life, and Clarice Starling (Jodie Foster) *in The Silence of the Lambs* is an FBI candidate (a little less ordinary, but still a student) when she is thrust into a situation to help capture a serial killer.

It is easier to write a strong bad guy than a strong good guy. Effective dramatic structure dictates that when you throw your protagonist and antagonist into the ring, it should be a fair battle. Plus, actors love to play compelling bad guys. For every Atticus Finch (*To Kill a Mockingbird*), there are multiple Norman Bates-like (*Psycho*) characters actors want to play.

Many of the greatest characters in cinema are a mixture of saint and sinner. Isn't there a mixture of Jekyll and Hyde in all of us? Don't we love to go to movies and watch complex characters wrestle with life, with themselves? Showing that struggle is part of what makes your characters engaging and memorable. It gives your characters dimensionality.

What is it about your characters that make them memorable? What obstacles are they trying to overcome? How do they respond to setbacks?

Great characters are not lukewarm.

GOOD BAD PEOPLE

"The better the villain, the better the picture."
—Alfred Hitchcock

"Your bad guy must always be taking action. He's always plotting. Planning, stealing, killing, wounding, belittling, or scraping cheese off your pizza. If the bad guy isn't constantly making (more and more clever) moves, he's not much of a bad guy."
—William M. Akers
Your Screenplay Sucks!: 100 Ways to Make it Great

"The antagonist must be as strong as the protagonist. The wills of conflicting personalities must clash."
—Lajos Egri

Egri says this strong unity of opposites creates an "unbreakable bond" that leads to the climax of your story. One of the best bad guys in modern cinema is Col. Hans Landa (Christopher Waltz) in *Inglourious Basterds*.

ORPHAN CHARACTERS

"When a hero starts his life as an orphan, it is to show he has nothing to lose. He is unattached and unencumbered by family ties and social obligations, so he is usually portrayed as an orphan to indicate that he is not saddled with the normal attachments the rest of us have."
—Michael Chase Walker
Power Screenwriting

Michael Chase Walker's *Power Screenwriting* provides a concise and instructive 1-page summary of the role of orphans in literature and the movies (Walker, in turn, points to Carol Pearson's *The Hero Within* for many of his insights). Walker helped me realize that there are orphans running all over the place in cinematic history. While the orphan can literally be an orphan, he or she usually isn't. Walker clarifies, "The orphan/hero today is created by giving your main character a single and footloose status. He may be divorced, widowed, abandoned, handicapped or a maverick. It doesn't matter. The point is that the heroes and heroines must be free to seek their destiny and reclaim their birthright."

Think of how these characters and/or movies represent orphans, literally or figuratively:

Annie
Babette's Feast
Bambi
Batman
C.C. "Bud' Baxter (*The Apartment*)
Cinderella
Charles Foster Kane (*Citizen Kane)*
Don Draper (*Man Men*)
Dorothy (*The Wizard of Oz*)
Elf
Elsa (Frozen)
E.T.
Erin Brockovich
The Firm
Forrest Gump
Gladiator
Harry Potter
Heidi
Jane Eyre
James Bond
Jerry Maguire
The Lion King
Luke Skywalker
Neo (*The Maxtrix*)
Rocky
Seabiscuit
Snow White
Spiderman

Tarzan
Viktor Vavorski (Tom Hanks's character in *The Terminal*)
Will Hunting (*Good Will Hunting*)
The Wrestler

Note: Clint Eastwood made a career out of playing orphan characters.

Orphans in movies are often lost and alone as they begin their journey. They can't phone home because there is no one home. Is there any wonder that audiences connect with such characters? Novelist Charles Dickens had great success with many orphan characters including Pip, David Copperfield, and Oliver Twist.

STAY WITH THE MONEY

"'Stay with the money.' The audience came to see the star. The star is the hero; the drama consists solely in the quest of the hero."
—David Mamet
Bambi vs. Godzilla

One of the great things about watching films repeatedly is you begin to notice little details and see patterns emerge. Ideally the first time you watch a movie you are simply engaged in the story and entertained. Then you go back as a screenwriter looking for clues as to what made the film work, and more importantly how this can make you become a better screenwriter and filmmaker.

One thing you'll notice in many character-driven films—*The Verdict, A Beautiful Mind, Erin Brockovich, Juno,* and *Nightcrawler* come to mind—is that the main characters are in every scene (or almost every scene) in the movie. And if they're not in the scene, chances are good that scene is still about them.

WRITING ACTOR BAIT

"Producers and directors buy a property because they like the story.

Actors buy it because they see them-selves in a part. "
—Jerry Lewis
The Total Film-Maker

"If you want to attach a star, then you really need to have a great protagonist. A protagonist who is really active, who is really initiating the action of the movie, who's responsible for the forward momentum of the narrative."
—Christopher Lockhart, WME Story Editor
Script magazine, January/February 2012

If you want to see Lockhart's words in action, watch *Flight* starring Denzel Washington. It's not hard to understand why Oscar-winner Washington was attracted to the script by John Gatins. In an interview with Miki Turner in *The Root,* Washington said of his pilot role, "The complexity was wonderful to play. . . . [T]his was an adventure. Starting with the screenplay and the collaboration with the filmmaker, getting a chance to fly around in flight simulators, hanging upside down in a plane and playing a drunk."

Not every film is a Hollywood film, but if you want to attract a name actor to your script, you have to consider what kind of bait you are using. Having meaningful conflict and a solid concept is a great start. Having a three-dimensional lead character with a narrative arc is desired.

When Kevin Costner was at or near the peak of his movie star power, he was offered the lead role in *Field of Dreams.* Having just made the baseball movie *Bull Durham,* he was apprehensive about doing another baseball-related movie. But there was one scene in the script that made him say yes to doing the movie. It's the scene at the end of the film when Costner's character asked his dad (who is one of the ghost players) if he'd like to play catch. Reading that moment in the script made him catch his breath.

"I get so much credit for this, but Phil Robinson is the guy who wrote [the *Field of Dreams* script]. I never would have done that movie based on a pitch. I did it based on the script. And I knew the script had gold dust on it. I didn't know obviously that it would become part of the vocabulary. I didn't know 30 years later it would find its way into the hearts of the people the way it did. But it found its way into my heart, and that's why I said I'm going to do this movie in the corn."
—Kevin Costner
Interview on *The Bill Simmons Podcast*

He did do the movie set in a cornfield, and that visceral response that Costner had when he read the script also made the hair stand up on the backs of millions of viewers and caused grownups to weep. My guess is it had less to do with Costner's character and more to do with plenty of people who would love to have an opportunity to reconnect with a deceased parent one last time, and perhaps patch up some unfinished business.

And why even more than 30 years after the movie's release that people still flock to the *Field of Dreams* movie site in eastern Iowa. Keep in mind that you can even write actor bait for your non-lead roles.

"If you make your minor characters as interesting as you possibly can in the space that you've got, better actors will play them. And your film has more chance commercially."
—Nick Hornby (*An Education, Brooklyn*)
The Q&A with Jeff Goldsmith

Of course, there are various reasons why a star or name actor says yes to a role, including one actor who said he did a movie because it was being shot in a cool location that would seem like a vacation.

THE ART OF DRAMATIC WRITING

"The pivotal character knows what he wants . . . without him the story flounders . . . in fact, there is no story."
—Lajos Egri

One of the hang-ups that some people have with the classic writing book *The Art of Dramatic Writing* by Lajos Egri is that its focus is on theater. And while some of the references remain well-known plays today, others are more obscure.

So I've decided to give the 50+year old book a little contemporary injection by connecting Egri's thoughts to a more recent film. He starts his book by discussing premise and follows it by considering character.

What some people call the protagonist, hero, or main character, Egri also calls "the pivotal character."

"A pivotal character must not merely desire something. He must want it so badly that he will destroy or be destroyed in the effort to attain his goal. . . . A good character must have something very vital at stake."
—Lajos Egri

Getting back to Chuck Nolan, the plane crashed pilot in *Cast Away*, screenwriter William Broyles Jr. gave Nolan plenty at stake. First there is just the survival issue of living on a deserted island, yearning for home and willing to risk his life to return to it. Additionally, though, there is also the issue of his fiancé back home. Even if he survives and returns home, will his fiancé have waited for him or assumed he died in the accident?

"A pivotal character is a driving force, not because he decided to be one. He becomes what he is for the simple reason that some inner or outer necessity forces him to act; there is something at stake for him, honor, health, money, protection, vengeance, or a mighty passion."

Later in the chapter Egri applies this point to those who have a desire to write, act, sing, or paint by saying that 99% of them are driven by caprice or whim. Egri writes, "Ninety-nine percent usually give up before they have a chance to achieve anything. They have no perseverance, no stamina, no physical or mental strength, the inner urge to create is not strong enough."

So write strong, willful pivotal characters. And be one yourself.

SIMPLE STORIES/COMPLEX CHARACTERS

"I like simple stories and complex characters."

—Oscar-winning screenwriter Billy Bob Thornton (*Sling Blade*)
Roger Ebert, "Filmmaker Fills Simple Stories with Complex Folks"

Recently I watched two modern classics, *Deliverance* and *Scent of a Woman*, and read the script again for *Juno*. Although these movies are different in genre and were made in three different decades, they have at least one thing in common: they are simple stories.

Four guys on a canoe trip in a remote area are attacked and tormented by sadistic locals. A prep school kid takes a short-term caretaker job and has a life-changing experience with a retired Army Lieutenant Colonel. A teenage girl gets pregnant. Simple.

While *Deliverance, Scent of a Woman,* and *Juno* are simple stories, certainly the main characters are complex. Revisit the scripts of those films written by James Dickey, Bo Goldman, and Diablo Cody to see how they weaved their craft.

But don't confuse simplicity with being simplistic, though.

Robert McKee writes in *Story,* "My advice to most writers is to design relatively simple but complex stories. 'Relatively simple,' doesn't mean simplistic." He points to the French toast scene in *Kramer vs. Kramer* as a simple but complex scene. On the surface it's a scene with a father making breakfast for his son. But it's really a complex scene as Dustin Hoffman's character is in conflict with himself (inner-personal conflict), his son who is telling him he's doing it wrong (personal conflict), the kitchen (environment/extra-personal), and he's even at conflict with his wife who is absent from the scene but also the main reason he's having all these other conflicts.

"Plot is just not my gift. I'm fascinated with complex characters, and that doesn't mix well with complex plots."
—Oscar-nominated Taylor Sheridan (*Hell or High Water, Yellowstone*)

"I'm a big fan of simple stories, complex characters. I love when stories get from here to here. I know then I'll have room for great character stuff to go on."
—Screenwriter Stuart Beattie (*Collateral*)

Stuart Beattie's screenplay for *Collateral* tells a simple story. A hit man catches a cab at night with the goal of killing five people before taking a morning flight out of LAX. That simplicity allowed Beattie to add complexity to the characters played by Tom Cruise and Jamie Foxx. For example, Cruise's character is a hit man who also has a knowledge and appreciation of jazz music. One of his hits takes place in a jazz club.

"[The jazz scene] is modeled after two favorite scenes of mine, *True Romance* with Christopher Walken and Dennis Hopper . . . and the

Luc Besson movie *La Femme Nikita* when he takes her to the restaurant and you think, oh great—he's finally taking her out. And here's the gun, here are the people. And the whole thing changes on a dime. I love those kind of scenes and I wanted that kind of scene in *Collateral*."

—Stuart Beattie
The Dialogue: Learning from the Masters interview with Mike De Luca

In *Schindler's List*, Ralph Fiennes' character Amon Goeth (known as the "Butcher of Plaszów") is depicted as someone who is moved by classical music yet has no problem standing on his balcony and casually shooting Jews in a forced labor camp. Comparable to Cruise's hitman in *Collateral*, a violent character is made more compelling as a character by giving him a soulful, musical side.

Beattie admires screenwriter Steve Zaillian, who won an Oscar for writing *Schindler's List*. The chances are good that *Schindler's List* is in what Beattie calls his "personal reference library."

THE ACTIVE PROTAGONIST

"One of the hardest concepts for new screenwriters to master is the active protagonist. Passive protagonists populate the pages of countless screenplays."
—Linda Cowgill
"Creating Characters Who Work for You, Not Against You"
Now Write! Screenwriting, edited by Sherry Ellis and Laurie Lamson

A great example of an active protagonist is 17-year-old Ree Dolly (Jennifer Lawrence) in *Winter's Bone* (screenplay by Debra Granik and Anne Rosellini, based on a novel by Daniel Woodrell).

Dolly needs to find her missing father or risk losing the family's house. So she actively sets out to find where her father is, despite this taking her to some ugly places. (Ugly places = Conflict.)

A look at any list of popular movie characters will be full of active protagonists. (And active antagonists.)

Aron Ralston (*127 Hours*)
Axel Foley (*Beverly Hills Cop*)
The Bride (*Kill Bill: Vol. 1*)
Chris Washington (*Get Out*)
Darth Vader
Dorothy Gale (*The Wizard of Oz*)
Django (*Django Unchained*)
Ferris Bueller
Indiana Jones
Iron Man
Leigh Anne Tuohy, (*The Blind Side*)
Michael Corleone
Norman Bates
Scarlett O'Hara

CHARACTER WOUND

"Most of us have some old pain or hurt that we don't think about all the time, but which is always vulnerable on some level of awareness. . . . To humanize a hero or any character, give her a wound, a visible, physical injury or deep emotional wound."
—Christopher Vogler
The Writer's Journey

"All characters are wounded souls, and the stories we tell are merely an acting out of the healing process. They are the closing of open wounds, the scabbing-over process."
—Richard Krevolin
Screenwriting from the Soul

There are many ways a wound can be expressed in a character. It can be a physical wound like "Ratso" Rizzo's limp in *Midnight Cowboy*, the daughter's hearing in *A Quiet Place,* and Nemo's damaged fin in *Finding Nemo*. But, as in those cases, there are internal wounds are well.

CHARACTER FLAWS 101

"Well, nobody's perfect."
Classic last line from *Some Like it Hot*

"The main character's persona is plagued with a flaw, and as this flaw is tested throughout the story, the main character integrates a greater understanding of overcoming the flaw through the lessons of life that are expressed by the story."

—Kate Wright
Screenwriting is Storytelling

Nothing quite sells news like a fallen hero. Every year the list grows of famous and accomplished politicians, entertainers, and athletes who we eventually learn are not flawless people. The world (or your local community) recently discovered that _____ _____ is not perfect. The news of imperfection—of character flaws—still makes the news. It always has, and always will.

"Who is it that can tell me who I am?"
King Lear in Shakespeare's *King Lear*

"I've never known a better seaman, but as a man, he's a snake. He doesn't punish for discipline. He likes to see men crawl. Sometime, I'd like to push his poison down his own throat."
Lt. Fletcher Christian regarding Captain Bligh
Mutiny on the Bounty (1935)

"One of the things that made Captain Bligh in *Mutiny on the Bounty* an unforgettable character was the way in which his chief qualities— cruelty and hardness—were stressed even to the point of having him order the continued flogging of a man who died under the lash. The character who has no dominating trait or traits offers nothing of dramatic value."
—Screenwriter Frances Marion
How to Write and Sell Film Stories

Flaws can be external and/or internal so they offer ample room for conflict.

Character flaws in movies are not always spelled out as clearly as they are in *The Wizard of Oz*, but it's hard not to have a flawed character in a film because the cornerstone of drama is conflict.

Protagonists and antagonists both have flaws. The major difference tends to be the protagonist/hero generally must overcome his or her flaw for growth, whereas the antagonist is often defeated due to his or her great flaw. Even in tragic endings where protagonists do not learn from their mistakes, grow as people, or defeat evil (*Death of a Salesman, Chinatown, Citizen Kane, Scarface*), there is a warning shot felt in the heart of the viewer.

Here's a list of key character flaws in some well-known movies:

Anger: Billy Beane (Brad Pitt) in *Moneyball*, Ron Kovic (Tom Cruise) in *Born on the Fourth of July*, Harry Callahan (Clint Eastwood) in *Dirty Harry*, Ike Turner (Laurence Fishburne) in *What's Love Got to Do with It*, Tommy DeVito (Joe Pesci) in *Goodfellas*

Dishonesty: Fletcher Reede (Jim Carrey) in *Liar! Liar!*, Alonzo (Denzel Washington) in *Training Day*, Frank Abagnale Jr. (Leonardo DiCaprio) in *Catch Me If You Can, Keyser Söze* (Kevin Spacey) *in The Usual Suspects*

Drug/alcohol dependence: Frank Galvin (Paul Newman) in *The Verdict*, Gwen Cummings (Sandra Bullock) in *28 Days*, Ben Sanderson (Nicolas Cage) in *Leaving Las Vegas*, Don Birnam (Ray Milland) in *The Lost Weekend*, Whip Whitaker (Denzel Washington) in *Flight, Rick Dalton* (Leonardo DiCaprio) in *Once Upon a Time … in Hollywood*

Greed/hunger for power: Darth Vader in *Star Wars*, Gordon Gekko (Michael Douglas) and Bud Fox (Charlie Sheen) in *Wall Street*, Miranda Priestley (*The Devil Wears Prada*)

Infidelity: *The Graduate, Body Heat, Unfaithful, One Night Stand*

Manipulative: Catherine Tramell (Sharon Stone) in *Basic Instinct*, Terence Fletcher (*J.K. Simmons*) in *Whiplash*, Hannibal (Anthony Hopkins) in *The Silence of the Lambs*

Mental illness: John Nash (Russell Crowe) in *A Beautiful Mind*, Norman Bates (Anthony Perkins) in *Psycho*, Jack Torrance (*Jack Nicholson*) *in The Shining*, Captain Queeg (Humphrey Bogart) in *The Caine Mutiny*, Blanche DuBois (Vivien Leigh) in *A Streetcar Named Desire*, Colonel Kurtz (Marlon Brando) in *Apocalypse Now*, Alex (Glenn Close) in *Fatal Attraction*

Obsessiveness: Melvin Udall (Jack Nicholson) in *As Good as it Gets)*, Sally Albright (Meg Ryan) in *When Harry Met Sally*, Bob Wiley (Brian Murray) in *What About Bob?*, Joan Crawford *(Faye Dunaway) in Mommie Dearest*, Felix Unger *(Jack Lemmon) in The Odd Couple*, Howard Hughes (Leonardo DeCaprio*) in The Aviator*

Pride/arrogance: Hud Bannon (Paul Newman) in *Hud*, Maverick (Tom Cruise) in *Top Gun*, Lightning McQueen (Owen Wilson) in *Cars*, Jordan Belfort (Leonardo DiCaprio) in *The Wolf of Wall Street*

You could keep making list after list of character flaws (naiveté, narcissism, meekness, recklessness, promiscuity, etc.) and the only thing you'd find in common is that flaws play well on screen and have provided many memorable roles. And explains why Leonardo DiCaprio is mentioned four times in the above lists.

Why? Because flaws equal conflict.

And if you drill deeper, you'll notice that many Oscar nominated and Oscar winning roles have characters that have a combination of flaws.

In his documentary *Baseball: A Film by Ken Burns* (1994), and his 2010 follow-up with Lynn Novick, *Baseball: The Tenth Inning*, Burns addressed baseball heroes and their flaws. Gambling and drug-use are two of the flaws that haunt some of baseball's greatest legends.

"Loving contradictions is saying you love life. All our heroes have dark sides. Only in modern media culture would heroism mean perfection. The Greeks have told us heroism is a negotiation between strength and weakness. That defines heroism."
—Ken Burns
Orlando Sentinel article by Hal Boedeker

Many a writer has started with a strong character in mind. And if that character starts out in a world of conflict (or falls into it soon after the movie begins), and has a clear goal, then that strong character is on his or her way to driving a good story.

"Greek classical drama frequently afflicted the hero with a blind spot that prevented that character from seeing the error of his or her ways. This strategy still shows in films that range from character studies to epics, to action stories."
—Paul Lucey
Story Sense

Human flaws are one of the chief topics of concern throughout the history of both philosophy and religion. Where do our flaws come from, and what do we do about them? Why is it that every person and civilization since the beginning of time seems to be so messed up? Are we not born good? If flaws and sins are an inherent part of the human condition, what are the ramifications of this? These are huge questions.

For writers, though, what this means in practice is ultimately clear: this is a messed-up world with a whole cast of real-life flawed characters.

We're all trying to figure out why we're wired the way we're wired. We go to the movies, in part, to help answer this question. The side-benefit to writing flawed characters is that the audience not only identifies with them, but also actors love to play them. Great characters with flaws tend to be appreciated at the box office and at award time. It's a win-win approach.

Scott Beck, Bryan Woods, and John Krasinski not only use two flaws brilliantly in *A Quiet Place*, but they pay them off at the climax and conclusion of the film. The first is the father's inability to tell his daughter that he loves her until a key moment in the movie. And the second is when the daughter's (Millicent Simmonds) weakness—her deafness turns into a double strength as she uses it to defeat the creatures terrorizing her family.

"I always look for amazing characters who I find are fascinating, charming, flawed, romantic and in trouble."
—Oscar-winning writer/director David O. Russell

And that moment when your main character is in trouble is usually the catalyst that propels your story forward. That catalyst is so essential that it often leads to the ending that Aristotle said was surprising and inevitable.

4 CATALYST

HOW TO JUMP START YOUR STORY

"My psychological state when I start a screenplay is always the same. It's a mix of fear, anxiety, and insecurity."
—Oscar-winning screenwriter Akiva Goldsman (*A Beautiful Mind*)

Q. American Film: What is your philosophy on what constitutes good drama?
Steven Spielberg: For me, it's someone — a protagonist —who is no longer in control of his life, who loses control and then has to somehow regain it. That's good drama. All of my pictures have had external forces working on the protagonist. In almost every Hitchcock film, the protagonist loses control early in the first act. Then he not only has to get it back, he has to address the situation. That theme has to follow me through my films, too.
American Film magazine, June 1988

How do you start your story? Something must happen to set your story in motion. Some call this an inciting incident, an exciting incident, a hook, the call to adventure, or a catalyst. Author Margaret Atwood calls it a "break in the pattern." When this event or situation happens, it disrupts the life of your protagonist. It sets them on a quest.

"Whatever its nature, the inciting incident is an event that forces the future protagonist to take action. Think of the inciting incident as an electroshock."
—Yves Lavandier
Constructing a Story

It must be a dynamic event. It should rock the protagonist's world and they must fight to overcome it. Most of the time the catalyst is easy to spot.

Juno finds out she's pregnant (*Juno*).

E.T. misses his ride and gets stranded on earth (*E.T.*).

The Italian Stallion is picked to fight the champ (*Rocky*).

A shark eats a girl on a late-night swim in the ocean (*Jaws*).

A sports agent writes a controversial mission statement (*Jerry Maguire*).

Zack Mayo signs up for officer training (*An Officer and a Gentleman*).

Dr. Richard Kimble's wife is killed (*The Fugitive*).

Just before taking vows become a nun, a women learns she's Jewish (*Ida*).

Charlie Kane dies just after saying "Rosebud" (*Citizen Kane*).

A boyfriend dumps his girlfriend (*Legally Blond*).

Nemo is captured by a scuba diver (*Finding Nemo*).

A solider needs rescued in World War II (*Saving Private Ryan*).

A helicopter is shot down (*Black Hawk Down*).

Ferris decides to take the day off (*Ferris Bueller's Day Off*).

Will solves a difficult mathematical equation (*Good Will Hunting*).

An oven breaks on Thanksgiving Day (*Pieces of April*).

A large family goes on vacation but forgets one of the kids (*Home Alone*).

A law school grad takes an offer for a *seemingly* perfect job (*The Firm*)

A man floats face down in water, dead (*Sunset Boulevard*).

A man floats face down in water, alive (*The Bourne Identity*).

A boy's wish to become bigger is magically granted (*Big*).

A farmer hears a voice telling him "If you build it he will come" (*Field of Dreams*).

A special spider bites a high school student (*Spider-Man*).

A Japanese bureaucrat discovers he has terminal cancer (*Iriku*).

A marshal gets news that the bad guys are coming to town (*High Noon*).

"The overwhelming majority of stories are based on a need, a problem, or an unusual situation."
—Director Edward Dmytryk (*The Caine Mutiny*)

Often inciting incidents boil down to the worst things that can happen in your life:

Aging (*City Slickers*)
Divorce (*Kramer vs. Kramer*)
Fatal diagnosis (*The Bucket List*)
Financial crisis (*The Perfect Storm*)
Helicopter crash (*Black Hawk Down*)
Hijacking (*Captain Phillips*)
Illness (*The Doctor*)
Kidnapping (*All the Money in the World*)
Murder (*Witness*)
Natural disaster (*The Wizard of Oz*)
Plane crash (*Cast Away*)
Quitting a job (*Lost in America*)
Recession (*Indecent Proposal*)
Getting Shot (*Regarding Henry*)
Taking the seemingly perfect job (*The Firm*)
War (*Platoon*)

Like a boxer's one-two punch, there is often a set-up and then a payoff:

Jerry Maguire writes mission statement—then gets fired (*Jerry Maguire*).

Jack wins a ticket—then saves Rose from jumping to her death (*Titanic*).

Dr. Richard Kimble is falsely charged with his wife's murder—then decides to flee a wrecked bus and track down the real killer.

A shark attacks a young woman—the sheriff finds her body, or an arm at least.

Charlie Babbitt in *Rain Man* learns that he's basically been left out of his dead father's will. He does get a classic car and the award winning rose bushes, but not the money he hoped for. He then sets out to find out who the primary "beneficiary" is of his father's $3 million dollar estate.

Charlie Kane dies and a reporter sets out to discover the meaning of Kane's last word, "Rosebud." (Never mind that nobody is around to actually hear the word being said.)

You could argue in *Jaws* that if the girl dies in the ocean without her body being discovered, the case is written off as a drunken girl drowning. So is the inciting incident the attack or the discovered arm? Let's not get hung up on technical things or we'll say the beer she drank is the inciting incident . . . or the moment the beer was bought. Chalk it up to a cause and effect. Find your inciting incident, your catalyst, and get on with writing your story.

If the inciting incident doesn't happen, the movie doesn't happen. Writer Skip Press asks, "Will this event put my main character on a path to his ultimate goal from which there is no turning back?"

Sometimes this event happens in the first scene, often within the first ten pages, and 99.9% of the time it occurs within the story's first act. Apollo Creed chooses to fight Rocky at the 30-minute mark of the movie, making it a relatively late inciting incident.

When Syd Field studied scripts by Joe Eszterhas, he noticed, "In most cases . . . the inciting incident was a cinematic tool he used to set up the story from page one, word one."

If you've ever found yourself watching a movie and wondering when it's going to start, it's usually because the storytellers spent too much time setting up the inciting incident. This moment needs to come when it will have the most impact, but in our advertising saturated culture it can be hard for viewers (and studio readers) to wait too long for the inciting incident.

why screenwriting teachers repeatedly emphasize the first 10 pages of your script. It sets the tone of your story, and provides an indication of who the main characters are and what they want.

The inciting incident ideally happens on screen and must be dynamic. It gets our attention and the attention of our protagonist. If our protagonist doesn't react to this, then there is no story.

The climax of the film will ideally be tied to your inciting incident. Think of the catalyst and the climax like bookends that hold your story in place. Rocky is picked to fight Apollo Creed and the climax occurs when the fight concludes.

An inciting incident arouses a desire in the protagonist to go to the end of the line to resolve it. Rocky can't say, "I don't even have a locker. I'm a bum. Maybe I should take my life into a different direction." Well he could, but it's a different movie.

Your audience wants to know what your story is about. They want to be entertained. And they want to watch your characters wrestle with life issues. This is the real reason why we go to the movies. Human dramas are lived out on the screen in ways that help us with our own dramas.

Your inciting incident is what sets your protagonist in motion.

"As long as the protagonist wants something, the audience will want something."
—David Mamet (*The Verdict*)

"Find a character who's obsessed and you have a real driving line."
—Oscar-winning screenwriter Ron Bass (*Rain Man*)

Stephen King says he likes to put characters in "some sort of predicament and then watch them try to work themselves free."

THE MAJOR OR CENTRAL DRAMATIC QUESTION

"The MDQ [Major Dramatic Question] is the linchpin of the dramatic narrative – the purpose for which the story is being told."
—Christopher Lockhart

"Hunger for the answer to the Major Dramatic Question grips the audience's interest, holding it to the last act's climax."
—Robert McKee
Story

The inciting incident also sets up the script's major dramatic question. This whole concept of a Major Dramatic Question (MDQ)—some refer to it as a central dramatic question—is so important it could be page one of any screenwriting book. Kenneth Rowe writes about it in his book *Write that Play*, which was published in 1939, so even the term has been a staple of dramatic writing for a long time.

While I started this book with a chapter on conflict—and the importance of not boring the audience— you could argue that the major dramatic question is the overarching conflict of your story and what holds your audience's attention. When you watch the movie *Speed* the MDQ is "Is everyone on the bus going to survive?"

"The MDQ is the thing that keeps us watching, wondering how things will turn out. By the end of the movie, there will be—there must be—an answer to the MDQ. A 'yes' or a 'no.'"
—Daniel Noah
Writing Movies: The Practical Guide to Creating Stellar Screenplays
Gotham Writers' Workshop edited by Alexander Steele

According to the writers at Gotham Writers' Workshop, the way to find your MDQ is through your protagonist, who has a tangible goal with obstacles that present conflict in achieving that goal. Here are some MDQ examples they give:

Will Scarlet win Ashley? (*Gone with the Wind*)
Will Indy obtain the legendary Ark of the Covenant? (*Raiders of the Lost Ark*)
Will Clarice catch Buffalo Bill? (*The Silence of the Lambs*)
Will John McClane free the hostages? (*Die Hard*)

While a single MDQ isn't always clear (and sometimes it even shifts within the story—as it does in *Pyscho*), here are a broad range of films that come to mind when I think of the MDQ:

Will Rea (Jennifer Lawrence) find her father? (*Winter's Bone*)

Will Marlin find his son? (*Finding Nemo*)

Will Kramer be able to keep custody of his son? (*Kramer vs. Kramer*)

Will a freed slave find his wife? (*Django Unchained*)

Will the troops find Ryan before he's killed? (*Saving Private Ryan*)

Will Pee Wee find his bike? (*Pee Wee's Big Adventure*)

Will Phil (Bill Murray) find a way to stop reliving the same day over and over? (*Groundhog Day*)

Will E.T. get home? (*E.T.*)

Will Scotland find freedom from tyranny? (*Braveheart*)

Will three buddies find their friend—before his wedding? (*The Hangover*)

Will a man survive being buried alive? (*Buried*)

Will Josh complete his mission of replacing his dad's La-Z-Boy chair? (*The Puffy Chair*)

Will Neal (Steve Martin) make it home for Thanksgiving? (*Planes, Trains & Automobiles*)

Will a stranger protect a small western town against outlaws? (*High Plains Drifter*)

Will a sheriff protect a small western town against outlaws? (*High Noon*)

Will Erin bring justice to a small town? (*Erin Brockovich*)

Will Matt Damon's character reach his potential? (*Good Will Hunting*)

Will Ida return to the convent and become a nun? (*Ida*)

Will Butch, Sundance, and Etta make it to Bolivia and relive their heydays? (*Butch Cassidy and the Sundance Kid*)

Will C.C. Baxter (Jack Lemmon) get a promotion? (*The Apartment*)

Who killed the under-employed screenwriter? (*Sunset Blvd.*)

Who is Keyser Söze? (*The Usual Suspect*)

What is Rosebud? (*Citizen Kane*)

Will the drummer Ruben regain his hearing (*Sound of Metal*)

WME Story Editor Christopher Lockhart, in his blog post "Screenwriting 101," gives these examples:

Will Dorothy get back to Kansas? (The *Wizard of Oz*)

Will Sheriff Brody kill the shark? (*Jaws*)

Will Galvin win the case? (*The Verdict*)

Lockhart adds that while the MDQ tends to be external (physical), a connected internal dilemma (psychological) can be proposed in the form of minor dramatic question.

Will Galvin win back self-respect? (*The Verdict*)
Will Dorothy find her place in the world? (*The Wizard of Oz*)

Playing off of Lockhart's physical/psychological idea, let me consider two of my favorite films and ponder whether you can ask a single-layered, mashed-up question. Will Rocky beat Apollo Creed (physical/external) or at least go the distance with him, and thereby prove to himself that he's not a bum (internal/psychological)?

Is it possible for the MDQ to have a one-two punch?

Will Jerry land a large contract for his client and save his business, and get the girl? (*Jerry Maguire*)

In the indie film *Pieces of April*, "Will April find a way to cook a turkey for Thanksgiving AND make amends with her family?" Now we're tying in theme and climax into the MDQ, a powerful combination.

But it's the MDQ that drives the story and is tied to the major goal of your hero/protagonist. Lockhart drives home the importance of The Major Dramatic Question:

"The MDQ is the THROUGHLINE. It carries us from the END OF THE FIRST ACT through to the CLIMAX. The dramatic narrative builds to the climax – which is the dramatic and emotional pinnacle of the story. It is the moment of cathartic release."

There are always exceptions, and biopics and ensemble movies frequently seem to be the trickiest in terms of Major Dramatic Question. For instance, in both *Apollo 1* and *Schindler's List* the MDQ is not "Will the astronauts survive?" and "Will Schindler save lives in Nazi concentration camps" but a question of how they were accomplished.

The MDQ gives you, your story, and the audience a track to run on. Advancing the plot is simply moving toward answering the MDQ.

A REALLY SIMPLE WRITING RULE (VIA TREY PARKER)

"What should happen between every beat that you've written down, is either the word 'therefore' or 'but'. So you come up with an idea and write 'and this happens…and then this happens…' no, no, no. It should be 'this happens and therefore, this happens'. '*But,* this happens, *therefore,* this happens. . . .'"
—Trey Parker (*South Park*)
mtvU, "Stand In at NYU"

Parker's quote addresses causality, change, and conflict. It's not that Clarice Starling (Jodie Foster) in *The Silence of the Lambs* goes for a jog *and then* has a meeting with Jack Crawford (Scott Glenn). Rather, Clarice is on a run training to be an FBI agent *but* her run is disrupted with news that she has to meet with Crawford, *therefore* she learns about a serial killer that they want her to help capture. Something caused a change in the scene.

Randy Olson's book *Houston, We Have a Narrative* refines Parker's thought down to "ABT" (*and, but, therefore*). Olson gives credit to Frank Daniel for originally developing the concept of replacing "and" with "but" and "therefore."

Czechoslovakia-born Daniel's directed the Oscar-winning film *The Shop on Main Street* (1965), taught at FAMU film school in Prague, later taught screenwriting at USC, and became the first dean of the American Film Institute. David Lynch said of Daniel, "no one understood the art of film-making as he did." His approach to teaching continues at universities today in what is known as Daniel Methodology.

So far, we've looked at the importance of conflict, concept, characters, and catalyst. If you want to see all of that boiled down to a single getting hit with brass knuckles moment in a movie, watch the scene in *Dallas Buyers Club* just before the ten-minute mark.

That's when a doctor tells Ron Woodroof (Matthew McConaughey) that he's HIV positive. The doctor adds, "We estimate you have 30 days left to put your affairs in order." The screenplay by Craig Borten and Melisa Wallack deals with how Woodroof fights with that imminent death sentence.

5 CONSTRUCTION

"SCREENPLAYS ARE STRUCTURE."
—William Goldman
Adventures in the Screen Trade
(Goldman used all caps intentionally.)

"Poor plot construction is the bane of many a beginner. . . . [A] usual defect is a too weak conflict which, of course, results in a weak climax."
—Frances Marion

"Every scene should be an arrow pointing to the next scene."
—Ernest Lehman

William Goldman said, "writing a screenplay is in many ways similar to executing a piece of carpentry." David Mamet expanded that thought in *On Film Directing* when he wrote in detail how his hand-built house was two hundred years old and—if catastrophe free—would still be standing for another two hundred years.

He contrasted this with the counter-cultural architecture trends of the 1960s. Just 30 years later those houses that eschewed traditional design (and common sense) "fell down or are falling down or should be torn down."

Aaron Sorkin said that when he was writing the screenplay based on his play *A Few Good Men*, he'd not only never written a screenplay before, but he'd never even seen one. Nor was he versed in movies, because he was focused on theater. This was his crash course in learning screenwriting:

"I read as many screenplays as I could. I started to pay attention to movies, and I tried to figure out how to kind of crowbar this story into a three-act structure, which I was told movies have to be. So I fiddled around with the placement of some emotional climaxes in the story and then managed to turn it into three acts."
—Aaron Sorkin (*The Social Network*)
Zen and the Art of Screenwriting by William Froug

Sorkin also said he read William Goldman's classic screenwriting book *Adventures in the Screen Trade* as he was forming his early understanding of screenwriting. Sorkin considers Goldman "the dean of American screenwriters."

To borrow poet Robert Frost's words about writing in free verse, you are free to "play tennis without a net" and ignore structure in your screenwriting, skipping this entire chapter.

"Structure seems antithetical to the free-wheeling creative process we associate with creating fresh art. But it's essential to understand structure."
—Writer/director Rian Johnson (*Brick, Star Wars: The Last Jedi*)
Moviemaker magazine

Not everyone believes in three-act structure, or what one would consider a traditional narrative arc. There are movies that contain mini-plots or no plot at all. Movies like *Nashville, Boyhood, Blow-Up, Detroit, Wild Strawberries, Roma,* and *The Florida Project* fall into a less structured, more meandering category.

"I don't know what the hell a third act is. It's not a concern of mine."
—Oscar-winning screenwriter Charlie Kaufman (*Eternal Sunshine of the Spotless Mind*)

"Regarding [the structure of *The Florida Project*] my co-screenwriter Chris Bergosh . . . is actually very structured in his writing, he likes the three-act structure. I come from the other side of the spectrum where I can have a 10-minute Tarkovsky tracking shot that I'm intrigued by. We sort of meet somewhere in the middle."
—Writer/director Sean Baker
The Director's Cut podcast interview with Paul Schrader

One of my favorite films is *Tender Mercies.* I consider it to have a mini-plot, but I think what makes it work is that it hits you on an emotional level. Robert Duvall won his sole Academy Award for his role as a down and out country singer in this character study written by Horton Foote. (Foote also won an Academy Award for his script.) The downside is that mini-plot and non-plot movies tend to be less broadly acceptable and attract smaller audiences.

Non-plot and mini-plot films tend to be lower-budget art house films or government-funded global cinema. One of the conventions of art house movies is an offbeat flavor. They aim to use non-traditional, non-arc plot techniques to tell more abstract stories.

"In *Roma* there was only one draft. Because I decided what I was going to do was sit and start writing without any consideration to length, [without] any consideration to character structure, [and without] any kind of structure."
—Alfonso Cuarón (who wrote *Roma* in three weeks)

The epitome of a non-plot film in the United States is Andy Warhol's 1964 experimental film *Empire,* which originally had a run time of eight hours and five minutes. The black and white silent film included a five-minute stationary shot of the Empire State Building.

If Warhol's eight-hour film strikes you as extravagant, consider Swedish director Anders Weberg's 2016 release of a 7-hour trailer for his 720-hour (30-day) experimental film *Ambiancé.* But for the broadest audience, I think the following quote from an Oscar winner is a balanced look at structure:

"When I first started writing I don't think I paid much attention to structure, I relied more on inspiration. I thought inspiration was all that mattered and that structure would work itself out. Looking back on things I've done, I noticed there is a structure that I wasn't really aware of when I was doing it, which leads me to believe there's kind of a natural structure to storytelling that's inherent in almost all kinds of stories. Traditional stories anyway.
—Steve Zaillian (*Schindler's List*)

THE IMPORTANCE OF PAGE 1

"The most important and the most difficult page any new screenwriter will ever write is page one. The bald truth is that this page is your entrance into the world of professionals in the motion picture and/or television community."
—William Froug
Screenwriting Tricks of the Trade

People who read scripts for a living say they can usually tell the skill of a writer by reading just the first few pages of a script. Some go as far as saying they make a judgment on the script based on just the first page. At that point they are not evaluating things like plot or characters, but just the way you set up the story. How you handle the first scene description.

SCREENWRITING BY NUMBERS

"The length of a film should be directly related to the endurance of the human bladder."
—Alfred Hitchcock

Numbers play a key part in every production, from the slate that keeps track of takes to the crew's mileage. Screenplays are not exempt.

When you were a child, the chances are good that at some point you used one of those paint-by-numbers kits. You were supposed to use blue for number 1, yellow for number 2, and so on. When you finished painting in all the numbers you actually had a decent little painting (for a five-year-old).

That's not a bad way to approach writing, no matter your age. This might sound too cold, calculated, or superficial, but hang with me for a moment. It's easy to get confused about the numbers game. Advice from books, magazines, and blogs can be conflicting and confusing.

Screenwriting-by-numbers is simply a way to think about basic story structure, a way to demystify the process. Think of it like playing or watching a sport: it helps to know the game's parameters. Where are the court's boundaries? How high is the rim or the net? How are points scored? Or consider cooking, if you prefer. What amounts of each ingredient does the recipe require? To what degree can you improvise and change some of the ingredients and amounts, adding your own flourishes?

Attending to numbers takes nothing away from your originality, nothing away from the story you have a burning desire to tell. It does not diminish the status of a great athlete to shoot a basketball at the same ten-foot hoop everyone uses; rather it enhances her status. Understanding the game's limitations allows her greatness to emerge.

"Limitation stimulates the imagination."
—Graphic designer Milton Glaser

The idea of limits is one of my favorite aspects of screenwriting to consider. It's like pulling back the veil. It's easy to grasp and easy to follow, yet it's a hang-up for many writers because they overlook it. As Clint Eastwood says in *Dirty Harry*, "A man's got to know his limitations."

Part of knowing one's limitations is embracing a particular form for your script. For instance, how long can a short film be and still be eligible for an Oscar? According to the Academy "A short film is defined as a motion picture that is not more than 40 minutes in running time (including all credits)." The total run time of a 30-minute broadcast sitcom is around 22 minutes.

How long should a feature film script be? A coy but unhelpful response would be, "as long as it needs to be." In the feature film world (especially for the new screenwriter), the real answer is that most screenplays tend to fall between 90 and 120 pages.

You can rebel against that all you want (go ahead and point out the exceptions) but in reality, at roughly a page per minute, the majority of movies fall between an hour and a half and two hours in length. Why fight that? There is great freedom there.

A mighty river is powerful only if it has banks to contain it. Look at these highly regarded films from a variety of genres that fall within the 100-120 minute parameters:

The African Queen —105 minutes
The Bourne Ultimatum — 115 minutes
Casablanca — 102 minutes

Citizen Kane — 119 minutes
Finding Nemo —100 minutes
On the Waterfront — 109 minutes
Pretty Woman — 117 minutes
Psycho — 108 minutes
Raiders of the Lost Ark — 115 minutes
Sunset Boulevard —110 minutes

That's a pretty good list of films, but what about those under 100 minutes? You'll find more comedy and horror films here because if you can scare people or make them laugh for an hour and a half you've done your job. You'll also find low-budget films here because it's simply cheaper to make a film closer to 90 minutes than one that is 120 minutes. Films with small sets also tend to land in this timeframe.

Annie Hall — 94 minutes
The Farewell —98 minutes
Halloween — 91 minutes
Juno — 96 minutes
Monsters, Inc. — 92 minutes
A Quiet Place — 90 minutes
Reservoir Dogs — 99 minutes
Tiny Furniture—98 minutes
Twelve Angry Men —95 minutes
When Harry Met Sally — 95 minutes

Many other films are shorter than 90 minutes. Common in old B-Movie Westerns that played on double features and exploitation movies that were intended for drive in audiences, as well as classic horror and comedies.

Airplane — *88 minutes*
Bambi —68 minutes
Great Stagecoach Robbery — 64 minutes
The Bullfighters — 60 minutes (Laurel and Hardy)
The Cameraman — 76 minutes (Buster Keaton)
The Gold Rush — 82 minutes (Charlie Chaplin)
High Noon — 84 minutes
The Lion King – 88 minutes
The Raven — 86 minutes (Roger Corman)

She's Gotta Have It — 84 minutes
Stand by Me — 89 minutes
Stranger than Paradise — 89 minutes (using only master shots)
This is Spinal Tap — 82 minutes
Toy Story — 80 minutes

Perhaps you are the stubborn type and want to point out all the great films that are well over the two-hour mark. Let's deal with some of them.

Ben-Hur (1959) — 212 minutes
Dances with Wolves — 181 minutes
The Godfather — 175 minutes
Gone with the Wind — 201 minutes
Lord of the Rings: The Return of the King — 210 minutes
Titanic — 194 minutes

Most of those films just listed were all best-selling books first, so they had a built-in audience. And *Titanic* was based on a well-documented historic event. Even these films, though, fall between 3 and 4 hours. That's a relatively broad limitation, but a limitation nonetheless.

It's hard enough to get any film made, so if you're really interested in getting produced, why not improve your odds by writing a 90-minute screenplay? Keep in mind that low-budget producers are trying to keep their costs down. In Hollywood there are readers who get paid by the number of scripts they review. Human nature suggests that they'll choose to read the 90-page script before the 150-page script.

Embrace your limitations (especially if you're not an established writer).

THE 90-PAGE SCRIPT

So let's say you're setting out to write a 90-page script. Now what?

1-3 page scenes

Here's an interesting observation I've made simply from reading scripts and watching movies. Most scenes are between one and three pages in length. If that averages out to two pages per scene, the result is a 90-minute movie with 45 scenes.

Do you see the freedom here? Many writers could stop reading this right now and write down 45 scenes from their childhoods, or odd things that have happened to them at work. I'm not saying that you have a screenplay yet, but you may have an outline. Just 45 scenes. That's doable, right? There's nothing magical about 45 scenes, but it's a good number to shoot for. I hope you're beginning to see the freedom in writing-by-numbers.

When I first started writing screenplays, I wondered how to keep track of all my characters. Perhaps unsurprisingly, script readers have the same problem when reading scripts. This is why most screenplays only have four to six main characters. There's just not much room to develop strong characters beyond that.

One Protagonist/ One Antagonist

Limit yourself to one main protagonist and one main antagonist.

When you write your script, either your protagonist or antagonist should be in every scene (or at least have a really good reason why they're not there). Once I tuned into this, I've watched with awe how some writers include the protagonist in every scene. It's easy to find yourself going off on little tangents and subplots involving side characters. In general, resist this temptation.

Lots of White Space

When you read a screenplay of your favorite movie, the chances are good that there will be a lot of white on the page. Top screenwriters often write sparingly. You generally don't find big chunks of scene descriptions and thick lines of dialogue.

The Law of Three

I've read many great scripts that basically applied what I call the law of three. As you watch movies from now on, I think you too will see the pattern.

Three lines or fewer of dialogue.

Three characters or fewer per scene.

"It's difficult to have a lot of characters."
—Francis Ford Coppola

Most scenes involve three characters or fewer. There may be other characters around, but the main conversation is limited to three. It is hard to write—and hard to follow—more than three characters talking.

Three Subplots or Fewer

Generally, you are limited to three subplots in a story because, again, you have limited time to develop them.

As you watch films with the Law of Three in mind, I think you'll find that it is followed pretty closely.

How long does it take to write a screenplay? The answer is all over the place, but if you want some motivation to write quickly, recall that it took Sylvester Stallone only three and a half days to write *Rocky*.

Even if true, though, Stallone's claim is a little misleading. He went on to say of that first speed draft that "ninety percent was not good, but at least it had a beginning and a middle. I had something to work on."

It would take 20 more drafts of *Rocky* before the producers were ready to make the movie.

Additionally, in an interview with Kam Williams of *The Aquarian*, Stallone said, "My first eight to 10 scripts were pretty horrendous, but I stayed at it, and stayed at it, until I eventually found a voice and a subject like Rocky that people were interested in."

Stallone wrote eight to ten scripts before he did a vomit draft of *Rocky* in three and a half days. After the vomit draft of *Rocky*, his process became all about revisions.

AVERAGE LENGTH OF A MOVIE

Author and professor David Bordwell did research on the average length of movie scenes over the last 50 years.

"In films made after 1961 most scenes run between 1.5 and 3 minutes. The practice reflects the contemporary screenwriter's rule of thumb that a scene should consume no more than two or three pages (with a page counting as a minute of screen time)."
—David Bordwell
The Way Hollywood Tells It

Bordwell's average would be even shorter if we just looked at films produced over the last decade.

I imagine that, thanks to the internet, the average attention span today favors shorter scenes that average between one and two minutes. The opening scenes of *The Social Network* (over six minutes) and *Inglourious Basterds* (over 14 minutes) are exceptions.

IS 110 THE NEW 120?

"Is 110 the new 120? — *Up In The Air* **may clock in at 124 pages but that's because Jason Reitman only has to impress himself . . . If you're writing a drama, you can eek into 110+ territory. But I'd still look to keep it under 110. Readers are just used to it."**
—Carson Reeves
Scriptshadow (July 13, 2009)

If you're planning on making your own film and are on a limited budget, the best reason to aim for a 90 pages is 90 pages is a legitimate length for a feature and the less pages you have to shoot, the less the film costs to make.

WHAT IS ESSENTIAL?

I picked up the book *The Technique of Screenplay Writing* (1944) by Eugene Vale many years ago at a used bookstore in Baltimore, Maryland. Since there's much to admire from many movies from the '30s and '40s, it's good every now and then to see the kind of thinking that was kicking around Hollywood during that golden era.

"What is essential? In reducing the total information to that which is important, the good writer can tell a story in a smaller amount of space than the writer who is not capable of picking out the essential facts. . . . While the means of expression must be handled in the most economical way, the amount of information must not be sparse but adequate."

—Eugene Vale
The Technique of Screenplay Writing

SHOW, DON'T TELL

"Ultimately, it all comes down to one of the grand old rules of screenwriting: whenever possible – show, don't tell."

—Ray Morton

A good example of "show, don't tell" is in the movie *As Good as it Gets*. Melvin (Jack Nicholson) repeatedly locks and unlocks his apartment door five times in a row, and then washes his hands three times in succession. We get the hint that he's neurotic.

Screenwriters Mark Andrus and James L. Brooks could have written a scene explaining Melvin's OCD, but it's much more interesting and effective to just show his character in action.

Here's an example of "show, don't tell" from *The Verdict* screenplay by David Mamet

INT. COFFEE SHOP - DAY

Galvin sitting in the deserted coffee shop in his raincoat.

Reading a section of the paper. He picks up his teacup, drinks.

Lowers it to the table.

ANGLE - INSERT

Galvin twists tea bag around a spoon to extract
last drops of tea. His hand moves to his felt pen
lying on the table. He moves his hand to the
paper, open at the obituary section. We SEE
several names crossed out. He circles one funeral
listing.

ANGLE

Galvin sitting raises cup of tea to his lips.
Looks around a deserted coffee shop. Sighs.

In the movie version they made one significant change: there's no teacup.
Either Mamet, director Sidney Lumet, or somebody else said, "This guy's
an alcoholic — what better way of showing that than to have him knocking
back a stiff one with his morning donut?" The breakfast of champions.

Newman's performance in that scene shows you the desperate state his
character is in without a word being spoken. In fact, the whole opening
sequence of the film shows you a man in need of redemption.

**"IF YOU PRETEND THE CHARACTERS CAN'T SPEAK, AND
WRITE A SILENT MOVIE, YOU WILL BE WRITING GREAT
DRAMA. IF YOU DEPRIVE YOURSELF OF THE CRUTCH OF
NARRATION, EXPOSITION, INDEED, OF *SPEECH*, YOU
WILL BE FORGED TO WORK IN A NEW MEDIUM —
TELLING STORIES IN PICTURES (ALSO KNOWN AS
SCREENWRITING).**
—David Mamet BOLD memo to *The Unit* writers

**"This is age-old screenwriting advice but it's so true. SHOW don't
TELL. I can't tell you how much more impactful it is on a reader to
SEE a character take on an issue as opposed to being told of an
issue. It would be like Han Solo saying 'I'm a badass,' instead of
SHOWING him kill Greedo."**
—Carson Reeves

"Remember, the first rule of film is Show Don't Tell."
—William C. Martell

Wait, I thought the first rule was "Don't be boring"? See what I mean about getting contradictory advice? Well, it's boring to tell instead of show. So the two rules actually complement each other.

FOUR BASIC FUNTIONS OF DIALOGUE

The dialogue must serve four basic functions:

To move the storyline forward.

To reveal aspects of character not otherwise seen.

To present exposition and particulars of past events.

To set the tone for the film.
—Irwin R. Blacker
The Elements of Screenwriting

SCREENWRITING AND EXPOSITION

"Primary exposition is telling and showing to the audience the time and place of the story, the names and relationships of the characters, and the nature of the conflict."
—Irwin R. Blacker
The Elements of Screenwriting

Dramatically speaking, exposition is simply the way you convey information so the audience can follow the story. Exposition delivered via dialogue or action without killing momentum is invaluable.

Exposition works best in films when it is sprinkled here and there and doesn't *feel* like exposition. An argument is a good place to sneak in exposition. In the movie *Steve Jobs* written by Aaron Sorkin there is a computer problem just before the Mac launch in front of a live audience. When Andy Herzfeld tells Steve Jobs in a heated exchange that his development team isn't a pit crew at a Daytona race that can fix the problem in seconds.

                    STEVE
          You didn't have seconds you had
          three weeks. The universe was
          created in a third of that time.

                    ANDY
          Well someday you'll have to tell us
          Well someday you'll have to tell us
          how you did it.

The audience concludes that some of the Apple team feel like Jobs has a God-complex. Throughout the film the audience is exposed to what's known as Jobs' "reality distortion field."

Think of exposition like exposure in photography. It reveals a subject. When you take a picture of someone on film you expose a part of them. And every angle gives you a little different exposure or insight into the person. In a close-up you might see a small scar on their face, from the side you might see a tattoo on their arm, and from behind you might see that their hair is thinning.

In real life people are constantly giving us exposition. Two pieces of real-life expo that come to mind were in the form of warnings about other people. The first one came years ago when I was young and began a job wide-eyed and excited. A fellow who had been at the company for many years warned me about the president of the company: "Be careful, there's a trail of broken relationships behind him."

That was a great bit of exposition given in a way that was fresh and allowed me to fill in the blanks without knowing the details. Another person I worked with said of someone we knew, "I know there is a good person in there wanting to come out." Great line.

I once did a video interview with someone who told me, "The memories of my father could be put on the back of a postage stamp." That one line told me more about his relationship with his father than a multi-page monologue could have accomplished. Keep track of how exposition is given to you in real life and in movies and TV shows you watch.

In screenwriting, it's best if your exposition is almost invisible so the audience doesn't feel they are being spoon-fed information. But even Shakespeare and Christopher Nolan (*Inception*) tend to be exposition heavy at times. (Though Nolan's *Dunkirk* was so light on exposition that on first viewing I had trouble following the story.)

Detective shows on network TV are some of the worst at dumping exposition on an audience. They have to frontload information because they need to grab your attention early before you change the channel. "Okay, we think Joe did this because his girlfriend just broke up with him and he lost his job at the factory where he works, and he has a hunting rifle that uses the same caliber bullet that was used in the murder." Then they often dump more exposition right at the end to explain what happened.

Consider these lines and exchanges from movies that convey exposition in an excellent and minimalistic way:

"Jerry lies, lies, lies—he's an agent. He lies."
(Bachelor party video in *Jerry Maguire*.)

"Are you late for something?" —"Always."
(*My Favorite Year*)

"Is there anything I should know?" (Referring to the Mexican drug cartel.) —"You're asking me how a watch is made."
(*Sicario*)

A key to writing good exposition is to only reveal what you have to reveal. The opening graphic of *A Quiet Place* is simply, "DAY 89." It instantly pulls the audience into the story without any explanation. In real life, people withhold information for various reasons. It's the guy who says after the fifth date, "Have I told you I have a kid?"

In *Butch Cassidy and the Sundance Kid*, timely exposition comes just before a shootout when Butch says to Sundance, "Kid, I think there's something I ought to tell you. I never shot anybody before." Sundance replies, "One hell of a time to tell me." At 90 minutes into the film, it is one hell of a time to reveal this little nugget about the notorious outlaw and bank robber.

" A lot of time, there's no excitement under the exposition. It's just

something you have to get past."
—William Goldman

Writers often use exposition early in the film to set the stage. In *Jerry Maguire,* Jerry explains what a sports agent does. Later, Cameron Crowe avoids the usual spill-your-guts exposition trap when Dorothy tells Jerry, "Let's not tell all our sad stories."

The opening hip hop song from *Hamilton: An American Musical* used exposition to get our attention. The lyrics proclaim founding father Alexander Hamilton as a "bastard, orphan, son of a whore," letting the audience know this won't be a traditional history lesson.

The writing you use to set up your story is what some call "laying pipe."

"'Laying Pipe,' is about how much screen time you must use to set up your story. In my opinion, audiences will only stand for so much of that."
—Blake Snyder

"Overt exposition is another of a screenplay's great sins."
—Edward Dmytryk

Overt exposition is the kind thing you might find on a bad police procedural in TV. Here's a slightly exaggerated version:

```
        DETECTIVE EXPOSITION
        (looking down at tire tracks)
    This accident wasn't an accident.
    These tire tracks indicate that the
    car was a red 1972 Chevy Impala
    driven by a 28-year-old unemployed
    white male with brown hair who lives
    with his mother and has daddy issues.
```

A great example of not spelling out everything is in the *Nightcrawler* screenplay by Dan Gilroy.

LOU

steps out ... scanning the empty alley before taking a

WRENCH

from his car and moving to a line of open garages where the

MAYHEM VIDEO VAN

is parked ... beat before

LOU

slides under the van ... squeak of bolts turning and CUT TO

A MOONLIT CANYON

There is no setup of what Lou (Jake Gyllenhaal) did. We don't even see what he did. Just "squeak of bolts turning." In the next scene the Mayhem Van is "wrapped around a telephone poll" and a cameraman (his main video competition) is put into an ambulance.

But there's no exposition explaining that Lou is so devious that he uses a torque wrench to adjust the metal calipers and loosens a screw on the van's disc brakes reducing the ability of the break pads to function properly, essentially setting up the van to wreck

Screenwriters get lost in the weeds by having complex setups that go on and on about how complicated a computer setup is and keep laying pipe because they want the audience to understand what's going on. The audience doesn't usually care. Just show a guy going under a car with a wrench—or a woman connecting some wires— and the audience will get it.

Here is a nice and concise bit of exposition used humorously in *The Princess Bride*: "What you do not smell is called iocane powder. It is odorless, tasteless, dissolves instantly in liquid, and is among the more deadlier poisons known to man." Mystery Man on Film wrote on his blog of this line of exposition: "Perfect the pipe is laid; the audience knows how this scene is going to work —one of the men will die from ingesting the poison."

In *Field of Dreams,* Kevin Costner's character says, "Dad was a Yankees fan then, so of course I rooted for Brooklyn. But in '58 the Dodgers moved away so we had to find other things to fight about." The two sentences sum up his relationship with his father. (And sets up that ending I wrote about in chapter three that made Costner want to do the film.)

"But you have to be careful that your characters are not talking only in order to get information out. If you need to give the audience a bit of information, make sure to give the character his own reason to tell us about it. That's called making the dialogue organic to the character."

—Alex Epstein

Save the best exposition for last. Of course, one of the outstanding examples of this is when Darth Vader says, "Luke, I am your father." I was at a midnight showing in Hollywood when I first heard that line uttered, and it was a great personal movie moment. Other great memorable lines of powerful expo include "I see dead people" (*The Sixth Sense*) and "She's my sister and my daughter" (*Chinatown*).

Good exposition doesn't need to be spoken, either. In *Good Will Hunting,* Matt Damon's character reads books in a room filled with books. We get a clue that he reads a lot. That's simple and effective visual exposition.

Sometimes you can use false exposition to lead the characters and audience astray, as Norman Bates does in *Psycho.* Just because someone tells you something (and even believes it himself) doesn't mean it's true.

Subtext is another way of masking exposition. Actors love to talk about playing subtext. That's what is being said beyond the words. Think of the many ways someone can say "I love you," and all of the different meanings that phrase can convey—including even "I hate you."

As you're writing and rewriting your script, be aware of how exposition is being conveyed. Make every effort to make the exposition seamless, and make sure it's there for a good reason.

FLASHBACKS AND EXPOSITION

Flashbacks are usually a form of exposition in that they are telling audiences something from the past that informs the story taking place in the present. Flashbacks are sometimes frowned upon in screenplays because they often function as graceless info dumps rather than integral parts of the story. But flashbacks can be handled well.

You don't watch *Citizen Kane, Casablanca, or Rashomon* and say, "Wow, those would have been better films without those nagging flashbacks." But it is best if your flashbacks move your story forward.

STARS DON'T DO EXPOSITION —OR DO THEY?

"Primary exposition is telling and showing to the audience the time and place of the story, the names and relationships of the characters, and the nature of the conflict."
—Irwin R. Blacker

While watching the film *Charade* I heard a phrase on the audio commentary attributed to Cary Grant: "Stars don't do exposition." Stars prefer to say lines like Clark Gable did in *Gone with the Wind*:

"Frankly, my dear I don't give a damn."

Short. Pithy. Memorable. So memorable that it was voted as the top American movie quote by the American Film Institute.

William Goldman said, "Stars without exception, hate carrying the plot . . . If you can give the exposition to a secondary character, do it. It's just another way of protecting the star."

If you're writing a script for a movie star, you might want to go through your script and double-check those places when he or she is dishing out exposition.

But there are exceptions. One of the most repeated lines of expo in recent years was given by Liam Neeson in *Taken*:

"I don't know who you are. I don't know what you want. If you are looking for ransom, I can tell you I don't have money. But what I do have are a very particular set of skills, skills I have acquired over a very long career. Skills that make me a nightmare for people like you. If you let my daughter go now, that'll be the end of it. I will not look for you, I will not pursue you. But if you don't, I will look for you, I will find you, and I will kill you."

In the movie *8 Mile,* B-Rabbit *(Eminem)* battles Papa Doc (Anthony Mackie) in a freestyle rap contest where B-Rabbit says early in his song, " I know everything he has against me" and proceeds to do an expositional dump about himself in quite an engaging way.

The opposite of telling an audience more than they need to know is not telling them enough.

"The marks of the artsy-craftsy film are withholding basic exposition and leaving the viewer confused. The illusion of profundity is not the same as being profound."
—Irwin R. Blacker
The Elements of Screenwriting

We've all seen movies and television shows where we're lost in the story. The trick is to give the audience enough to want them wondering what's going to happen next, but not so much that the outcome seemed spoon-feed to us.

SCREENWRITING AND COINCIDENCE

"Coincidence. It's a screenwriter's stock in trade. It lies at the very heart of storytelling; it's been around even before Oedipus slept with his mother. It's the essence of the 'what if.' Coincidence comes into play for inciting incidents, chance meetings, clever plot twists, and surprising revelations. It's a very necessary dramatic tool."
—Screenwriter Terry Rossio *(Pirates of the Caribbean)*

One time I spent two days in a town I had never been in before. Both mornings I went to the same Starbucks at different times in the morning. And both times the same person was standing behind me in line. What are the odds? It's hard to miss that kind of coincidence.

All of us have real stories of coincidence ranging from simple to complex.

A song you haven't heard in years plays on the radio simultaneously on two different stations. The person next to you on your flight is a high school friend you haven't seen for twenty years.

Coincidence is a part of life, so we shouldn't be surprised when it shows up in movies. In general, though, coincidence should not be used *throughout* your story unless you are writing a farce (*Groundhog Day*) or a story where coincidence is otherwise integral to the story. For instance, we expect *Forrest Gump* to bump shoulders with Elvis, John F. Kennedy and John Lennon. It's an intentional choice in the script, and part of the fun.

Here's the best quote I've found on how to use coincidence:

"Use coincidence to get characters into trouble, not out of trouble."
—Writer/director Alexander Mackendrick (*The Man in the White Suit*)

Example: Steve Martin in *The Jerk* is thrilled to see his name, Navin Johnson, in the phone book because now he's a "somebody." The next cut shows a psychopath with a rifle who randomly picks a name from the phone book and lands on "Navin Johnson."

Also avoid using coincidence at important moments in your script. One theory is that coincidence is best used in the first act, as early as possible. Sure, it's a coincidence that the swimmer in *Jaws* just happens to take a swim during feeding time. But something has to start the story. The inciting incident is often a fitting place for a coincidence.

The worst time to use coincidence is at the end of the film. As Robert McKee writes in *Story*, "Never use coincidence to turn an ending. This is deus ex machina, the writer's greatest sin." This phrase from ancient Greek theater refers to when a god would be lowered onto the stage to fix everything.

You will find coincidence abuse across every genre. Perhaps the biggest offenders are romantic comedies, as writers work to get two people together. Could there be a bigger coincidence (or heavy-handed metaphor) than a recently widowed man falling in love with the recipient of his dead wife's transplanted heart? Critics used words like "gimmick," "contrived," and "creepy" to refer to the plot of *Return to Me*.

You can overcome heavy-handed coincidence, but it takes work to avoid it. The real secret of using coincidence is to sneak it in where it is needed. Avoid using coincidence at key moments of the story.

Terry Rossio wrote in his *Wordplay* column:

"One of the classic rules of coincidence is that fate—if it must be present — should always favor the antagonist. If our hero has a gun on the villain and the hero's gun jams, it's called drama. If the villain has our hero dead in his sights, and the villain's gun jams, it's called a lousy cheat, a not very inventive way to sneak the hero out of his predicament."

When the audience rolls their eyes and has one of those "you've-got-to be-kidding" moments, you know that coincidence has been misused.

It's best when the audience doesn't even realize the coincidence has occurred. In *Mystic River*, the story starts and ends with coincidence, but the story is so compelling that it's not a stumbling block. Sean Penn's daughter is killed on the same night that his friend Tim Robbins kills a man—big coincidence. And Sean Penn kills Robbins thinking he killed his daughter on the same night that detectives arrest the real killers of Penn's daughter–another big coincidence.

Coincidence is like subtext, exposition, and other tricks of the trade in that it can be dealt with well or poorly. The best way to handle coincidence in your scripts is to do so organically. For instance, it is not just a coincidence at the end of *Jaws* that Chief Brody (Roy Scheider) has a gun and knows how to use it (he is the police chief), or that there is an oxygen tank on the boat. Those props were organically built in early to the story.

Coincidence should be used sparingly. As usual, though, there are exceptions.

At least one great filmmaker didn't flinch at the opportunity to add coincidence. Alfred Hitchcock's *The Birds* doesn't try to hide it or downplay it in any way. He even highlighted it in a key part of the script, and then used it as an exposition dump.

The crazy thing is that he pulled it off, like a car theft in front of a police station. I guess when you are known as "The Master of Suspense," you can pull off things that mere mortals can't.

The scene in question takes place in a restaurant after children have been attacked by birds at a school yard. There just happens to be a woman at the restaurant who at the right moment overhears a conversation about birds and says, "Ornithology happens to be my avocation."

Spielberg and his writing team handled this more smoothly in *Jaws*. A shark expert (Richard Dreyfuss) is drawn to the town because of the shark attacks. He doesn't just happen to be there; he is a scientist who therefore has a believable motivation to show up and stick around. He also becomes the perfect character to organically deliver exposition regarding shark behavior.

By contrast, Hitchcock had a lady buying a pack of cigarettes in a restaurant who just happens to be a bird expert. Hitchcock was asked about why the bird expert was there. He basically replied that it would be a fun break between all of the suspense, and that people wouldn't notice.

I guess the key lesson here is that if you do use coincidence (or more egregiously, a coincidence on top of an expositional dump), make sure the rest of your film is good enough that no one notices or cares.

TICKING CLOCK

"Always helps to have a ticking clock."
—William M. Akers
Your Screenplay Sucks

"The purpose of a ticking clock: to inject urgency and tension into the story or an individual scene."
—Screenwriter Doug Eboch (*Sweet Home Alabama*)
Let's Schmooze blog

Once Upon a Time … in Hollywood is a movie built around a ticking clock.

The ticking clock is a device writers use to create a sense of urgency—in both the characters and the audience. It's not found in every film and TV show, but there are plenty of examples of stories across all genres that show it's something worthwhile to have in your toolbox.

Sometimes the ticking clock is used in a single scene, and other times it basically spans the entire film. Two examples include *Back to the Future* and *Taken*. Major stakes are on the line, and the conflict must be resolved within a specific time frame.

A literal clock does not have to tick (although it certainly can), but it must be clear to the characters and audience that there will be dire consequences if the something isn't accomplished before time runs out.

"An example of a ticking clock would be the movie *Armageddon*, where the team had only a short time to blow up the asteroid, or all of mankind would be destroyed when it hit Earth. This gives an underlying tension to the entire movie"
—Emmy-winning writer/producer Stephen J. Cannell (*21 Jump Street*)

"[A ticking clock] is most common in action stories (*Speed*), thrillers (*Outbreak*), caper stories (where the characters pull off some kind of heist, as in *Ocean's Eleven*), and suicide mission stories (*The Guns of Navarone, The Dirty Dozen*)."
—John Truby
The Anatomy of Story

But ticking clocks can also be found in comedies and other genres. Some examples include *48 Hours, The Blues Brothers, The Hangover, Happy Gilmore, The Hunt for Red October, United 93, Notorious, The Silence of the Lambs, Little Miss Sunshine, High Noon, Unstoppable,* and *The African Queen.*

One of my favorite examples is *127 Hours,* where a solo adventurer must find a way to get his arm released from being wedged in a rock crevasse before he dies from lack of food and water.

An example of what a ticking clock looks like on the page can be found in Drew Goddard's *The Martian* (based on Andy Weir's book). This scene starts on page 16 after astronaut Mark Watney (Matt Damon) survives being stranded on Mars.

INT. HAB - DAWN

Mark sits in the darkness. We get the sense he hasn't moved much in the night. He stares into the middle distance.

Then.

He makes the decision. Get up, *Mark*. He gets to his feet. Moves with purpose as he rummages through the hab. Looking for something. Where is it? There.

A pencil.

He pulls a notecard free from one of his manuals. *Paper*.

Back to basics. He sits at the table. And begins writing math equations.

> MARK
> Let's do the math...

Mark address camera. He looks less-terrible than he did before.

> MARK (CON'T)
> Our surface mission here was
> supposed to take thirty-one days.
> For redundancy, they sent enough
> food for sixty-eight days. For six
> people. So for just me, it'll last
> three-hundred days. And I figure I
> can stretch that to four hundred if
> I ration. So. . . I've still gotta
> figure out how to grow three years worth
> of food. Here. On a planet where nothing
> grows. Luckily, I'm the botanist.

Mark holds up one of his mission briefs. Points to the word "Botanist" under "Watney." Look at us like, *impressed?*

<pre>
                    MARK (CON'T)
          Mars will come to fear my botany powers.
</pre>

Even the terrific indie films *Winter's Bone, Buried*, and *Ida* have ticking clocks. TV programs like *Breaking Bad* and *Empire* have ticking clocks related to the health of the lead characters.

Like any technique, there are times when its use can seem heavy-handed and forced—even a cliché. But this doesn't negate that—when used well—it is time-trusted (pun intended) way to produce a sense of urgency.

Remember in *Saving Private Ryan* when Tom Hanks and his troop are charged with finding (and returning) Private Ryan before he's killed on the battlefield? That qualifies as a ticking clock. As does finding (and killing) the shark in *Jaws* before it wrecks the town's tourist economy. Spielberg apparently loves the technique, as is also evident in *Raiders of the Lost Ark, Jurassic Park, E.T.,* and *Schindler's List*. If Spielberg doesn't shy away from ticking clocks, why should you?

DEALING WITH THE PASSING OF TIME

"Play it, Sam. Play *As Time Goes By*."
Rick Blaine (Humphrey Bogart) in *Casablanca*

Did you know that the movie *Three Days of the Condor* was based on the novel *Six Days of the Condor*?

Why do you think the screenwriters Lorenzo Semple and David Rayfiel compressed the novel by James Grady? I haven't read any comments by the writers, or from the star Robert Redford, or by director Sydney Pollack on why this was done, but I have a pretty good hunch as to why.

More often than not, films will compress time for the sake of moving the story forward and keeping audiences enthralled.

Screenwriters often talk of a time lock or a ticking clock on a film. This refers to a specific period of time in the story during which something must happen or else. ("If you don't get the heck out of Dodge by sunset, there will be hell to pay.") It sets the parameters for the story. Here are some films that have a time-lock: *High Noon, Speed, 48 Hours, Apollo 13*.

Lew Hunter in his book *Screenwriting 434* says when you use a time lock "you inject an urgency into your story that can give it additional drive to heighten audience involvement and anxiety." Of course, it's best if your time lock is organic to the story.

Some movies deal with time by placing the story within a single day, a single night, or even in real time (the length of the film):

American Graffiti
Before Sunrise (and its sequels)
Buried
Clerks
Halloween
Phone Booth
Rope
Russian Ark
The Breakfast Club
Timecode

I once heard John Irving give a talk at the Iowa Writers' Workshop. He spoke about the limitations that film has in showing the passing of time. When he's writing a novel, he can take a person from a baby to old age and it's no problem for the reader, but in movies it doesn't work as well. He explained that if your main character is a child for the first 30 minutes of the film, audiences have a certain emotional investment in that character; to age them too rapidly can cause a disconcerting jolt.

This may be one of the problems Irving is facing in bringing the story of Dan Gable to the screen. Gable had a great wrestling high school and college wrestling career before winning a gold medal in the 1972 Olympics. He then went on to win 15 NCAA Championships as head wrestling coach at the University of Iowa.

How do you tell this story in an hour-and-a-half or two-hour movie? And even if you found a way, can you really have the same person play Gable as a 15-year-old high school freshman, as a 23-year-old Olympic wrestler, and as a 49-year-old coach? See the problem there?

The digital world can help the aging process, or even reverse it as in *The Curious Case of Benjamin Button*. Hollywood has found other creative ways to deal with the passing of time when needed. For instance, in *Forrest Gump* we are introduced to Forrest (Tom Hanks) as an adult in the opening scene. Although we then go on to see Forrest as a child, during most of the film he is an adult. It helps our investment in the adult Forrest that we were introduced to him so early in the film.

In *The Natural,* (written by Roger Towne and Phil Dusenberry) director Barry Levinson chose to have Robert Redford play not only the thirtysomething Roy Hobbs, but also Roy Hobbs as a teenager. They used soft lighting and shadows (not to mention Redford's ever-youthful appearance) to create believability for the audience.

The remarkable TV movie *The Autobiography of Miss Jane Pittman* won eight primetime Emmys, including two for actress Cicely Tyson. Tyson's portrayal of a 110-year-old woman reflecting on her life was amazing, and greatly aided by makeup and costume design (both of which also won Emmys), and a whole creative team that brought Ernest J. Gaines' novel to life.

One major problem with the passing of time is the high cost of conveying different eras. Consider the expense of the cars alone to indicate the time periods of a story set across different decades. It's been done before, but if you are starting out it may be best to avoid that hurdle. A short time frame also favors lower-budget films since there are fewer continuity issues to worry about. This is especially helpful if you can't afford a script supervisor.

DESCRIBING SCENES AND CHARACTERS

"Good description usually consists of a few well chosen details that will stand for everything else."
—Stephen King

When you break down the core aspects of a screenplay, you have scene headings (INT. HOSPITAL ROOM – DAY), dialogue ("I'm walking here!"), and what is called scene description, action, or narrative. Scene description is the little blurb that sets up the scene, explains what's going on in-between the dialogue, and introduces and describes characters as economically as possible.

Character introductions are usually just one to three sentences in length.

At the head of the party is an American, INDIANA JONES. He wears a short leather jacket, a flapped holster, and a brimmed felt hat with a weird feather stuck in the band.

Indiana Jones, written by Lawrence Kasdan

CLOSE - RON STALLWORTH
Black, 21, Handsome, Intelligent, sporting a good sized Afro, rebellious but straight laced by most 1970's standards gets out of his Ford Pinto staring at the cavernous opening to Norad.

BlacKkKlansman written by Charlie Wachtel & David Rabinowitz, and Kevin Willmott & Spike Lee

JUNO MacGUFF stands on a placid street in a nondescript subdivision, facing the curb. It's FALL. Juno is sixteen years old, an artfully bedraggled burnout kid.

Juno, written by Diablo Cody

ERIN BROCKOVICH. How to describe her? A beauty queen would come to mind — which, in fact, she was. Tall in a mini skirt, legs crossed, tight top, beautiful – but clearly from a social class and geographical orientation whose standards for displaying beauty are not based on subtlety.

Erin Brockovich, written by Susannah Grant

Some would argue that writing, "A beauty queen would come to mind — which, in fact, she was" is a cheat. You're *telling* the reader something on the page that is not *shown* on the screen. *Show, don't tell* is a great concept, but many successful writers sneak in little details to help those reading the script to understand their intentions. Oscar-winner Tony Gilroy (*Michael Clayton*) goes as far as telling you what a character is thinking or feeling if he thinks it is necessary.

Remember that you're trying to get a busy, possibly jaded reader with a large stack of scripts to get excited about your script. It's savvy to do what you can to help them out.

DESCRIBING ACTION

The action, or narrative, is simply what's supposed to be happening on the screen. More often than not, it involves a few brief comments rather than thick paragraphs. If there is a lot of action, it's best if you can break it down into short paragraphs. Keeping the action to a minimum keeps the screenplay vertical—lots of white space on the side, rather than large blocks of text—which helps the reader of your script heading down the page. Here are what some memorable action scenes look like on the page. Notice that it only takes a few words to convey a great deal about the scenes:

```
INT. GARAGE

Cameron has kicked the Ferrari off the Jack. It
squeals out of the garage in a cloud of blue smoke. A
$50,000 unmanned investment heading backwards down a
driveway.
```
Ferris Bueller's Day Off, by John Hughes

```
EXT. ART MUSEUM STAIRS - DAY

It is twilight and Rocky is alone at the very bottom
of a huge flight of steps that seem to stretch into
the heavens . . . Rocky takes a deep breath and
sprints up the never ending stairs . . . Halfway up,
his body shows the strain. Nearing the top, Rocky
pumps with all his strength and arrives at the very
top...He looks down the steep stairs and swells with
pride...He is ready.
```
Rocky, by Sylvester Stallone

```
As ANNIE swings, the sledgehammer makes contact with
the ankle. It breaks with a sharp CRACK

CUT TO: PAUL: CLOSE UP, shrieking
```
Misery, by William Goldman

```
He wades upstream, ripping his clothes from his
body. He gets his shirt off, spins it through the
air over his head, flings the shirt away. He
```

raises his arm to the sky, turning slowly,
feeling the rain washing him clean. Exultant.
Triumphant. A FLASH OF LIGHTNING arcs from
horizon to horizon.

The Shawkshank Redemption, by Frank Darabont

DESCRIBING SETTINGS

Three well-known movies exemplify good practices for describing settings:

INT. MEMPHIS SUPERHUB–NIGHT–LATER

Our executives work amid the army of EMPLOYEES
sorting the rivers of Christmas packages that
flow relentlessly into the Hub. Some still have
ties on, others have on Christmas hats. It's
incredibly complex; the work is demanding,
intense. Like "Modern Times": on overdrive. Above

them is a COUNTDOWN clock approaching 00:15:00.

Cast Away, by William Broyles, Jr.

INT. GORDON GEKKO'S OFFICE (JOE'S POV) – DAY

Furnishings in hypermodern gray and black
lacquer, Modern Art range from field paintings by
Art Reinhardt to the smashed dishes of Julian
Schnabel. Nautilus equipment, hi-tech gadgets are
in evidence, including a splendid Howard Miller
World Time Clock, and a world map…

Three of Gekko's people, young MBA's dressed for
success, are scattered about the room, on phones,

calculators, coming in and out.

Wall Street, by Oliver Stone & Stanley Weiser

Here are excerpts from two different script versions of the same scene from
Jaws written by Peter Benchley and Carl Gottlieb.

QUINT'S HOUSE - DAY

Brody and Hooper are approaching Quint's house.
They enter through the big wooden doors, into
another circle of Hell. Smoke and steam from two
big oil drums sitting over fires fills the air.
Quint and his mate, Herschel, are grinding pieces
of pilot whale into chum. The whale lies bloody
on the floor, its ruined carcass adding to the
stench of other sharks being boiled in the drums,
their tails suspended in the air.

INT. QUINT'S RESIDENCE - NIGHT

Entering Quint's abode is not unlike a spooky
ride at Disneyland...the placement of objects,
the dungeon lighting, the tendrils of smoke and
dust in the air makes a visitor wish he were
carrying a 100-watt bulb.

There is gear everywhere. The walls are adorned
with jerky shark hides, coiled ropes dangle like
serpents above a galley stove that leaks smoke
and holds two weeks' worth of filthy dishes.

Stephen King says that when it comes to scene descriptions in novels, "a
meal is as good as a feast." Some novelists clearly disagree (with some
descriptions filling several pages), but King's sentiment generally applies
well to screenplays.

Screenplays evolve over time trying to build to the most impactful climax
and conclusion. And climax/conclusions are what our next chapter is all
about.

6. CLIMAX/CONCLUSIONS

"The main thing in writing a movie is to have a good ending."
—Oscar-winning screenwriter Christopher McQuarrie (*The Usual Suspects*)

"The plot must have a definite as an ending as it had a beginning."
—John Emerson and Anita Loos
How to Write Photoplays (1920)

"If you remember the plot, it's not a great movie. You remember moments."
—Martin Scorsese

"Endings, frankly, are a bitch."
—Two-time Oscar winning screenwriter William Goldman

At the end of this chapter, I'll hit on how to write what Michael Arndt calls the *Insanely Great Ending*. First, though, let's consider the different kinds of movie endings.

HAPPY, SAD, IRONIC, AND AMBIGUOUS ENDINGS

Writer, director, and actor Charlie Chaplin said that *The Gold Rush* was "the picture that I want to be remembered by." It has not just one but *two* happy endings. One version of the film shows the Little Tramp and a saloon girl he's fallen in love with standing by an old house. The other version of the film ends when they kiss. Anytime the guy and girl end up together, plenty of cynics are ready to cry "Cliché!"

"I'm not afraid of doing a cliché, if it's right. We don't wade through our existence with any sort of originality. We all live and die and eat people say, that's been done before. So what?"
—Charlie Chaplin
Charlie Chaplin Interviews, edited by Kevin Hayes

An Officer and a Gentleman (1982), written by Douglas Day Stewart, has a memorable ending. Zack Mayo (Richard Gere) struts into the factory where Paula Pokrifki (Debra Winger) works and literally sweeps her off her feet to the tune of "Up Where We Belong," and carries her out to hopefully live happily ever. Cue the audience's tears. Numerous critics cried "Cliché!" and hammered the movie for it.

But I wasn't a jaded film critic when I first saw that film. I was a 20-year-old film school student working in a factory that summer. I worked alongside people who had spent ten, twenty, or even thirty years of their lives on assembly lines making boat windshields. One co-worker told me that if he didn't take Quaaludes, he wouldn't make it through the day.

Work in a factory can be boring, but the workers themselves are fascinating. I found the ending exhilarating and couldn't care less whether it qualified as a cliché. Decades later Gere said that he didn't even want to shoot that scene because it was "the dopiest ending." But when he saw the finished cut with the music, he said he "got chills on the back of my neck."

Only later did I come to fully appreciate what director Taylor Hackford and screenwriter Douglas Day Stewart had pulled off in that film. Not only were they working with a limited budget, but they flipped the internal, external, and philosophical stakes of the main character (I will explain what I mean by stakes later in the chapter).

Mayo's goal is to get past officer training and become a pilot. Halfway into the movie, though, he is asked to drop out. We sense that he's had plenty of raw sex, but he's never had a real relationship with a woman. To top it off, he's self-centered.

At the climax of the film, though, what looks like sure defeat results in victory. He ends up graduating and is on his way to becoming a pilot. He sacrifices a record run to help another recruit get over a wall. And then, in the famous ending, he literally sweeps the woman he loves off of her feet.

It was a hit with audiences, and time has been good to *An Officer and a Gentleman*. Critic Roger Ebert was an early champion of the film. If Hackford and Stewart had been more worried about clichés, it's unlikely that this much-loved movie moment would have ever happened.

> *"An Officer and a Gentleman* is the best movie about love that I've seen in a long time…This is a wonderful movie precisely because it's so willing to deal with matters of the heart."
> —Roger Ebert, review of *An Officer and a Gentleman*

There are four main ways to end your screenplay: happy ending, sad ending, ambiguous ending, or ironic ending.

Happy: *Back to the Future, It's a Wonderful Life, Lion (2016), The Shawshank Redemption.* The lovers unite, paradise is found, the shark is killed, order is restored.

Sad: *Buried, Chinatown, No Country for Old Men, The Perfect Storm.* These are down endings, often where a key protagonist dies. Injustice, hardship, or evil prevails.

Sometimes what's stated is just the hard realities of life; at other times the filmmakers are explicitly advocating nihilism. Director Ingmar Bergman once said, "We are trapped in the senseless illusion of human history and we realize at the end that all hope is gone." Less depressingly, sad endings can function like Greek tragedies, serving as cautionary tales that reveal something key about human weakness.

Sad or tragic endings are especially common in indie and foreign films. Apart from the last shot, *The Florida Project* had a down ending. But the $2 million film wasn't looking for a superhero box office.

Ironic: *La La Land, Rocky, Toy Story 3, The Silence of the Lambs.* Good irony is at the core of many great endings. Typically, the hero doesn't get her intended goal, but gains something greater instead. Or perhaps she *does* get her goal but loses something else in the process. Rocky loses the fight, but gains Adrian and a sense of self-esteem. Clarice catches the serial killer Buffalo Bill, but psychopath Hannibal escapes. Jack saves Rose's life in *Titanic* but sacrifices his own life in the process.

Ambiguous: *The Graduate, Memento, The Wrestler, 2001: A Space Odyssey.* This ending invites viewers to "choose their own adventure." The audience essentially has to decide what happened to the characters. Filmmakers who favor ambiguous endings tend to say things like, "I think it's best if audiences bring their own conclusion to what happened to the main characters." Many times audiences walk out confused . . . or lost. The TV show *Lost* was a mystery series that ended with a massive unsolved mystery. The controversial finale still has fans arguing over its meaning.

Ambiguous endings can be tough at the box office because they don't lend themselves to word-of-mouth praise. If you are less concerned with box office returns, though, that opens the door to more ambiguous endings as in *Roma*.

CAST AWAY ENDING — CASE STUDY

Let's consider the ending of the modern-day classic *Cast Away* and explore not only how it ended—but how it could have ended.

Most films clearly end with one of the four types just discussed. There is an outlier, though, another rarely used option. Just as there are cross-genre movies, there are at least a few movies that have mixed endings.

In *Cast Away*, Tom Hanks stars as a FedEx executive Chuck Nolan who becomes a modern-day Robinson Crusoe when a plane crash leaves him stranded on a deserted island. *Cast Away* contains a mixture of ending types. Consider:

Happy: Chuck survives years on the deserted island, and finally reunites with his fiancé Kelly (Helen Hunt) . . .

Sad: . . .*but* discovers that Kelly is now married and has a daughter . . . (Bummer!)

Ironic: . . .*but* it turns out that they still have deep feelings for each other, and they end up kissing. Sitting in his old jeep, Chuck tells Kelly, "It's time to go home." Just when we think they're going to ride off into the sunset (even though it's at night and raining), he pulls into her driveway and sends her back to her new family. They love each other but can't be together.

His goal of reuniting with the woman he loves is crushed. But he's grateful for that love because the hope of being with her kept him alive all those years as he fought for survival on a deserted island.

Ambiguous: Now what's Chuck going to do? Where's he going to go? There's a blip of hope that he'll end up with the artist the audience was introduced to at the beginning of the film, because he has a package to deliver to her at the end of the film. But she's not home, so he leaves the package and a note.

Where's he going to go now? His jeep sits at a four-way intersection in the middle of remote Texas. The back of the truck in front of him has angel wings on it, indicating that its driver is the very same artist whose package he just dropped off! I believe that most audience members are probably begging Chuck, at this point, to at least explore that possibility. Zemeckis, Hanks, and every executive at Twentieth Century Fox had to know that this is what the audience wanted. They may have even shot the scene where, after some contemplation, he at least heads his Jeep down the dirt road toward the woman's house.

Which way does he go? This is the last sentence from *Cast Away — The Shooting Script:*

```
It doesn't really matter which way he goes. At
some point in life's grand journey you just have
to let go of the oars and have faith. His new
life begins...now. The end is just the beginning.
```

The last shot fades out on a close-up of Chuck contemplating where to go next. My guess is that the filmmakers decided to end with ambiguity to avoid the happy ending cliché.

Cast Away screenwriter William Broyles Jr. later said, "Chuck's first word of dialogue in the movie is 'time.' Time runs his life and for six years and time ran our lives as we made this movie. His last words are 'thank you,' an expression of gratitude which defines his transformation."

The danger of ambiguous endings is that they can leave the audience emotionally unsatisfied. Even if this is the writer's intention, it is a risky choice.

Would Chuck getting in his Jeep and heading down the dirt road toward the artist's truck have been a better ending? We'll never know. But I did find a version of the script (marked "3rd draft") where Chuck ends up in a remote area talking to (ironically) a FedEx driver named Erica.

> ERICA
> What brings you out to the sticks?

> CHUCK
> Had a package to deliver.

> ERICA
> You? Personally?

> CHUCK
> I had it on the island with me.

> ERICA
> Must be a story there.

There's a connection building here, effortlessly.

EXT.   BEACH - MOMENTS LATER

We are wide on the beach, watching the truck move along the water, kicking up wisps of sand.

> CHUCK (V.O.)
> Yeah, a long one.

> ERICA (V.O.)
> I've got lots of time.

> CHUCK (V.O.)
> So do I.

The truck goes down the beach and then turns inland, away from the ocean. Away from all that.

> CHUCK (V.O.)
> So do I.

And we pull back, taking in the sweep of the beach, the estuaries, and the green forest stretching back into America.

The end is the beginning.

That ending is a little less ambiguous. It took six years to make *Cast Away*, and it would be fascinating to learn how the filmmakers wrestled with the ending.

One critic thought that the Chuck and Kelly relationship was unresolved and left audiences hanging. But I think it was resolved in the way *Casablanca* was resolved. Both Chuck and Rick (Humphrey Bogart) took the high road in parting with the woman they loved for a greater good.

Writer/director Frank Darabont said on the 20th Anniversary DVD of *The Shawshank Redemption* that he wanted to end *Shawshank* simply by showing Red (Morgan Freeman's character) being freed from prison and riding off on a bus. Fade to black. Ambiguous. But the producers pushed for him to at least shoot a sequence where Red and Andy are reunited on a beautiful island paradise with his friend, an ending the audience yearned for. Darabont basically said that if they had used his ambiguous ending, *Shawshank* would not be the highly regarded film it is today, and he wouldn't be doing a 20th anniversary commentary.

EARN YOUR ENDING

The Christmas classic *It's a Wonderful Life* is a dark film in many ways. George Bailey (Jimmy Stewart) is suicidal. Seconds after sitting at a bar praying, "I'm at the end of my rope. Show me the way, oh God," Bailey gets punched in the face.

"My favorite Christmas film is *It's a Wonderful Life* and I think Capra did a great job of balancing the light and the dark, the comedic and the dramatic—but George Bailey from the mid-point on he's got to go through some really tough, dark stuff. And I think the reason that that film lives on today, and the reason every time you watch it is you get choked up at the end is because—I don't care how tough you are—it's because it's earned."
—Filmmaker Edward Burns (*The Brothers McMullen*)
The Q&A with Jeff Goldsmith

Capra always gets a lot of credit for *It's a Wonderful Life*, and justifiably so, but consider the film's other writers:

Francis Goodrich (screenplay),
Albert Hackett (screenplay), and
Frank Capra (screenplay)
Jo Swerling (additional scenes),
Philip Van Doren Stern (story),
Michael Wilson, contributor to screenplay (uncredited)

Goodrich and Hackett won the 1956 Pulitzer Prize for Drama for their play *The Diary of Anne Frank*. They both also received 4 Oscar nominations, including their script for *The Father of the Bride* (1950). Swerling, who was born in Ukraine, was a Tony-Award winning writer and lyricist who received an Oscar nomination for co-writing *The Pride of the Yankees*. Stern was born in Wyalusing, Pennsylvania and was an accomplished historian who wrote over 40 books. There was a lot of talent behind the story and script of *It's a Wonderful Life*.

Let's dig deeper and see what makes movie endings special.

IT'S THE RELATIONSHIPS, STUPID!

"Positive relationships trump positive accomplishments."
—Lindsay Doran

"If you just see two fighters pounding each other into unconsciousness, it doesn't pull you in as emotionally as seeing who they are fighting for."
—Sylvester Stallone

It is important to distinguish between the climax and the ending of your story. The distinction may be as subtle as a single shot, but it can make all the difference. To borrow Mark Twain's phrasing, there is a huge difference between the right ending and the almost-right ending.

The *almost-right* ending to *Rocky* occurs after the fight with Apollo Creed is over. Although Rocky loses the fight, he accomplishes his goal of going 15

rounds with the champ. The *right* ending, though, is when Rocky clutches Adrian in his arms in the ring just as Creed is announced the winner. Rocky's scene with Adrian was actually filmed during a reshoot with a small crew. Stallone had doubts that hugging Adrian would work as the ending, until he saw the final edit with Bill Conti's music playing. It wasn't the music alone, though, that made it such a fulfilling ending. It was the relationship, the embrace, and the proclamation of love.

Lindsay Doran, producer and former president of United Artists, points out in her TED Talk "Saving the World vs. Kissing the Girl" that movies like *Dirty Dancing, The Karate Kid,* and *The King's Speech* are not just about a triumphant dance, fight, or speech. Doran points out that the important moment arrives *after* their accomplishments— when it's shared with someone the hero loves. It's Jennifer Grey reconciling with her father, Ralph Macchio sharing his victory with his mother and Mr. Miyagi, and the ending graphic of *The King's Speech* stating, "Lionel and Bertie remained friends for the rest of their lives."

"What's being celebrated at the ends of those movies is each other. It's the tenderness and the kindness and the comfort of each other."
—Lindsay Doran

That certainly explains the ending of *It's a Wonderful Life.* I think the main story climax to *It's a Wonderful Life* is when the formerly suicidal George Bailey says he wants to live and then realizes he's alive. The film could have ended when he jumped for joy into the policeman's arms, but it wouldn't have been as fulfilling.

You could argue that what make *It's a Wonderful Life* such a wonderful ending is it has multiple climaxes. It doesn't just have an ending that ties up a few loose ends before it fades to black. There is an emotional climax when George reunites with his wife and kids. But wait there's more! Many people in town show up to give money to help George pay a debt and end up singing together. They could have faded to black there. But wait there's even more!

Michael Arndt points out that even after George Bailey solves his internal issues ("I want to live") and external issues (he doesn't owe a large debt), he still feels like a loser. He never went to the big city and found financial fortunes like Mr. Potter (the richest man in Bedford Falls). But that changed for the family man, by changing the meaning of a single word.

"[George] never became a rich man like Mr. Potter—until his war hero brother flies through a blizzard, raises a toast and goes, 'To George Bailey, the richest man in town.' And now you're inverting the meaning of what riches are. . . . A lot of time your hero's epiphany is just changing the meaning of a single word."
—Michael Arndt
OnWriting, WGA East podcast interview

And that's what made for an *Insanely Great Ending.*

INSANELY GREAT ENDINGS

Since 2006, Oscar-winning screenwriter Michael Arndt (*Little Miss Sunshine*) has occasionally given a talk called *Endings: The Good, The Bad, and The Insanely Great* at places like Pixar, Warner Brothers, Sundance, and various film festivals around the world. For years, you could only find cryptic bootleg notes from the talk on the internet. But now Arndt has the 90-minute presentation—in all its glory— online for free. I think it's one of the best screenwriting presentations ever.

Arndt breaks down film endings into three simple categories:

Bad = Positive . . . but Predictable
Good = Positive and . . . Surprising
Insanely Great = Positive, Surprising and . . . Meaningful (and Emotional)

Movies (and a book) that he says qualify for the Insanely Great Ending are:

8 ½
Catch-22 (the book)
Casablanca
Little Miss Sunshine
Rocky
Star Wars
The Bad News Bears (1976)
The Graduate

"I'm a huge believer that your story is all about your ending. So I would never write a story without knowing exactly, on a moment-by-moment basis, what's going to happen at the climax of your story. . . . And then you reverse engineer your story from there."
—Screenwriter Michael Arndt (*Little Miss Sunshine*)

So how do you get a meaningful ending?

Arndt says that the key is having three stakes—*internal, external,* and *philosophical.* That these three stakes need to come together in the final two minutes of the movie. Most movies have external stakes (get the money, win the fight, save the world), and internal stakes are quite common as well (romantic love, parent/child love, friendship), but philosophical stakes—the underlying *values* at stake in a movie—are harder to find.

Arndt thinks that the word theme obscures that philosophical stakes really are about conflicting values. It's a case of *the dominant values* vs. *the underdog values.* In *Casablanca,* for example, the conflicting values are community vs. individual.

The secret to an *insanely great ending* is as follows: a crisis forces the conflicting values to collide; the collision leads to a climax; the climax leads to a resolution in which "you're resolving all the stakes of your story all at the same time."

I will use one of my favorite all-time movie endings to explain what I think Arndt means. This is a natural example since it was written by Arndt (with a healthy assist from the Pixar brain trust).

Toy Story 3 could have ended at the 90-minute mark with Andy unselfishly giving his toys to Bonnie (the little girl at the end) and driving off to college with Woody. It would have been a good but bittersweet ending. The toys end up in a caring home and Woody is in his favored place with Andy.

Here's how the movie ends, though. As Andy finishes giving his toys (except Woody) to the little girl, the audience thinks Woody is safely in the car, in the box marked "college." But when the little girl looks in a box that the audience thinks is empty, she notices something. Her surprised glance begins a three-minute ending that pushes *Toy Story 3* into the *Insanely Great Ending* stratosphere.

00:00-00:27—It's Woody in the box. Andy is perplexed as he takes Woody out of the box. When the little girl reaches for Woody, Andy pulls Woody toward him. He's not sure he's ready to part with Woody.

00:28-01:29—He reflects on Woody and how special he is. After making sure she'll take care of Woody, he hands Woody to the little girl. They then play with the toys until it's time for him to leave.

01:30-3:00—After the young girl goes inside with her mother, Woody and the other toys sit up and watch Andy drive away. Woody says, "So long partner." Buzz Lightyear puts his arm around Woody to comfort him. Tilt up to clouds and fade to black.

External stakes: The toys are spared from doom (furnace, day care, attic) and have a new home with a caring person who will enjoy playing with them.

Internal stakes: Andy confirms that Woody was his oldest toy and has a special place in his heart.

Philosophical stakes: Woody sacrifices his special place with Andy to keep the old team together. He chooses community over self, as does Andy.

This tension between community and self also happens to be the central dilemma in both *Star Wars* and *Casablanca*.

A more recent example of an *Insanely Great Ending* is found in *A Quiet Place*. In terms of external stakes, the family is spared from the creatures. In terms of internal stakes, the father tells his daughter (via sign language) "I have always loved you." Philosophically, the question is "How far would you go to protect your children?"

In *A Quiet Place*, all these stakes reach a climax in the final 10 minutes. Although not everyone survives, the resolution of the philosophical stakes leads to a satisfactory ending for the audience. Without that philosophical resolution, I doubt it would have been such a huge hit.

One take-away from *Casablanca*, *Star Wars*, *Toy Story 3*, and *A Quiet Place* is that this formula for an *Insanely Great Ending* works whether the film is a classic drama, an action movie, a family film, or a horror film.

Arndt also makes clear that this isn't the only way to end a film. In fact, his favorite film (Ozu's *Late Spring*) does not have what he would consider an *Insanely Great Ending*. Nor do other favorites of his: Isao Takahata's *My Neighbors the Yamadas*, Satyajit Ray's *Panther Panchali,* or Guillermo del Toro's *Pan's Labyrinth.*

Arndt recommends *Taxi Driver* screenwriter Paul Schrader's book *Transcendent Film Style* to explore another kind of ending—the slow ending. Which is an aspect of slow cinema.

"'Slow cinema' is a fairly recent term used to designate a branch of art cinema which features minimal narrative, little action or camera movement and long running times."
—Paul Schrader

Other aspects of slow cinema are images preferred over dialogue, a visual flatness, and non-acting. Because slow cinema tends to move away from traditional narrative forms, today you will find examples in museums.

But along with Schrader's own *First Reformed*, other filmmakers from around the world who followed a "slow cinema" approach are Robert Bresson (*Pickpocket*), Carl Dryer (*The Passion of Joan of Arc*), Yasujirō Ozu (*Tokyo Story*), Roberto Rossellini (*Voyage in Italy*), and Andrei Tarkovsky (*Nostalgia*).

Schrader says the Tarkovsky's long shots are so long that they're meditative. We've all had that experience where a last shot stays on the screen riveting our attention and causing us to ponder what we've just experienced.

What supercharges an ending with meaning is an emotional release, a sense of clarity, seeing the world with "new eyes," and having an understanding that "life is actually pretty good."

That emotional release that Arndt talks about is what dramatic storytelling specializes in. A closely packed climax and conclusion can be powerful, and when done well can even bring about a catharsis.

7 CATHARSIS

"We all yearn for reconciliation, for catharsis."
Cobb (Leonardo DiCaprio)
Inception written by Christopher Nolan

"I made mistakes in drama. I thought drama was when actors cried. But drama is when the audience cries."
—Oscar-winning director Frank Capra (*You Can't Take It With You*)

"Story is an emotional journey. That's all it is."
—Oscar winning screenwriter Christopher McQuarrie (*The Usual Suspects*)
The Inside Pitch interview with Christopher Lockhart

"Everyone wants to find a way out of pain."
—Alex Blumberg
CreativeLive class *Power Your Podcast with Storytelling*

One of the most emotional scenes I've ever seen in a movie is when an adult Jenny in *Forrest Gump* throws rocks at her childhood home until she collapses in exhaustion. Forrest says in the voice over, "Sometimes there just aren't enough rocks." I've never experienced the abuse and trauma that Jenny had, but that scene makes my eyes water just thinking about it.

Movies that stir a strong emotional response personally are *Good Will Hunting, The Shawshank Redemption,* and *Tender Mercies.* For others it's *The Karate Kid, Titanic,* and *The Princess Bride.*

Studies show that movies have an ability to respond to heartbreak, death, and justice in ways that seem real. They also somehow have the ability to make us happy even when we're sad.

"I just started with the emotion I wanted to create in an audience, the emotion that a great drum solo can create for me. . . . I knew [*Whiplash*] was not going to be a subtle, quiet movie. This needed to be a movie that moved like a bullet train and hit the audience in the gut."
—Writer/director Damien Chazelle (*Whiplash*)
Go Into the Story interview with Tim Wainwright

AIM FOR THE HEART

Before Cal Fussman interviewed Mikhail Gorbachev for *Esquire* magazine, he was told he would only have 10 minutes with the one-time leader of the Soviet Union. Instead of jumping in with a question about nuclear disarmament, the Cold War, or Ronald Reagan, he asked this question:

"What's the best lesson your father ever taught you?"

This question prompted a long answer about how Gorbachev's father took his family to get ice cream before he went off to serve in World War II. When the publicist showed up ten minutes later, Gorbachev wasn't even finished with the story, much less answers to Fussman's other questions. Fussman thought he'd blown his opportunity.

But Gorbachev said he wanted to speak with Fussman further and ended up connecting the ice cream story—and fears that his father could be killed during the war— to President Reagan and ending the Cold War.

Fussman learned the power of that first question going to the heart and not the head. Fussman's view was that once you engaged the heart, you would connect with the head, and that would give you a "pathway to the soul."

Many great films and plays deal with core emotions like joy, sadness, fear, and anticipation. Sadness due to a loss, in fact, is one of the major emotional themes running throughout the history of drama.

August: Osage County (Tracy Letts)

Buried Child (Sam Shepard)

Crimes of the Heart (Beth Henley)

The Cherry Orchard (Chekhov)

Death of a Salesman (Miller)

Equus (Peter Shaffer)

Fences (August Wilson)

The Glass Menagerie (Tennessee Williams)

Glengarry Glen Ross (David Mamet)

Hedda Gabbler (Ibsen)

Juno and the Paycheck (Sean O'Casey)

Hamilton (Lin-Manuel Miranda)

King Lear (Shakespeare)

The Little Foxes (Lillian Hellman)

Long Day's Journey Into Night (O'Neil)

Medea (Euripides)

Miss Julie (Strindberg)

'Night Mother (Marsha Norman)

The Odd Couple (Neil Simon)

Oedipus Rex (Sophocles)

Prometheus Bound (Aeschylus)

Pygmalion (George Bernard Shaw)

A Raisin in the Sun (Lorraine Hansberry)

Ruined (Lynn Nottage)

A Trip to Bountiful (Horton Foote)

The Visit (Friedrich Durrenmatt)

Who's Afraid of Virginia Woolf? (Edward Albee)

"Sorrow is one of the vibrations that prove the fact of living."
— Antoine de Saint-Exupery

When exploring why emotions, and particularly sadness, seem to get so much stage time throughout theatrical history, it's hard not to dwell on the great American playwright Eugene O'Neill (1888-1953). O'Neill wrote his share of downbeat stories (*Long Day's Journey Into Night, The Iceman Cometh*). In 1936, he was the first American playwright to win the Nobel Prize for Literature.

In the 1922 article *Making Plays with a Tragic End: An Intimate Interview with Eugene O'Neill,* Malcolm Mollan had this exchange with O'Neill:

Malcolm Mollan: Have you any present purpose, or expectations, of writing a play with an out-and-out happy ending? You'll grant, I suppose, that there are interesting situations in life, even dramatic situations, out of which genuine happiness sometimes issues?

Eugene O'Neill: Sure, I'll write about happiness, if I ever happen to meet up with that luxury, and find it sufficiently dramatic and in harmony with any deep rhythm of life. But happiness is a word. What does it mean? Exaltation: an intensified feeling of the significant worth of man's being and becoming? Well, if it means that—and not a mere smirking contentment with one's lot—I know there is more of it in tragedy than in all the happy-ending plays ever written.

See here, it's a sheer present-day judgment to think tragedy as unhappy! The Greeks and the Elizabethans knew better. They felt the tremendous lift to it. It roused them spiritually to a deeper understanding of life. Through it they found release from the petty considerations of everyday existence. They saw their lives ennobled by it.

My mother died on a beautiful spring day following 10 days of ugly medical procedures in intensive care. At one point she looked at me near the end of her long life and said, "How long?" because her body was shutting down and she was ready to leave this world.

The moment she died my sister and I were by her side each holding one of her hands. It was the first and only time I've felt someone's pulse stop and watched their breathing cease. It was tragically beautiful. It was spiritual.

Is there ever a time in your life when you feel more mixed emotions then when someone close to you dies? That's often a time of experiencing both joy and sadness resulting in a melancholy state of being.

To have *tears of joy* is a cathartic experience. The term catharsis comes from the Greek word meaning purification or cleansing. Movies and theater have a unique ability to give us a metaphoric purification. Perhaps that's why David Mamet says, "Drama is the stepchild of religion."

PITY, FEAR, AND CATHARSIS

"Aristotle described the formula [in *Poetics*]. He did that two and a half thousand years ago. Not only did it work then, it still works today. So actually anyone who says there is no formula is wrong; there is. And Aristotle did it in a way that makes it incredibly easy to remember . . . pity, fear, and catharsis."
—Agent Julian Friedman
The Mystery of Storytelling

Friedman unpacks Aristotle's teaching by saying that audiences feel pity for a character when they watch a character go through misfortunes, often underserved.

I think the universal (and ongoing) appeal of the original *Rocky* movie is that the audience emotionally becomes Rocky. They go through the hard times with him. Friedman adds, "When you release the character from the jeopardy—or whatever the situation they're in—the audience experiences a catharsis. Pity, fear, catharsis."

"Pity, Fear, and Catharsis" is a useful and proven schema that screenwriters are wise to recall as they work to bring emotional power to their own scripts.

"I can remember very vividly in high school getting my heart broken and it was like a physical pain. I was physically nauseous. And anytime there is an emotion that is that strong, or that I can remember or feel that strongly in the present day, it's worth hanging a movie around."
—Writer/Director Jeff Nichols (*Mud*)

EMOTIONALLY MOVING THE AUDIENCE

"Storytelling is innate to the human condition. Its underpinnings are cerebral, emotional, communal, and psychological. One of the storyteller's main responsibilities is to resonate in the audience's psyche a certain something at the end of it all, to emotionally move the audience, to compel the audience to 'get it' on a visceral level."
—Oscar-nominated director Arthur Hiller (*Love Story*)
(Hiller also directed *The Hospital* for which Paddy Chayefsky won an Oscar for his script.)

Writer/director James Cameron has directed two of the biggest box office movies ever (*Titanic, Avatar*), but it's not just his special effects that attract a wide audience around the world.

"[James Cameron] gets a lot of points for being a techno-brat, but he is a very emotional storyteller."
—Steven Spielberg

"Cameron has long claimed that *Titanic* was at its core a love story. Or at least that's how he approached the venture. It's great to have a story with huge scope and stakes, but writers have to provide points of emotional connection for the reader in order for them to become invested in that bigger story."
—Scott Myers

Cameron co-wrote the script for *Terminator 2: Judgment Day* (*T2*) with William Wisher and directed the film that made over $500 million when it was released in 1991. It was the top box office film that year, and while it did win four Academy Awards—including visual effects—Cameron points to something deeper that he was after.

"Getting the audience to cry for the Terminator at the end of *T2*, for me that was the whole purpose of making the film. If you can get the audience to feel emotion for a character that in the previous film you despised utterly and were terrified by, then that's a cinematic arc."
—James Cameron

NO EMOTION? "YOUR SCREENPLAY SUCKS"

"Give the reader an emotional experience or you're wasting your time. It doesn't matter what emotion it is, but make damn sure he or she feels something."
—William M. Akers
Your Screenplay Sucks! : 100 Ways to Make It Great

One of the 100 Ways to make your script great in Akers' book is this:
"You don't give the reader enough emotion!

Emotion can be anything. Laughter. Fear. Compassion. Heartache. Lust."

One of Akers' illustrations is the scene in *E.T* when Elliott and E.T. fly for the first time, silhouetted against the moon.

Other emotional scenes that continue to be audience favorites include the "mad as hell" scene from *Network*, the filibuster scene in *Mr. Smith Goes to Washington*, Judy Garland singing "Somewhere Over the Rainbow" in *The Wizard of Oz*, the spaghetti scene from *Lady and the Tramp*, and the ending of *Toy Story 3*.

Is it even possible to have a memorable scene that isn't emotional?

EMOTIONAL MANIPULATION

"Isn't the whole point of making a trip to the movie theater that you're actually hoping to be emotionally manipulated? Because you want someone to tell you a story that will then make you laugh or cry?"
—Jim Hill

"Today, many film-makers are afraid to deal with sentiment, dismissing it as sentimentality. But the ability to properly handle sentiment and its underlying emotion, to get the most out of it without going over the line into mawkishness, is the trademark of the true dramatist."
—Director Edward Dmytryk (*The Caine Mutiny*)
On Screen Writing (published in 1985)

Not everyone is a fan of movies that have a more emotional bent. The chief argument is usually that they don't like being manipulated.

Here's what animation historian Michael Barrier said about the beloved Pixar movies:

"There's a sentimentality in most Pixar pictures that are very manipulative and completely unconvincing to me. They are congratulating their audience for feeling these synthetic emotions and, to me, that's offensive."

I recently heard an interview with an accomplished economist who said that he experienced neither great highs or great lows. He said that he knew some people struggled with depression, but that was totally foreign to him. He said he also knew that some people experienced euphoric highs, but that was something that he did not experience.

This fellow seemed to have a phlegmatic personality. The stable, calm, even-keeled type that is often stereotyped by accountants and engineers. "Just the facts, ma'am," as Sergeant Joe Friday said on *Dragnet*. That's okay. We're all wired differently.

I can't speak for Barrier, but I've met plenty of people over the years who don't like fantasy stories in general or specifically Disney films. I had one acting teacher who despised Spielberg's *E.T.* because he thought it was overly sentimental. You can't please everyone all the time, but the timeless and global acceptance of movie franchises like *Star Wars* and *Toy Story* tell us that the filmmakers are tapping into something there that connects with a wide audience.

If you want to have a theater that's only open when it rains— so you know you'll get a committed audience (as does Bill Murray's character in *Tootsie*)— that's your prerogative.

A distinctive characteristic of many independent and foreign films is that they are more cerebral than a typical Hollywood mainstream film. They appeal more to the intellect (and professional film critics and film scholars tend to be on the intellectual side). But if some emotional films come off as sappy, it's fair to say that many intellectual films come off as cold. It's a balance that must be determined by the filmmakers.

Contrary to critics like Barrier, I would argue that *Toy Story 3* has both a heart and a head. It not only earned over one billion dollars, but it also won the Academy Award for best Animated Film and earned a rare 100% approval rating from top critics on Rotten Tomatoes. I think *Toy Story 3* is a great film to study and works on many layers without being "grotesquely sentimental."

Sentimental? Yes. Grotesquely? Nah. I find nothing repulsive or distorted in *Toy Story 3*. The simple truth is we go to films *in order* to be manipulated. A lot of time, effort, skill, and money goes into picking the right voice, sound effects, music, lighting, camera moves, wardrobe, and props that the performers can capture an audience's emotions with a story. There are plenty of people yearning for a well-told story to take them on an emotional journey. That's why they're buying a ticket.

A GYMNASIUM FOR THE SENSES

"I'm in a glass case of emotion."
Ron Burgundy (Will Ferrell), *The Anchorman*

Richard Walter has a whole chapter in his book *Essentials of Screenwriting* simply titled "Emotion."

"Film is for feeling. . . . Frighten the folks, make them cry, make them angry; they will stand in line to see your movie. Human beings need regularly to experience strong emotions; it's how we know we are alive."
—Richard Walter

Walter added that we should consider the movie theater a "gymnasium for the senses" which is great imagery. And advice that resonates with advice written way back in 1937.

"In writing the film story, keep in mind that the object is to make the reader or spectator *feel*. The object of all drama is to move an audience to some definite feeling; to make an impression not on the intellect, but on the senses."
—Francis Marion
How to Write and Sell Film Stories

And here's the same sentiment from the writer of the Oscar nominated screenplay *Lion*. (The story of a five-year-old boy in India accidently separated from his family at age five, who searches for his family as an adult.)

"The movie [*Lion*] is primarily an emotional journey, and the movies that matter to me, you experience them here, in the heart and the gut. They're not such intellectual exercises as visceral and emotional experiences."
—Screenwriter Luke Davies
Moviemaker

It is worth noting that in ancient Greece gymnasiums were also a place that not only stressed physical pursuits, but scholarly and philosophical ones as well. But I think it's fair to say that movies and emotion are a powerful combination.

AESTHETIC EMOTION

"Aestheticism is a search after the signs of the beautiful. It is the science of the beautiful through which men seek the correlation of the arts. It is, to speak more exactly, the search after the secret of life."
—Oscar Wilde

One way screenwriters can help generate emotional connections in their audiences is simply through beautiful imagery, skillfully conveyed. Audiences are frequently moved by elements of the story itself. For example, someone dies, a romance falls apart, or lovers reunite. But sometimes emotional responses have more to do with a striking image, sound, situation, etc. The reason for the response may be difficult to articulate; a beautiful image is shared, and the beauty itself seems to catalyze the emotional response. The moment feels *sublime*.

An example from a movie during which the characters experience aesthetic emotion occurs in *The Shawshank Redemption*, when Mozart's music is played in the prison courtyard. Red observes;

"I have no idea to this day what those two Italian ladies were singing

about. Truth is—I don't want to know, some things are best left unsaid. I like to think they were singing about something so beautiful that it can't be expressed in words and makes your heart ache because of it."

Beyond elements of plot or character that are likely to elicit emotional responses for more obvious reasons—the audience can relate to them in some meaningful way—screenwriters can also look for opportunities to move audiences with beauty itself, generating idiosyncratic and memorable movie moments.

EMOTIONAL STUCTURE

"Plot is more than a pattern of events, it is the ordering of emotions."
—Irwin Blacker
Elements of Screenwriting

"Without understanding Emotional Structure, the beginning, the middle, and the end of your script have a 100 percent chance of becoming the beginning, the muddle, and the end. Because emotions rule the central, most misunderstood and most feared element of a screenplay: that of the story's underlying meaning."
—Emmy Award-winner and UCLA instructor Peter Dunne
Emotional Structure: Creating the Story Beneath the Plot

"Directors don't make pictures, directors make things that you are supposed to get an emotional hit off of. You're supposed to feel something."
—Director David Fincher (*Se7en, Fight Club*)

"Doesn't everyone feel in the same language? Emotion, which equals great writing, transcends genres, ages, economic classes, and political boundaries."
—Karl Iglesias

"There's no movie that can't be told through its emotions. And there's no movie that succeeds that is told any other way."
—Screenwriter Billy Ray (*Captain Phillips*)

Your hero's goal is not really what the film should be about; rather, you should focus on the hero's *emotional transformation* as she pursues that goal. This is where emotional structure intersects with theme, or the philosophical stakes. Here's a quick overview of how this has played out in some classic films from the last few decades:

1960s: *The Apartment* is about more than the plot of Jack Lemmon's character getting his apartment back. It's about him standing up for himself and becoming a man with a backbone. He becomes a more complete person.

1970s: *Rocky* is about more than the plot of trying to become a champion boxer. It's really about him becoming a more complete person. Early in the movie his old trainer calls him a loser and that concept is what he's fighting against the whole movie.

1980s: The plot of *Die Hard* is about a cop who wants to stop terrorists, but emotionally it's about reconciling with his estranged wife.

1990s: The plot of *Schindler's List* is about an imperfect man trying to save people from concentration camps, but as we watch him stand up to evil and become a more selfless man, the emotional lesson for the viewer is that they can do the same.

2000s: The plot of *Erin Brockovich* is a woman leading a legal crusade against a corporate giant, but emotionally and thematically it's about a woman overcoming tremendous odds to provide for her family and become whole.

2010s: The plot of *Toy Story 3* involves a gang of toys trying to physically survive destruction after being accidentally being put in the trash, but emotionally and thematically it's about surviving change and finding new purposes in life.

2020s: The plot of *Sound of Metal* is about a drummer hoping to regain his loss of hearing, but it's also emotionally and thematically about surviving change and finding a new purpose in life. (Echoes of *Toy Story 3*.)

Notice that the short list of films above not only have strong emotional structures, but they all span different decades and genres. They are primal and universal stories, widely enjoyed by audiences and critics.

There are films in which characters are transformed by difficult situations that finish with a sense of completeness and harmony that they didn't have at the start of the movie. It's not hard to understand why this connects with moviegoers; the urge to overcome our own flaws and become better people while making the world a better place is found universally, across eras and cultures.

"Witness **is a great little film that works on all levels. The ending of one thing is always the beginning of something else."**
—Syd Field

The 1985 movie *Witness* sparks a wide range of emotions in the viewer. It elicits happiness, sadness, disgust, surprise, anticipation, love, trust, excitement, tenderness, anger, and fear. Perhaps part of the explanation for the film's success (and an enduring favorite to be discussed in screenwriting circles) is that all these feelings can be experienced in the first act alone, as they organically emerge from the events of the story.

The writers of *Witness* (William Kelly, Earl K. Wallace, and Pam Wallace) won an Academy Award for their script and story (Peter Weir—director of *Witness*—also had an uncredited hand in shaping the script.) Beyond the first act, they continued to build emotionally poignant moments into the story: feelings of affection, pride, passion, nervousness, sadness, shame, shock, alienation, disappointment, panic, hope, courage, and others as well.

Peter Dunne, in his book *Emotional Structure,* writes that the opening scene of *Witness* would look like this on an index card:

Opening in AMISH COUNTRY

A FUNERAL. The COMMUNITY DRESSED IN TRADITIONAL AMISH CLOTHES. Then a gathering AT RACHEL'S FAMILY FARMHOUSE.

We SEE the CULTURE and the PEOPLE. It is A GENTLE WORLD, SINCERE AND SWEET even at an emotional time as this.

WE MEET RACHEL, SAMUEL, ELI and the others. SET UP HER TRIP TO THE CITY

Many writers use index cards to help build their dramatic structure. They can help you envision the flow of the story. The twist Dunne suggests is writing out the emotional payoff of the scene on the back of the card.

Dunne writes, "We are creating an emotional structure for our screenplay, and this card is worthless unless it contains the emotional content and the emotional intent of the scene."

Here's my version of writing from the opening of Witness of what you might write on the back of your index card to address emotion intent:

"Sorrow and hurt fill the farmhouse as tears are shed at an Amish funeral that appears to be another time in another country—but is in fact current day rural Pennsylvania. The audience is disoriented by the Amish language and has compassion for a wife and young son who have lost a husband and a father."

Or you could write with more Sorkin-like brevity on the front of your index card: "Rural Amish Funeral. Tears and sorrow. Introduce widow and son."

Either way, you are now on your way to emotionally (on top of dramatically) structuring your film.

"Scene after scene you will build on those emotions until eventually even the smallest occurrences in the plot will have emotional impact. . . . [Y]our audience will begin to react viscerally to things late in the script that were introduced in the beginning of the script. . . ."
—Peter Dunne

Even if you aren't the type of writer who uses index cards or other visual aids to track your story, assessing the emotional impact of each scene is important in understanding the emotional structure of your film. Directors, actors, cinematographers, and editors all can benefit from working to determine the emotional thrust of each scene.

YOUR CHARACTER'S EMOTIONAL LIFE

"A character's emotional life helps the audience to identify with the character and understand his motivations. . . . When the emotional component of a story is left out, the characters seem flat and unreal."
—Linda J. Cowgill
The Art of Plotting

In *The Bourne Identity*, Jason Bourne (Matt Damon) has a problem: he doesn't know who he is because he suffers from amnesia. Even though it's an action-adventure movie with plenty of crafty fight scenes and thrilling car chases, the filmmakers take time to make an emotional connection between not only the main characters, but between Jason and the audience.

It doesn't necessarily require a lot of text to establish emotionally poignant moments for your characters. In one brief exchange between Jason and Marie (Franka Potente), as the two characters are about to part ways, Jason says, "Thanks for the ride." Marie replies, "Anytime." Damon's pause before responding indicates the emotion Jason feels at this moment. A few seconds later, he tells her she can wait for him, to which she responds, "You'd probably just forget me if I stayed here." Jason replies, "How could I forget about you? You're the only person I know." The entire scene is only a minute long, and the dialogue is sparse, but we its fine writing, acting, directing, and editing generate a rich exchange. That sort of attention to detail is part of what separates the film from standard roller coaster actions movies.

EMOTIONAL CATHARSIS — DIABLO CODY

In this exploration of emotions in screenwriting and filmmaking I've quoted other on the important role that emotions have on characters, audiences, and on script readers.. But I have yet to touch on the emotions *of the writer*.

"Everything I write is an emotional catharsis. It's my way of exorcising demons."
—Diablo Cody
Marie Claire interview by James Mottram

"I got into screenwriting for the best of all reasons: I got into it for self-therapy."
—Paul Schrader (*Taxi Driver, Raging Bull*)

"My body goes through the pain that I am going through in the writing. I feel the tenseness if I'm writing a scene between, let's say, a husband and wife who are having a fractious marriage."
—Neil Simon
Fresh Air interview with Terry Gross

I remember writing a scene once in which a dog died and being moved to tears. And when a reader of that script said she cried reading that scene I knew I had tapped into something special.

EMOTIONALLY SILENT DIALOGUE

"You'll find in times of great emotions in films, the characters almost always speak less words, not more. I count silence as a form of dialogue."
—David Freeman

"The perfect movie doesn't have any dialogue. So you should always be striving to make a silent movie."
—David Mamet
On Film Directing

There's a scene that comes to mind from *Cast Away* written by William Broyles, Jr. that's a great example of emotional silent dialogue. It occurs after Chuck (Tom Hanks) arrives home in Memphis after working his high-pressure FedEx job in Moscow, Russia and meets Kelly (Helen Hunt).

`INT. MEMPHIS STATE-BIOLOGY BLDG-NIGHT-MOMENTS LATER`

`Chuck walks down the hall toward where a WOMAN stands, her back to his, using a XEROX MACHINE. The clock above her says 1:35. A case of specimen jars along the wall.`

The woman is KELLY, hair up, glasses on, dressed in no-nonsense jeans. We see her face in the green intermittent light. She examines each page as it comes out, scanning the writing, making a quick note on one of the charts. We hear Ka-Chunk, Ka-Chunk of the machine.

For a long moment we are on Chuck's face as he stares at her. He's just come from talking to Stan about Mary and, by implication, the fragility of life. He's home from Russia. This is the woman he loves. Kelly senses his presence and turns to face him. A smile lights her face.

                    KELLY
          It's you...

She comes into his arms. As they hug, in the b.g. we hear the Ka-Chunk of the copier. Chuck begins to move to it, a slow, romantic dance to the beat of the Xerox. The machine stops. Kelley pushes a button. It starts again, and so does their dance.

And that's it. It's just a half page of writing—two spoken words in a broken sentence— but also so key to understanding their relationship. Christopher McQuarrie says that "Information is the death of emotion." That *Cast Away* scene could have been killed with, "When did you get back in town?"

EMOTIONAL CUES

"Great writers show how a character is angry by writing specific actions that suggest this action. They should never write, 'She is angry.' Instead, they should write, 'She throws a pot through a window.'"

—Karl Iglesias
Writing for Emotional Impact

An excellent example of emotional cues is a half-page scene from Mark Boal's *The Hurt Locker* script. This scene follows the explosion of

Improvised Explosive Device (IED) that killed a soldier on the streets of Baghdad.

INT CAMP VICTORY WAREHOUSE MORTUARY AFFAIRS - DAY

the wooden lid of a very white large box.

Inside, wrapped in plastic, are the remains of a soldier's life: a pair of boots, a toothbrush, a comb, an American flag.

Sanborn stares. Struggling to find meaning in objects.

Now we se that he's standing in a large warehouse, the mortuary affairs office, which is filled with rows and rows of many other identical white boxes.

> MORTUARY SOLDIER
> Anywhere is good.

Sanborn gently places Thompson's dog tags in the box.

> SOLIDER
> Is that everything?

> SANBORN
> Yeah.

The white box closes. Latches secure the lid.

And that's that. The soldier walks away.

Sanborn grips the box. He does not let go.

Notice that Boal doesn't come close to writing, "Sanborn is overcome with grief," or "Sanborn feels sad that his buddy is dead." Rather, he provides two short and simple sentences, "Sanborn grips the box. He does not let go." The emotional cues are quite subtle.

Later in the script, a soldier back from Iraq adjusts to civilian life as he shops in a U.S. supermarket.

CEREAL AISLE

James stares at the rows and rows of cereal boxes, a medley of different brands and containing the same sugar and coloring and starch

He looks this way and that.

Thrown by abundant choices after the starkness of Baghdad, he can't decide which brand is his.

He reaches for a box, then pulls back, still unsure of himself.

Giving up, he picks a box at random and tosses it into the cart.

Again, there is no hint of words like "confusion" or "disoriented." Boal doesn't write "He is overwhelmed by the many choices of American consumerism and feels lost and alone."

Boal wrote emotional cues— showing, not telling— and left plenty of room for the actors and directors to do their jobs. The film won six Oscars including one for Boal (Best Writing, Original Screenplay), one for Kathryn Bigelow (Best Director), and Best Motion Picture of the Year.

Another war movie that is full of emotional cues is *Saving Private Ryan*, which won five Oscars, and a nomination for screenwriter Robert Rodat. Of course, your screenplay doesn't have to be about war to have emotional cues. But war heightens reality and shows people in extreme situations, so it's no surprise that stories of war are full of emotional cues.

EMOTIONAL EVOLUTION/DEVOLUTION

"A relentless focus on the Inner Game is the key to writing a successful screenplay."
—Sandy Frank

Tiger Woods won a golf tournament in 2018 after a five-year drought of victories. Back in 2009 Tiger Woods was the most dominant player in the game and had won 71 PGA Golf Tournaments.

But at the end of November 2009 his personal life and professional golf game spiraled downward. A costly divorce and a loss of major sponsors followed. He went two years without a victory, and did rebound some, but injuries and age prevented him from regaining the stature he once had.

Tiger's well-published struggles are a fitting metaphor for a book *The Inner Game of Screenwriting* by Sandy Frank. Frank was a former Wall Street Corporate lawyer and four-time Emmy-winning writer for *The David Letterman Show*. Frank writes, "The Outer Game is what we usually think of as plot. It's what's going on onscreen, out in the world."

To continue the sports metaphor, Rocky wants to beat the champ (Outer) —but he also wants to prove to himself (Inner) that he's not the bum his ex-trainer said he was.

Frank wasn't the first writer to consider the inner/outer story. Here's how one screenwriting book unpacked it back in 1994:

"Screenplays often tell two main stories, The Outside/Action Story is driven by the goal. It is sometimes referred to as the spine. The Inside/Emotion Story usually derives from a relationship and is generally driven by the need. It is sometimes referred to as the heart of the story or the emotional through-line."
—David Trottier
The Screenwriter's Bible

Frank stressed the importance of the inner story and goes as far as saying, "The Head is important, but what really sells the film to an audience is the Heart." The subject of emotion is something that some books on screenwriting and filmmaking don't touch on at all. But if you're looking for a missing key to screenwriting, I think it's spelled e-m-o-t-i-o-n.

What I like most about Frank's book is where he says the three most common archetypes are Evolution, Devolution, and Staying the Course.

Tiger's story is one where he evolved professionally into one of the most dominant athletes ever, and then he professionally and personally devolved. That is what's so fascinating about his story. And we can relate to that to one degree or another.

"All of us human beings have flaws and try to overcome them. We watch movies to see characters struggle with that same ordeal."
—Sandy Frank

There have been plenty of movies that provide two hours of mindless, joyful entertainment, like an amusement park ride. These movies only have a solid Outer Story. But I think that the movies that stick with us—and the ones we return to again and again—do touch an emotional chord, and do so by having, "A relentless focus on the Inner Game."

Our great hope is that Humpty Dumpty can be put back together again. Especially when the Humpty Dumpty is us. In Tiger Woods' case, he did get put back together. In 2019, after four back surgeries in two years, he became the second oldest golfer to win the Masters Tournament. Headlines claimed his one-stroke victory and life rebound was "almost miraculous."

Gary Ross ends his screenplay for *Seabiscuit* with these words spoken by Red (Tobey Maguire): "You know, everybody thinks we found this broken-down horse and we fixed him, but we didn't . . . He fixed us. Every one of us. And, I guess in a way, we kind of fixed each other too."

MORPH ARCHETYPES

Here is an overview of what Sandy Frank writes about regarding what he called Morph Archetypes—Evolution, Devolution, and Staying the Course:

Evolution

The Evolution Archetype is the classic Hollywood ending where the main character overcomes a flaw, which leads to growth, which leads to a positive ending. Frank writes, "Whether or not he attains the goal of the Outer Game is almost beside the point, and in different movies that can go either way. The important thing is the growth expressed by the Inner Game."

It's easy to rattle off some of my favorite films over the last few decades that fit this category: *The Apartment, Babette's Feast, The Breakfast Club, Casablanca, Erin Brockovich, Good Will Hunting, It's a Wonderful Life, The Matrix, An Officer and A Gentleman, On the Waterfront, Rain Man, Schindler's List, Seabiscuit, The Shawshank Redemption, Star Wars, Tender Mercies, Tootsie, Toy Story, Wall Street, The Verdict,* and *Winter's Bone.*

Devolution

Frank writes, "In this type of story, the main character starts out healthy, but through the course of the screenplay he devolves or sinks, ending up at a lower level than where he was at the beginning."

Films that fit this pattern include *A Place in the Sun, Black Swan, Citizen Kane, Death of a Salesman, Joker, The Godfather, Psycho, Treasure of the Sierra Madre,* and *The Wrestler. Aguirre, the Wrath of God* is an example of a bad character getting even worse.

Staying the Course

Not all main characters change for better or worse.

This is an important distinction to make. People sometimes argue about who the main character is in a certain movie, and the claim is often made that the character who changes the most is the one the movie is about. I don't think that is always the case, though.

Recently I watched *Saving Private Ryan* again and I think the main character of the story is the Capt. John Miller (Tom Hanks). But he doesn't change much throughout the film. What he does do is follow the chain of command, and he changes those around him. They follow his lead and accomplish their mission.

Ferris Bueller's Day Off, Forrest Gump, Hud and *The Untouchables* all have main characters who stay the course and change the characters around them. Superheroes in general seem to fall into the staying-the-course group.

MAKING EMOTIONAL CONNECTIONS

Linda Cowgill, in her book *The Art of Plotting*, writes that emotions are hardest aspect of writing to teach because they are so difficult to deal with in a systematic way. It's easier to address things like intentions and conflict. Yet, she does a solid job of driving home how emotions work in stories.

"Great writers rake their heroes over the coals because this is how stories develop emotion, and emotion is how stories connect with their audience. . . . Emotion is the great universal that unites us in the human condition."
—Linda Cowgill

The following exchange between screenwriters Anne Spielberg and Gary Ross is from the expanded DVD edition of *Big*. The 1988 film brought the screenwriters an Oscar nomination. One of their goals in writing a script with lots of humor was trying not to be funny.

Ross: If there was a punchline on top of the situation where you could feel the writer, we'd yank it out. If you were organically laughing at the situation, then that was great. That's where the comedy should come from. If we went through pages and pages [in reading the script for *Big*] when you weren't laughing, that was okay.

Spielberg: And that's what gave the poignancy to it—that you're always on that edge of being a kid on his own, and he can't go home again. There's always that little moment of sadness just right around the corner.

Ross: And under a lot of the movie there is a lot of sadness. A loss of childhood is a wonderful and sad thing, and I think we respected both of those emotions. And I think one of the things we did that was good was when the story wasn't funny to us, but was true to the story—that was okay.

Writer/director Judd Apatow says people should think of comedies as dramas when they're writing. That the story should work even if there weren't any jokes. I think that is true of *Big* and his comedy classic *The 40-Year-Old Virgin*.

SORKIN'S EMOTIONAL DRIVE

When we think of climaxes in movies, it's easy to think of moments like the shark exploding at the end of *Jaws*. Less is said, though, about emotional climaxes. We're back in the realm of the outer story and the inner story. The outer story of *The Social Network*, written by Sorkin, has to do with a lawsuit surrounding Facebook. The inner emotional story, though, is what packs a punch in the last scene.

Sorkin sets up *The Social Network* story in the dynamic opening scene by showing Mark Zuckerberg's (played by Jesse Eisenberg) emotional mindset of wanting to be popular and accepted. I wouldn't be surprised if Sorkin wrote the opening and the closing scenes first, as they make such tidy bookends.

If *The Social Network* were a proverb it could be, "What shall it profit a man if he gains the world, but forfeits his friends?" The following comment by Sorkin gives some insight into how he went about developing the Zuckerberg character.

"Just because you have money, it's not like you no longer have emotions. [Zuckerberg] spends the first hour and 55 minutes of the movie being an anti-hero and the last five minutes being a tragic hero. I'm not judging, I want to respect and defend him so I locate the things in him that are most like myself . . . I'm awkward socially, and I've spent a lot of time with my nose pressed up against the glass feeling like an outsider."
—Aaron Sorkin

"I LOVE LUCY" LOVED EMOTION

It's hard to imagine that the small three-person writing team of Bob Carrol Jr., Madelyn Pugh Davis, and Jess Oppenheimer cranked out 30+ episodes each year for the first three seasons of *I Love Lucy*.

Lucille Ball called Oppenheimer "the brains" behind *I Love Lucy*. Davis and Carrol would meet with Oppenheimer to discuss story ideas and then go off and write the scripts together. Davis said one of the main questions they asked each week was "What emotion are we going to use this week?"

GIVING THE READER THE MOVIE EXPERIENCE

"People go to films to experience emotions."
—Paul Chitlik

Both Aaron Sorkin and Tony Gilroy said that one of the key things they learned from William Goldman about writing screenplays was that you should aim to give the reader as close as possible the *experience* of seeing the movie in theaters.

A non-traditional example of what Goldman called "readability" is found in his script *Butch Cassidy & the Sundance Kid* when he introduces the superposse in one line (in all caps): THE LONGEST TRAVELING SHOT IN THE HISTORY OF THE WORLD.

In his Oscar-winning script *Michael Clayton*, Gilroy didn't mind writing interior motivations and emotions of the lead character who pulls over in his Mercedes to stare at three horses in an open pasture, "the simplest thing to say is that this is a man who needs more than anything to see one pure, natural thing, and by some miracle has found his way to this place."

Gilroy says he's desperate to keep the overworked reader turning pages. Keep in mind that people reading your script are busy people.

"I've had clients write long scenes where it's just dialogue, ping-ponging back and forth between 2-3 characters. And as enjoyable as good dialogue can be, it can sometimes be hard to pick up the exact emotional nuance of what's going on in the scene. This is especially true if you're reading quickly because you have 12 other scripts to read that Sunday night. Which is often the case for execs and agents. It's not heartening to hear this, but it's a reality of the industry that work is rarely read in ideal circumstances."
—Literary Manager John Zaozirny (Bellevue Productions)

"I definitely have a thing from being an executive and reading so many scripts that I'm always afraid of kind of boring the reader."
—Screenwriter Pete Chiarelli (*The Proposal*)

Here's how others keep emotion at the forefront of their stories.

"The creative piece of writing—play, story, poem, rides on emotion. Usually on the emotion of the central character. By emotion I mean hunger, a desire, something burning under that character, humming and beating like a motor, sending him forward."
—Samson Raphaelson
The Human Nature of Playwriting

"What people really want to see, whether the character is a bookkeeper or a football player, is an emotional dramatic journey they can relate to."
—Writer/director Sylvester Stallone
Deadline interview with Mike Fleming Jr.

"I think all stories are emotionally based. From comedies to action adventures. If you don't have the emotional center of a piece then you lose everything else."
—Writer/director Paul Haggis (*Crash*)

"On the computer monitor on which I'm seeing your face right now, in big block letter across the top, it says WHAT IS THE SIMPLE EMOTIONAL JOURNEY? That's always the mantra for me. That's always the true north. Screenwriting is an intellectual exercise that's designed to illicit and emotional response."
—Screenwriter Billy Ray (*Shattered Glass*)
UCLA's *Story Break* interview with Simon Herbert and Chris Kyle

Ken Burns said the first time he saw his dad cry was when his dad was watching a movie. Burns decided at that point—as a 12-year-old in Ann Arbor, Michigan—that he wanted to be a filmmaker.

If there's one thing that helps give emotions some gravitas, it's having a controlling idea.

8 CONTROLLING IDEA

WRITING FROM THEME

"I was astounded at how really useful 'thematic thinking' turned out to be."
—Stephen King

"I think what makes a film stick to the brain is the theme."
—William C. Martell

"It took me time to realize plot, characters and all that were important, but it really had to be about something."
—Carl Foreman

"To produce a mighty work, you must choose a mighty theme."
—Herman Melville

There are many ways to attack writing your story. If you read enough of how writers ply their trade, you'll find produced writers who begin with different elements of the script in mind, for example plot, character, or situation. Another angle is to write from theme, or a controlling idea. Even those who don't start with theme usually discover one anyway at some point during their process.

I've read successful screenwriters and directors say some version of these contradictory things:

A) I never think in terms of theme.
B) I usually start with theme.
C) The theme reveals itself somewhere in the writing.
D) Theme is something the audience sees when the film hits the theaters.
E) I avoid writing from theme to avoid the story being message driven.
F) I have no clue what the word theme means.

Theme is not your story, but it is what your story is really about. The story of *Scarface* (1983) is a Cuban emigrant who rises from tent city to become a drug lord in Miami. The theme of *Scarface* is the old standard that crime doesn't pay; a life of excess and ruthless ambition will destroy you. Theme-wise, Tony Montana (Al Pacino) is in the same family as Shakespeare's *Macbeth*.

Variations of theme can pop up anywhere in the story. At the beginning of Oliver Stone's *Wall Street,* the first words out of Bud Fox's (Charlie Sheen) mouth when asked how he's doing are, "Any better and it'd be a sin." Bud Fox ends up doing much better. Not only is it a sin, but he also has to go to prison for it.

Stone uses the wiser, older Lou (Hal Holbrook) as the voice of reason when he tells Bud, "That's the problem with money — it makes you do things you don't want to do." Another time he tells Bud, "Enjoy it while it lasts — 'cause it never does."

That film takes place in '85, but the theme still resonates today: Crime doesn't pay, or a life of excess will destroy you, or even "the love of money is the root of all sorts of evil." Good themes are timeless and universal.

The big difference between *Scarface* and *Wall Street* is that Bud Fox doesn't get killed at the end like Tony Montana. Bud seems to have learned his lesson. There's a ray of hope for Fox at the end.

Speaking of hope . . . *The Shawshank Redemption* is all about hope, and screenwriter and director Frank Darabont finds many ways to express that theme. On page 63 of the script, Andy says while in prison "...there's a small place inside of us they never lock away, and that place is called hope."

The most often quoted line from the film is "Get busy living, or get busy dying."

Some writers post the theme on the wall where they write to keep them centered and focused. On the front page of *The Shawshank Redemption* script are the words, "Hope is a good thing, maybe the best of things, and no good thing ever dies . . . ." These words echo throughout the film and can stick with us long after we leave the theater.

The theme of hope is one of the major reasons people watch *The Shawshank Redemption* again and again. You don't have to have been in a state prison to know what it's like to live in your own personal prison. Or at least know what it's like to almost lose hope in difficult situations.

Theme is quite evident at the end of *Braveheart* when William Wallace (Mel Gibson) yells the last word of the film, "Freedom!" (or, as the screenplay says, "FREEEEE-DOMMMMMMM!"). Throughout the film, the theme "Live free or die" is clearly fleshed out.

"Great writers communicate theme through action and images, with good dialogue used sparingly. They prove their theme by showing it, not talking about it."
—Linda Seger
Making a Good Writer Great

"The most important decision I have to make: What is this movie about?. . . [W]hat is it about emotionally? What is the theme of the movie, the spine, the arc? What does the movie mean to me? Personalizing the movie is very important."
—Director Sidney Lumet
Making Movies

"The theme of [*Black Panther*] is, 'Am I my brother's keeper?' Each character has a different answer to that question and only one changes his answer. . . . My favorite action movies have themes that are deep, that you can chew on."
—Ryan Coogler

"Theme is the primary statement, the purpose of the story, the overall message, the truth behind the story."
—Robin U. Russin & William Missouri Downs
Writing the Picture

"The theme leads me to the character's flaw, but I remove the word 'flaw' and I replace it with the word "armor." Giving them a flaw makes me inherently judgmental of my characters. . . . That helps me into act two, which is like, 'How do I throw rocks at this armor?'"
—Screenwriter Anthony Grieco

"Theme is the most important element of a good screenplay. It's the driving intention behind the film. It's the message that the writer is trying to get across to the audience which, when effectively communicated, satisfies them, emotionally and analytically, and makes them feel they've just watched a good film."
—Emmy award-winning writer/producer Jeffrey Scott
The Importance of Theme in Screenwriting

"If your story isn't about anything—or your character just wants a pretty girl and a bag of money then it's not going to add up to anything. It may be funny—but most comedies are funny in the first act, they're funny in the second act, and then they either get sappy and sentimental in the third act or they just fall apart."
—Screenwriter Michael Arndt *(Toy Story 3)*
February 15, 2007 talk at Cody's Books in San Francisco

"When I construct my characters, I start by asking myself, 'What is the thematic value of my story?' Then I go, 'OK. Let's meet someone at the beginning of this story who doesn't believe in that value.' To me, a screenplay or a book, they're like a thesis. You're trying to either prove or disprove a value.
— Anthony Grieco
Scott Myers at the *Go Into the Story* blog

THOSE THAT LIKE STARTING FROM THEME

"So usually, for me, I have a thematic idea—an inspiration —and then I build everything around that."
—Writer/director Judd Apatow (*The 40-Year Old Virgin*)

I first became aware of Diane Frolov's writing back in the '90s when I saw her name in the credits for *Northern Exposure*. She and her writing partner and husband Andrew Schneider wrote and produced many episodes of the quirky show set in Cicely, Alaska. They won a Primetime Emmy for their episode "Seoul Mates."

Frolov's writing credits go back to TV programs *Magnum P.I.* and *The Incredible Hulk*. She was on *The Sopranos* team that won an Emmy in 2006 for Outstanding Drama Series.

William Froug interviewed Frolov (who was a student of Froug's at UCLA) and asked her to identify the most important thing to know before writing a screenplay. She replied,

"I would say theme. You really need to know what the piece is 'about' and you have to make sure that all plot turns and character arcs elucidate and project that theme."
—Diane Frolov

I've always been a *Northern Exposure* fan and put it up there with *The Twilight Zone* as television at its best. Consider the similarity between Frolov's response and the following quote from Rod Serling:

"In my case, first I think of a theme and then choose a story line or a plot to go with it. Once this is chosen, the characters fall into place."
—Rod Serling

"I'm personally a big fan of knowing what your theme is before starting. I think they can arise as you tell the story, but writing within and for a theme seems to me to help the process along."
—Screenwriter Kelly Marcel (*Saving Mr. Banks*)
Go Into the Story interview with Scott Myers

"Examine any good plot and you will find a theme embedded in it; it is the theme that gives the plot objective and purpose. A plot that does not prove anything is diffused and uninteresting. It 'doesn't get anywhere.' As a matter of fact, a plot is merely the more or less mechanical invention that gives opportunity to the characters to portray a theme; and the theme keeps the story from being just a series of episodes concerning the same characters."
—Frances Marion

"Is there a thematic narrative question that's being asked? And is it answered? Because without that it's not very fulfilling storytelling."
—Director Ron Howard (*A Beautiful Mind*)

"I will say like any time that we've gone off and written things where we haven't really honed in on any theme whatsoever, that's where you start getting into the weeds and you start losing your sight."
—Scott Beck (*A Quiet Place*)

In the book *Script Tease* by Dylan Callaghan, Diablo Cody was asked, "What guides you through a story if you don't outline? Is it character or a certain voice?":
"I like to pick a theme. I know that sounds stupid. It's not a super advanced technique. They pick a theme on *Laverne and Shirley*. I think about what the emotional core of the story is, what's something I can play on across multiple story lines, and I go from there."
—Diablo Cody

"The more you can find a theme that unites the plot and the character and think about that theme as you're writing, the better off you'll be determining the story's structure.
—Screenwriter Lawrence Konner (*Boardwalk Empire, Mona Lisa Smile*)
On Screenwriting

"I always work backwards from theme. . . . So once I know what that theme is about then I percolate on different ways to illustrate the theme. And every scene in the movie will be in service to supporting the theme."
—Writer/director Audrey Wells (*Under the Tuscan Sun*)
Anatomy of a Script

"The major theme is the heart and soul of your screenplay. Without a theme, your script will be hollow, empty."
—William Froug
Screenwriting Tricks of the Trade

"What I like best is a good moral story."
—Filmmaker Oscar Micheaux (*Within Our Gates*)
Micheaux (1884-1951) is regarded as the first black feature filmmaker.

Francis Ford Coppola not only differs from both Serling and others on starting from theme, but says he discovers the theme much later in the process.

"Sometimes you never really quite understand what the movie's about until you go into a matinée screening at the Oriental Theatre on a Thursday afternoon."
—Francis Ford Coppola
Lew Hunter's Screenwriting 434

And there are other writers who avoid theme altogether.

WRITERS WHO DON'T WRITE FROM THEME

"If somebody asks me about the themes of something I'm working on, I never have any idea what the themes are. . . . Somebody tells me the themes later. I sort of try to avoid developing themes. I want to just keep it a little bit more abstract."
—Writer/director Wes Anderson (*Rushmore, Moonrise Kingdom*)
Elvis Mitchell interview on KCRW's *The Treatment*

"After you've started shooting, producers come to you and ask, 'what is the theme of your picture?' They were very proud, you know, to have a theme. There's a kind of joke among us writers. You tell him, 'The theme? Don't you know? The theme of this is '*You can't eat soup with a fork.*' And he says, 'That's terrific.'"
—Billy Wilder
Conversations with the Great Moviemakers of Hollywood's Golden Age
Edited by George Stevens Jr.

"I never learned about themes. I'm not sure I know what themes are. I know English departments care about themes. So it's possible to look at my work, as I guess anybody's work, and infer a theme, but it's not something which concerns me."
—David Mamet
MasterClass

WRITERS WHO SAY A THEME EMERGES AT SOME POINT

"Every great work has something that's thematic about it. Not a message, because I don't think movies do messages very well. They fall flat. Socially, I mean, some great films were made back in the '30s and '40s and you can see that they were placed in the time they were made, but their themes are for all time. The biggest thing is the story, but within that you need some thematic element that gets the audience going, that reaches out to them."
—John Carpenter

"What I do is I try to figure out what the piece is about and link that to the story arc or the character arc. I always think there's two things going on in any script—there's the story and then there's the plot. The plot is the events. If it's a heist film, it's how they get in and out. But the story is why we're there, why we're watching the events. It's what's going on with the characters. And theme above that.
—Writer/director Shane Black
Creative Screenwriting interview by Peter Clines

"I try not to think about theme until later. If I'm adapting a book I'll extract a theme if I can from something that's already written, but if I'm writing something I don't say, 'Oh, here's the theme.' I feel like the movie's 'built' if you start with the theme ahead of time."
—Screenwriter Scott Frank (*Minority Report, Marley & Me*)
2012 BAFTA Lecture

PUT DOWN THE MEGAPHONE!

"You've got to find a way of saying it without saying it."
—Jazz musician Duke Ellington

Megaphones have a useful purpose. I used one when I had a job taking group photos of large sports teams; it was the only way I could make sure the players all heard me. But when writing screenplays, there are more subtle ways to be heard. Often all that's needed is just a simple action or a single sentence. The danger of pulling out your megaphone in a movie theater is that it tends to keep people out of the theater.

Here are a couple more quotes to throw into the mix as you walk that fine line in your own scripts between subtle theme and overt propaganda.

Not all writers agree that you should start from theme. Some even argue that the writer should never even be aware of the story's theme. Others say that starting with the theme before the story puts the cart before the horse.

The danger of starting with a theme or controlling idea (or "moral premise" as some call it) is that you can fall into didacticism or sermonizing. There are plenty of examples of heavy-handed themes weighing down stories. But perhaps that's a reflection of the talent and skill of the writer. Just because a Major League Baseball pitcher has an ineffective curveball, it doesn't mean curveballs are bad. Curveballs are a staple of baseball.

Films work best not as an intellectual exercise but as an emotional experience. Audiences want to be swept away by your story. They want to discover the theme, not have it handed to them.

"Here's the beautiful thing about theme, it's the underlying message that kind of unifies the story . . . Just like dialogue needs to have subtext and not be on the nose, you never want to be on the nose thematically. You don't want to be didactic, you don't want to be preachy, it'll put people to sleep."
—Filmmaker/teacher Jim Mercurio
Complete Screenwriting: From A to Z to A-List DVD course

"I think the really good movies are where you don't walk out going 'great message.' I think you walk out just feeling changed. Part of getting better at the craft is the seams don't show as much."
—Blake Snyder

"If a writer has a genuine story to tell, as opposed to a message to smuggle in, and is faithful to his storytelling and skillful in technique,

the audience may get a message. In fact, they may get more and deeper messages than the writer ever intended."
—K.L. Billingsley
The Seductive Image

"In life, we lead by example. In storytelling, we make our points by showing the world what's wrong with it through characters who say and do things that are so very wrong. Avoid speeches. Show things going wrong in your protag's world to make your points and create meaning."
—Mystery Man on Film blog
'Who is John Galt?" article at *The Story Department*

"Didactic screenplays sacrifice character and story to prove the theme correct. This results in propaganda, a story in which the characters are only mouthpieces for the author's message."
—Robin U. Russin and William Missouri Downs
Screenplay, Writing the Picture

"Don't have your hero come right out and say what he's learned. This is obvious and preachy and will turn off your audience. Instead you want to suggest your hero's insight by the actions he takes leading up to self-revelation."
—John Truby
The Anatomy of Story

"What the world needs now (besides love, sweet love) is more storytellers who thrill and entertain; and after you've been enthralled by the wondrous tale of the master yarn-spinner, you might find that the good storytelling also includes subtle messages which are covertly hung on the clothesline of compelling story."
—Richard Krevolin
Screenwriting for the Soul

THEME VS. STORY

"Time. We live by it, ladies and gentlemen, it doesn't live by us."
Chuck Nolan (Tom Hanks) in *Cast Away*

Back in the '90s when Tom Hanks first had the idea to make a movie about a modern-day Robinson Crusoe, the concept was intriguing to screenwriter William Broyles Jr.

It was Hanks' suggestion that the main character work for FedEx, which Broyles said turned out to be "the perfect symbol of a modern company" and just happened to have the motto, "The World on Time." From there, Broyles began to find ways to take a man deeply reliant on time and disconnect him from his modern life. His story asks, "What happens when your dreams don't come true?" and "What's truly important in life?"

"Wrestling with dramatic elements—and others about acceptance and fate and forces larger than ourselves–was an important part of the screenplay, but those battles tend to play out at subconscious levels. They're hard to write about explicitly, and to do so in a movie would be as self-defeating as it would be presumptuous to write about here. So while these thematic questions were constantly at work beneath the surface, they weren't the story, and that's what a movie has to be."
—William Broyles Jr.
Cast Away: The Shooting Script, Introduction

It's healthy to ask whether your theme is overpowering your story. This is particularly true in scripts with strong political or religious themes. This is often where zealous filmmakers get into trouble and critics start making accusations of propaganda.

A great example of a film with a religious theme that doesn't overpower the story is *The Decalogue* (1989) — a series of ten one-hour films that explore each of the Ten Commandments—by Polish director Krzysztof Kieslowski, who co-wrote the scripts with Krzysztof Piesiewicz.

Stanley Kubrick wrote in 1991 about *The Decalogue*: "It should not be out of place to observe that they have the very rare ability to dramatize their ideas rather than just talking about them. By making their points through the dramatic action of the story they gain the added power of allowing the audience to discover what's really going on rather than being told. They do this with such dazzling skill, you never see the ideas coming and don't realize until much later how profoundly they have reached your heart."

OBLIGATORY SCENE — STORY'S THEME

"Is there a confrontation scene? In a well-constructed story the audience is held in expectation of what is called an obligatory scene brought about by a reversal (or indeed, a series of reversals). Note that the obligatory scene, usually the denouement of a story, classically expresses the theme. It is an expression of the story's central moral, the point expressed as a generalization as seen in character-in-action."
—Writer/director Alexander Mackendrick
On Film-making

The fight between Rocky and Apollo Creed in *Rocky* may be the longest obligatory scene in cinema since it lasts basically the entire third act. The reversal scene where Rocky realizes he can't beat the champ is one of the key things that elevates *Rocky* from most films about sports. Robert McKee says that "Rocky redefined winning." Rocky decides that if he can just go the distance with the champ—be on his feet when the fight is over—he will have an internal victory.

"All I wanna do is go the distance. Nobody's ever gone the distance with Creed, and if I can go that distance, you see, and that bell rings and I'm still standin', I'm gonna know for the first time in my life, see, that I weren't just another bum from the neighborhood."
Rocky written by Sylvester Stallone

This personal victory is the theme of Rocky. The climax of the obligatory scene is when Rocky remains standing at the end of the fight. He's proven to himself that he's not a bum. He's the flip side of Terry Malloy in *On the Waterfront*; Rocky is a somebody, a contender.

Sometimes the controlling idea is almost a throwaway line in the script. And sometimes it seems like there's a spotlight on it.

"I got a motto—like your job, love your wife."
Del Griffith (John Candy)
Trains, Planes & Automobiles

"Hope is a dangerous thing."
Red in *The Shawshank Redemption*

"When life gets you down, you know what you gotta do? Just keep swimming. Just keep swimming."
Dory in *Finding Nemo*

"You know Donkey, some things are more than they appear."
Shrek in *Shrek*

"I do not associate with people that blame the world for their problems. 'Cause you're your problem Annie. And you're also your solution."
Megan in *Bridesmaids*

"Theme is not only the spine and core of your movie but the Heart and Soul of your story. . . . Theme is expressed through your main character's transformational arc during the journey. . . . To express transformation, the need for transformation has to be established – hence the Character FLAW. Remember this: Theme is the opposite of the character's flaw."
—Tawnya Bhattacharya (*Perception*)
Scriptshadow interview

And what is transformation about if it's not about change? Which we'll look at more in depth in the next chapter.

9 CHANGE

"Toy Story 3 is about change. It's about embracing change. It's about people being faced with change and how they deal with it."
—*Toy Story 3* director Lee Unkrich

"The main character must CHANGE. A screenplay is a story, with a beginning, middle, and end. If nothing happens to the hero, then what's the point? We are watching this movie because it is a defining moment in this character's life that will forever affects them. A simple way to do this is have the character start out one way (say 'greedy') and end up the opposite ('a philanthropist'). That is the story of *A Christmas Carol*, in a nutshell."
—Stephen Moramarco

WHAT CHANGED?

"Every story, every scene, and every beat is about change—a change in knowledge caused by discoveries, and change in actions caused by character decisions."
—Karl Iglesias
Writing for Emotional Impact

And somewhere men are laughing,
and somewhere children shout,
But there is no joy in Mudville
—Mighty Casey has struck out.
Casey at the Bat
Poem by Ernest Lawrence Thayer

"Chemistry is—well, technically chemistry is the study of matter. But I prefer to see it as the study of change. Now just think about this, electrons—they change their energy levels. Molecules change their bonds. Elements they combine and change into compounds. Well, that's all of life, right? It's the constant. It's the cycle; solution, dissolution just over and over and over. It is growth and decay, and then transformation. It is fascinating, really."
Walter White (Bryan Cranston)
Breaking Bad pilot written by Vince Gilligan

The change from water to ice to steam is neither good nor bad, but as the same element moves from liquid, to solid, to vapor it can be dramatic. For every scene you write, step back and ask, "What's changed?"

When watching movies and reading scripts, it's easiest to see change within a scene when a major event takes place such as an inciting incident or act break.

For instance, around the 7-minute mark in *Jerry Maguire*, Jerry says, "I couldn't escape one simple thought—I hated myself . . . I hated my place in the world." Later, in a late-night breakdown/breakthrough, he writes a personal mission statement: "Fewer clients. Less money." This changes his personal outlook from how the scene started, and it also changes the whole direction of his life. By the end of the scene, he's decided to not be a sketchy sports agent only concerned about financial gain— he's become "the me I'd always wanted to be."

It starts out well—his coworkers applaud him—but soon afterwards he gets fired. He then loses almost all his clients, his girlfriend, and his financial stability. Conflict and change are working hand-in-hand.

Sometimes the change can be more significant, like a major accident (*Cast Away, The Martian, Gravity*) or break-up (*Legally Blonde*), but other times it can be quite subtle, like that oven that doesn't work (*Pieces of April*). But ticked inside those seemingly subtle moments is often other major issues.

"I guess what I like in my movies is where you see a character change by maybe two degrees as opposed to the traditional movie change of ninety degrees. I guess that always feels false to me in

movies because that doesn't truly happen."
—Writer/director Paul Thomas Anderson (*There Will Be Blood*)
Best of Creative Screenwriting Vol. 1 (1994—2000)

There are three main categories of change that need to be considered:

Intrapersonal (Self)

Interpersonal (Others)

Extrapersonal (The World)

These categories are referred to by other terms as well (for example, "Inner," "Internal," "Intragroup," "External"), but whatever you call them, the conflict is with either:

A) Yourself

B) Those close to you (family, friends, co-workers)

C) The larger society, world, or universe, or nature itself

A traditional literary way of talking about universal struggles throughout the human race is put this way (using the world man to mean mankind.)

A) Man vs. Self

B) Man vs. Man (or Others)

C) Man vs. Nature

Sometimes a category is added like Man vs. Supernatural. But I like to cap it at three and tucking supernatural conflict into Man vs. Others. In general, it's best if there's some kind of change in each scene you write.

Robert McKee suggests you look at the end of a scene you've written and see how it's different from the start of the scene. If the charge is the same in both instances (both positive or both negative), you need to ask, "Why is this scene in my script?"

In other words, "What's changed?" Because if nothing has changed, the chances are good that it didn't move the story forward. The change won't always be major, but it should move the needle up or down in some way.

A simple example of a scene where the charge moves from positive (+) to negative (-) is an early scene in *Rocky*. Rocky starts the scene upbeat having won a fight the night before, but when he arrives at the gym he finds out he's lost his locker to another fighter.

Rocky goes from victor to loser (or at least a boxer in decline because of his trainer's lack of faith in him).

There's a great change scene in *The Devil Wears Prada* (screenplay by Aline Brosh McKenna based on Lauren Weisberger's novel) where Andy (Anne Hathaway) is humiliated in a job interview by Miranda Priestly (Meryl Streep). Andy starts out confident and prepared, but the interview quickly goes downhill as Miranda points out all the reasons why Andy is unsuited for a job in the fashion industry. But before Andy leaves the building an assistant catches up to her and tells her she got the job. (It turned out that Miranda saw something different she liked about Andy.) In that case the scene starts out neutral, changes to negative, and ends up positive.

In *Scriptnotes* episode 219, John August and Craig Mazin discuss the importance of change as they consider a scene from *The Lookout*:

"At least one of these states — an internal state, an interpersonal state, an external state — at least one of them must be different at the end of my scene. Or this scene is not a scene. And it doesn't belong in my movie."
—Craig Mazin

Mazin goes on to say that there are times when you get change on all three levels. A scene that comes to mind is in Mazin's HBO miniseries *Chernobyl* where the men are given the dangerous task of pushing radioactive chunks of debris off the roof. There's a lot of conflict and change in just two and a half minutes.

THE HERO'S JOURNEY, CHANGE AND TRANSFORMATION

"A hero is someone who has given his or her life to something bigger than oneself."
Joseph Campbell

Joseph's Campbell's *The Hero with a Thousand Faces* focuses on the Monomyth, or what's commonly known as "The Hero's Journey." Campbell's book was first published in 1949 and builds on the work of psychiatrist Carl Jung and anthropologist Adolf Bastian. The book eventually influenced George Lucas as he wrote *Star Wars*.

For our present purposes, let me condense the hero's journey into just four steps:

1. The call to adventure (which causes one to leave the ordinary world) with assistance from a supernatural aid or a mentor (for example, Obi-Wan Kenobi)

2. Tests, temptations, and entrance into the belly of the beast

3. Capturing the prize

4. Return to the ordinary world (home) with new insights

Not every film fits perfectly into *The Hero's Journey* template, but Campbell seems to have hit on a deep truth, a pattern in storytelling that strongly resonates with humans' hopes and dreams.

To use producer Joel Silver's phrase, there is something "uniquely familiar" about storytelling across eras and cultures. The narrative structure identified by Campbell is evident in the following stories, to name just a few:

The Epic Gilgamesh
Homer's *Odyssey*
The life and parables of Jesus
Moses in the book of *Exodus*
On the Waterfront
Schindler's List
Snow White and the Seven Dwarfs

"Most myths center around characters and — and a hero — and it's about how you conduct yourself as you go through the hero's journey, which everyone goes through."
—George Lucas
Interview with Bill Moyers

Read *The Writer's Journey* by Christopher Vogler and *Myths and the Movies* by Stuart Voytilla to see Campbell's teachings applied to cinema.

"Myths help you to have your own hero's journey, find your individuality, find your place in the world, but hopefully remind you that you're part of a whole, and that you must also be part of the community, and think of the welfare of the community above the welfare of yourself."
—George Lucas

DAN HARMON'S STORY CIRCLE

"I'm trying to communicate with people the best way I can."
—Dan Harmon

According to a *Wired Magazine* article by Brian Raftery, writer Dan Harmon grew up in Wisconsin as a class clown who loved watching reruns of *Taxi*. He got his start doing stand-up comedy in Milwaukee. When Oliver Stone optioned a screenplay Harmon wrote with Rob Schrab *(Scud: The Disposable Assassin)*, Harmon moved to L.A. He eventually started the video website *Channel 101*. After taking a Spanish class at a community college in L.A., he pitched the TV show *Community*. The sitcom premiered in 2009 and ran for 110 episodes on NBC and Yahoo!

Here is Harmon's story circle (with a hint of Joseph Campbell). He says this is "tattooed on my brain" and shaped every episode of *Community*. Harmon actually writes the character arcs in a circle—like a clock—on a chalkboard in the writing room.

1. A character is in a zone of comfort

2. But they want something

3. They enter an unfamiliar situation

4. Adapt to it

5. Get what they wanted

6. Pay a heavy price for it

7. They return to their familiar situation

8. Having changed

SLAVERY TO FREEDOM

"In the vast majority of stories, the hero's overall change moves from slavery to freedom."
—John Truby
The Anatomy of Story

Truby uses the word slavery to mean a way of life that is out of balance. One can be enslaved by money, a career, an illness, another person, a significant loss, a worldview, a prison, etc.

Several films— across many genres—that demonstrate Truby's trajectory:

12 Years a Slave
A Christmas Carol
Erin Brockovich
Good Will Hunting
Home Alone
On the Waterfront
Rain Man
Rocky
Seabiscuit
The Shawshank Redemption

Think about the script you're writing and ask whether/how your main character is enslaved. What is the path to freedom?

MAJOR REVERSALS

"Reversals are a more compelling form of discoveries or revelations because they turn the story upside down."
—Karl Iglesias

Sports and politics are two areas where we can observe dramatic reversals on the world stage. It's election night after the polls close and the underdog ends up victorious. It's the ending of the NFL Super Bowl when the quarterback throws an interception at the goal line costing them a victory. Reversals upend what everyone thought was going to happen.

In 2015, the University of Central Florida (UCF) football team finished the season 0-12. It was the worst season in school history, and the team finished last in the American Athletic Conference. The head coach resigned before the season ended. Two years later, the team finished with a Peach Bowl win against Auburn, and a 13-0 record. They not only won their conference, and finished in the top ten for the first time in major polls, but in The Colley Matrix they were listed as the 2017 National Champions.

Although such extreme reversals are uncommon in sports and otherwise, they happen often in the movies. This is probably a big part of why we watch movies. As Blake Snyder says, "All stories are about transformation."

**"A reversal changes the direction of the story 180 degrees . . .
Reversals can work physically or emotionally. They can reverse the
action or reverse a character's emotions."**
—Linda Seger
Making A Good Script Great

The two types of reversals are distinguishable by their scope and magnitude. In *Rocky*, when Adrian finally accepts a date from Rocky, it's a minor reversal in their relationship up to that point. When Rocky loses his locker, that's a bigger reversal. But when Rocky, a low-level club boxer, is chosen to fight the champion Apollo Creed, that is a major reversal in the story. That reversal is so major that it even spawned five more Rocky movies, and several *Creed* spin-offs.

If Rocky isn't chosen for that fight, perhaps he realizes that boxing really isn't his calling. Maybe he takes a factory job. But Rocky fought the champ, and it resulted in a movie franchise that's made well over a billion dollars at the box office.

There are five places in a script where major reversals are not only common, but necessary:

The catalyst/inciting incident. (Also known as the "Knock at the door," or "Exciting Incident") A reversal here sets your story in motion.

Act 1 turning point

Midpoint conflict

Act 2 turning point

Crisis/climax toward the end of your story

Many memorable movie scenes are major reversals that take place during one of these moments in the story.

Here are some major reversals:

"I see dead people" in *The Sixth Sense*

The sister/daughter complication in *Chinatown*

The tornado arrives in *The Wizard of Oz*.

The plane crashes in *Cast Away*.

The super posse shows up in *Butch Cassidy and the Sundance Kid*.

Mark Watney (Matt Damon) gets stranded on Mars in *The Martian*.

In *Gravity*, Ryan Stone (Sandra Bullock) gets lost in space.

A command module malfunctions in *Apollo 13*.
(Apparently, a lot of things can go wrong in space.)

Jerry Maguire gets fired.

The warden throws a rock through a Raquel Welch poster in *Shawshank*.

Woody is in the box at the end of *Toy Story 3*.

The head is in the box in *Se7en*.

The audience learns that the main character has a mental illness. (*Fight Club* and *A Beautiful Mind*)

Keyser Söze is revealed at the end of *The Usual Suspects*.

The "You can't handle the truth" scene in *A Few Good Men*.

A black police officer joins a white supremacy group *in BlacKkKlansman*.

A drummer loses his hearing in *Sound of Metal*.

The Manson Family decides at the last minute to change plans and invade Rick's house in *Once Upon a Time … in Hollywood*.

PIRATES, RAIDERS, AND REVERSALS

"The audience will come to 'know' the character through their actions. When characters can make decisions that run counter to expectations, bringing immediate reversals into the story, that's of immediate interest. [When Indiana Jones] ties up Marion instead of releasing her [in *Raiders of the Lost Ark*], it's a marvelous reversal, and we gain huge insights into Indy's character by that one action."
—Screenwriters Terry Rossio & Ted Elliott (*Pirates of the Caribbean*) *Wordplay* column, *"Plot Devices"*

The classic opening of *Raiders of the Lost Ark*, when Indy is confronted by Belloq, is also a great reversal that moves from positive to negative.

Speaking of Rossio and Elliot, consider this reversal from their *Pirates of the Caribbean: The Curse of the Black Pearl* script: From "You are without a doubt the worst pirate I've ever heard of. . . ." to "That's got to be the best pirate I've ever seen" (as Jack Sparrow steals a ship).

SHARKS, GHOSTS, AND REVERSALS

"Reversals can work physically or emotionally. They can reverse the action or reverse a character's emotions. In *Ghostbusters*, our unemployed university professors reverse direction and start their own business."
—Linda Seger

The character Matt (Richard Dreyfuss) in *Jaws* says that he's leaving the next day to do shark research on a ship at sea for 18 months. Later, when he and Sheriff Brody cut open the first shark that was captured and they realize that it's not *the* shark they were looking for, he reverses his decision because (as he tells Brody) "you've still got a hell of a fish out there."

REVERSALS, ROADBLOCKS, AND COMPLICATIONS

"A relationship, I think, is like a shark. You know? It has to constantly move forward or it dies. And I think what we got on our hands is a dead shark."
—Alvy Singer (Woody Allen) in *Annie Hall*

Have you ever had a boyfriend or girlfriend break-up with you? It's a common occurrence.

The Social Network opens with a scene that builds to a break-up.

"You are probably going to be a very successful computer person. But you're going to go through life thinking that girls don't like you because you're a nerd. And I want you to know, from the bottom of my heart, that that won't be true. It'll be because you're an asshole."
—Erica Albright (Rooney Mara) in *The Social Network*
Screenplay by Aaron Sorkin

If your goal is to be in a healthy, loving relationship and your partner calls you an asshole right before they break up with you, you have three basic options:

—Work through those issues with that person (and perhaps yourself) and eventually kiss and make up.

—Shake the dust off your feet and move on to another relationship (or at least begin looking for one).

—Listen to the Phil Collins song *I Don't Care Anymore* 426 times, swear off personal relationships as impossible and get a dog, and throw yourself into your career.

We could call those three options complications, roadblocks, and reversals. On Scott Myers' screenwriting blog *Go Into the Story*, here's how he defines them:

Complication: An event or circumstance which slows the Protagonist's progress toward his goal.

Roadblock: An event or circumstance which stops the Protagonist's progress toward his goal.

Reversal: An event or circumstance, which reverses the Protagonist's progress toward his goal.

Screenwriters and screenwriting instructors have plenty of terms for various writing techniques, and they can get confusing. But I think *complications, roadblocks,* and *reversals* is a simple and helpful way to look at scenes you're writing.

In the fictitious movie version of Mark Zuckerberg's life, screenwriter Aaron Sorkin uses the break-up to change not only Zuckerberg's life, but also the lives of quite a few other people. In the movie, this break-up sparked a major reversal that ultimately changed the world.

After the break-up, Zuckerberg could have walked around campus and thought things over and then taken his ex some flowers and tried to make up. In that scenario, the break-up was just a complication.

Or, after the break-up he could have said, "Fine, there's more fish in the sea" and spent a few days or weeks looking for a new girlfriend. The break-up was just a roadblock in his quest for a healthy, loving relationship.

Instead, Sorkin had Zuckerberg head back to his dorm and with a little bit of computer know-how, a few beers, a couple of friends, and a lot of bitterness, Zuckerberg launched the "hot or not" website to get back at the woman who broke-up with him. The seeds of Facebook were planted.

EMOTIONAL CHANGE "[D]ramatic action pulls moviegoers to the edge of their seats. And yes, conflict, tension, suspense and curiosity hook moviegoers. Yet, no matter how exciting the action, the character's emotional reactions and emotional development

provide fascination. Any presentation with a strong human element increases the chances of audience identification."
—Martha Alderson
The Writers Store article *Character Emotion Makes the Plot*

When Howard Beale (Peter Finch) says he's "Mad as hell and not going to take it anymore" in *Network,* it's an emotional change that has resonated with new audiences for decades.

FIGHTS, SEDUCTIONS, AND NEGOTIATIONS

Before Mike Nichols won Oscar, Tony, and Emmy awards for his film, theater, and TV directing, he performed improv comedy and taught acting classes. He said he learned working with Elaine May that there were only three kinds of scenes—"Fights, seductions, and negotiations." Implicit in each of those is conflict and room for change throughout any scene.

Here are brief examples from two films Nichols directed, and one from writer/director Dan Gilroy.

Fight: "I hope that was an empty bottle, George! You can't afford to waste good liquor, not on your salary!" (*Who's Afraid of Virginia Woolf?*)

Seduction: "Mrs. Robinson – you're trying to seduce me. ... Aren't you?" (*The Graduate*) Negotiation: "You're the news director on the vampire shift at the lowest rated station in L.A. I have to think you're invested in this transaction." (*Nightcrawler*)

What makes that particular line from *Nightcrawler* such effective writing, and overall creepy, is it's part of a scene that is a fight, a twisted seduction, and negotiation rolled into one. A rare screenwriting trifecta.

GRACE NOTES

"If you could watch a movie about a person who's struggling and at the end they're a better person than at the beginning, it's hope for the end they're a better person than at the beginning, it's hope for yourself, it's hope for the people you love, it's hope for the human race, and I do think that's why people go to the movies."
—Judd Apatow

Judd Apatow likes James L. Brooks' use of "grace notes.' In music, a grace note is an extra note, a brief embellishment, at the end of a song. I think Apatow uses it here in the figurative sense, as a finishing touch.

An example Apatow gives is in the *Taxi* episode "Louie and the Blind Girl" where the gruff Louie (Danny DeVito) is dating a blind girl. She doesn't know that Louie is not a traditionally tall and handsome man. But she's having an operation and going to learn what he really looks like. He fears that she won't love him anymore. But when the big reveal moment comes and they take off her bandages it's clear that her love for him is real.

"It's very touching. And he leaves the room and one of his friends says, 'How'd it go?' and he basically says it went great. And then he takes this [cheap] ring that he got her and says, 'I guess I got to get her real ring' And to me that's perfect. It's just perfect storytelling. It got me emotionally, it touched my heart, and it has the funny, awful, edgy joke that stays true to character. And that's what I'm always trying to do, in some way find a James Brooks grace note."
—Judd Apatow
MasterClass

I think another grace note is in the James Brooks movie *As Good as It Gets*. When we are introduced to Melvin (Jack Nicholson) at the opening of the movie, we discover a man who drops a dog into a garbage bin. Toward the end of the movie, when Melvin tells Carol (Helen Hunt), "You make me want to be a better man," it is clear that he has changed.

"No character arc, no change, no movie."
—Richard Kevolin
Screenwriting in the Land of Oz

The final chapter in the book we'll be looking at ways you can build and sustain a career as a screenwriter, filmmaker, or content creator.

10. CAREERS AND COWS

"I think every writer harbors—secretly or not-so-secretly —delusions of grandeur. Still, when you're starting out, it's hard to imagine how you'll ever 'succeed.'"
—Michael Arndt

"I don't think there's any artist of any value who doesn't doubt what they're doing."
—Oscar winner Francis Ford Coppola (*The Godfather*)
Academy of Achievement Q&A

"A lot of filmmakers don't understand that you need to have a skill that pays you while you're chasing the dream."
—Alex Ferrari
Indie Film Hustle podcast # 403

"I am big, it's the pictures that got small."
Norma Desmond in *Sunset Boulevard* (1950)

The final chapter of this book will consider a variety of different opportunities for screenwriters, filmmakers, and content creators. We'll look at various routes creative people have taken on their road to success, their processes, and a word or two of encouragement for your journey. We'll close with a glance at a business in transition.

Let me start with the good news. There are lots of career opportunities in storytelling—if we use that term in the broadest sense. Think of it like a pyramid. At the top of the pyramid are a small group of wealthy feature filmmakers and TV show creators. At the bottom are a wide variety of people who are at the beginning or end of their career path, often working for little or no pay.

It's hard to nail down exactly how many people work in feature film or television business on a regular basis. But I've heard several professional filmmakers say that everyone in the business would have to quit for all the new film school graduates to have jobs in their field each year.

Even if you do not end up in Hollywood, the good news is that there are many other ways of making a living as a storyteller and content creator. As this chapter will attest, these unexpected detours often lead you to where you want to be.

Creative people have long held non-creative jobs to pay the bills. Rod Serling wrote fake product testimonials in Cincinnati before he created *The Twilight Zone.* Tennessee Williams worked in a shoe factory in St. Louis. Sam Shepard was a busboy. Nancy Meyers baked food she sold to restaurants. David Mamet sold carpets over the phone. Tony Gilroy was a bartender. Arthur Miller drove a truck. Diablo Cody was an administrative assistant in Minneapolis, and "a terrible assistant" by her own admission.

"I bartended in Broadway theaters, I dressed up as a moose and handed out leaflets. I drove a limousine, I delivered singing telegrams. I did all the kinds of things you're going to do, because it's unlikely that you're going to graduate and instantly be hired to do what you dream about doing."
—Aaron Sorkin *(The Social Network)* on his "survival jobs"
The Hollywood Reporter interview with Stephen Galloway

TV host Mike Rowe encourages people to not follow their dreams, but to follow their opportunities and to take their dreams with them.

There seems to be two schools of thought regarding how to survive the early stages of one's film career. The first is to get a job that leaves you with enough time and energy to write or create in your off hours. The second option is to take whatever job you can get in the production world.

Writer/director Sean Baker (*The Florida Project*) honed his craft by working on electronic press kits for a book publisher, and shooting/editing wedding videos. One large Russian wedding in particular gave him an idea for one of his unproduced screenplays.

"I would suggest to anybody who's striving to become a filmmaker to at least stay within the AV world. Because you're practicing on a daily basis. . . .you're still framing shots, you're still editing, you're understanding the technical side of things."
—Sean Baker
No Film School podcast interview

Callie Khouri started in the audio/visual world by working her way up at a production company that made commercials and music videos.

"Because I started literally answering the phone, and went to being the person that drives the film to the lab, and then to the person that orders the lighting package and the grip package, and the chairs, and just went through every single aspect of [production], I had a very firm understanding of what goes into making a film."
—Callie Khouri (who wrote her first screenplay, the Oscar winning screenplay *Thelma & Louise,* while working at that production company)
The Dialogue Series interview with Mike De Luca

Before Bruce Springsteen filled the Los Angeles Coliseum with around 100,000 people (at least, that's how I remember it) for the final concert of his 1985 *Born in the USA* tour (the greatest concert I ever attended), he had a humbler beginning playing smaller venues on the Jersey Shore. These included supermarket openings, bowling alleys, trailer parks, high school dances, weddings, fraternity parties, bar mitzvahs, and an Elks Lodge.

Content creators can work on a variety of productions: for educators, corporations, advertisers, news outlets, non-profits, churches/faith-based groups, magazines, TV stations, websites, social media, YouTube, college and professional sports, and countless other industries.

Content creators are in demand. Let's consider some of the routes that have been taken.

EDUCATION

There are four main ways that writers, filmmakers, and content creators get their education.

Top Film Schools: AFI (Darren Aronofsky), Cal Arts (Brad Bird), Columbia University (Kathryn Bigelow), Florida State University (Barry Jenkins), NYU (Spike Lee), Rhode Island School of Design (Gus Van Sant), UCLA (Francis Ford Coppola), USC (George Lucas), University of Texas at Austin (Robert Rodriguez), Wesleyan University (Joss Whedon, and Lin-Manuel Miranda was in the theater department there)
Note: Rodriguez left school after three years because his career took off. But after 13 films he returned to the classroom to finish his degree at UT.

Prestigious Private Schools: Barnard College (Greta Gerwig), Brown University (John Krasinski), Carnegie Mellon University (Steven Bochco), Dartmouth College (Shonda Rhimes), Emerson College (Norman Lear), Harvard University (Damien Chazelle), Northwestern University (Garry Marshall), Oberlin College (Lena Dunham), Sarah Lawrence College (Jordan Peele), Stanford University (Alexander Payne), Syracuse University (Aaron Sorkin)

Public Schools: University of Iowa (Diablo Cody, Tennessee Williams), University of Michigan (Lawrence Kasdan, Arthur Miller), University of Wisconsin—Madison (Michael Mann, Lorraine Hansberry). Screenwriter David Koepp (*Jurassic Park*) is kind of a hybrid who started at Madison and finished at the UCLA Film school.
Note: A full list of filmmakers from public colleges and universities would be long. But most don't have multiple accomplished people in film and TV that Iowa, Michigan and Wisconsin have produced.

Little or No College/Self-Educated: Paul Thomas Anderson, Peter Bogdanovich, Charlie Chaplin, Clint Eastwood, Frank Darabont, Moss Hart, Ben Hecht, Stanley Kubrick, Casey Neistat, Gordon Parks, Tyler Perry, Carl Reiner, Neil Simon, Steven Soderbergh, Kevin Smith, Steven Spielberg, Sylvester Stallone, (Both Stallone and Spielberg picked up bachelor's degrees later in life), Quentin Tarantino (who didn't even finish high school), Orson Welles

But even that last little or no college list is deceptive. There are a few geniuses tucked in that group. Spielberg was directing network TV programs at 21. Anderson went to a series of prep schools and academies and made his first movie at age eight. And Welles was performing Shakespeare at 14.

By the age of 22, Tarantino had probably seen more movies than 99.99% of film school graduates his age. It's a little like saying Mark Zuckerberg, Bill Gates, and Steve Jobs were college dropouts. Not quite the full story. Then there's Christopher Nolan (*Inception*) who learned production working on corporate videos and making short films on weekends. My takeaway from this is that successful filmmakers come from everywhere. But whatever route you take, know that the film business is not an easy one.

Writer/director Nora Ephron had the advantage of growing up in Beverly Hills with both of her parents (Henry and Phoebe Ephron) working as film and TV writers. She graduated from Wesleyan University and worked as a reporter for the *New York Post* before pursuing writing screenplays.

Yet she said, "For years, I just wrote scripts that didn't get made." Her first film (co-written with Alice Arlen) was *Silkwood* starring Meryl Streep, Cher, and Kurt Russell would be her first of three Oscar nominations.

"I think the most important thing you have to know is that it's a very, very hard business, full of rejection and setbacks. If you don't want to succeed really badly, you won't. But, of course, if you get a movie made and it works, there's nothing like it. Nothing."
—Nora Ephron (*When Harry Met Sally*)
Tales from the Script

Later in this chapter, we'll look a little more in-depth at the path several screenwriters took on their road to success. First, I'll share with you the secret screenwriting sauce from John Logan, who I think would echo Ephron's words about it being a very, very hard business.

"The reason that I am a writer today is Shakespeare."
—Three-time Oscar-nominated screenwriter John Logan (*Gladiator*)

Back in 2011 John Logan had a very good year. He wrote the script for *Hugo,* which led the field for the 2012 Oscars with a total of 11 nominations. But wait, there's more! He also wrote *Rango* (featuring Johnny Depp), which received an Oscar nomination for Animated Feature Film. But wait, there's still more! He also wrote *Coriolanus*, which was released in 2011 and picked up a BAFTA nomination for its director Ralph Fiennes.

He wasn't a newcomer, either. He had been nominated for an Academy Award twice before, for *The Aviator* (2004) and *Gladiator* (2000). His credits also include *Any Given Sunday, The Last Samurai*, and *Sweeney Todd.*

What's his secret? Be patient. It's coming.

"I graduated from Northwestern. I had no money. No one had any money. So I got a day job, shelving books at the Northwestern University Law Library. Every morning I would work from nine to five and shelve books, for ten years. Every single day for ten years."
—John Logan

He went home to his tiny apartment in Chicago and wrote plays. His plays were performed in condemned theaters, small church basements, or back alleys. After a decade of writing, he eventually landed an agent in L.A., Brian Siberell at CAA. He didn't have any assignments but moved to L.A. and took nine months to write his first screenplay, which eventually became *Any Given Sunday*—after he and Oliver Stone did a few re-writes first.

"We did 26 drafts of *Any Given Sunday*, one right after another, so I learned everything about the form from him. He was patient. I'd go to his house, he'd say, pick up that Oscar, hold it, it'll feel good, you'll enjoy it. And then we'd work. *Any Given Sunday*, like all these monstrous big movies, was hard to get made."
—John Logan

In case you missed it: *26 drafts*. That's after spending nine months writing and rewriting it on his own. After 10 years of writing plays in Chicago. After graduating from Northwestern. All that—then *26 drafts.*

Still with me? Still want to be a screenwriter? If so, here's some foundation work for you. From the lips of John Logan, here's the most powerful and potentially life-changing advice that you'll ever find for screenwriters:

"If you want to be a screenwriter—a successful screenwriter—here's the secret . . . This is what you have to do, it's great—don't tell anyone. You have to read *Hamlet*, and you have to read it again, and you have to read it until you understand every word."

Then Logan expands his reading list: Aristotle's *Poetics* (until you can quote it), Chekhov, *King Lear*, Ibsen, Tony Kushner, *Troilus and Cressida*, and Sophocles.

"You're going to understand the continuum of what it is to be a dramatist, so you have respect for the form in which you are trying to function. So you understand what comes before you. Then, if you choose, watch a couple of movies."
—John Logan

That doesn't even require a big financial commitment. You can pick up the entire major works of Shakespeare, Ibsen, and Chekhov for under $20 in a used bookstore, or a little more for all of them on Kindle. For a few more bucks you can add some Greek and contemporary writers. And of course, screenplays (for which I used to pay $15 per script) are now widely available on the internet for free.

One benefit of a school like Northwestern (as well as the top film schools and Ivy League school) is they have established pipelines into the industry. Many Hollywood executives come from Ivy League schools. Colleges like Harvard and Dartmouth have deep ties in Hollywood, and those preexisting social networks can make it more accessible for graduates to get introduced into the business.

College can be a great experience where you take classes with unique professors who challenge your thinking, where you're exposed to different cultures, crew each other's films, where you stay up all night having life-altering conversations with fellow students, and where life-long friendships and professional connections can be forged. But be wary of digging a hole with student loans that you can't crawl out of for two or three decades.

Writer/director Sam Esmail (*Mr. Robot*) went to NYU film school and AFI for his undergraduate work and MFA back when it was not near as expensive as it is today and said that he realized before his career took off that he was "either going to hit it big or die in debt." When asked before a WGA audience if film school is worth it today he said, "I don't know."

Grey's Anatomy show creator Shonda Rhimes went to Princeton University and USC School of Cinematic Arts a couple of decades ago and found her film school experience and contacts invaluable. Yet at the same time also warned others that you can't ignore the financial responsibilities.

"Student loans back when I went to school (because I'm an old lady) and going to school now are just different. So, to me, if you have to make the choice between going to film school, and coming out to L.A. and getting a job as a PA [production assistant] on a set, or a job as a PA in some writer's office or something like that, *get the job*."
—Shonda Rhimes
MasterClass

When Callie Khouri took the "get the job" route back in the '80s she wrote at night and on weekends, and because it was freelance production work, she also wrote on down days. It took her six months to write *Thelma & Louise*. A producer at the production company where she worked also paved the way for her script to find its way to Ridley Scott who eventually directed the film.

Rhimes is a big advocate for a college education, but said, "I'm not necessarily sure you need a film school education." Spike Lee said that his generation went to film school because it was one of the few places where young people could have access to equipment. That's no longer the case.

Writer/director Ava DuVernay (*Selma*) was a dual major at UCLA (English and African America studies) and worked as a film publicist for a decade before making her first short film over Christmas holiday in 2005.

"For my first five films I still worked my day job."
—Ava DuVernay

Because Scott Beck and Bryan Woods had been making films throughout middle school and high school, they majored in communications at Iowa rather than going the traditional film school route.

One filmmaker said after his film premiered at Sundance that his student loan was $330,000—as in three hundred and thirty thousand dollars. I hope his career takes off and he's able to pay that back. It's not hard to find other films school grads online regretting their $100,000 loans. I side with financial author and radio host Dave Ramsey that if you have a six-figure student loan you better have Dr. in front of your name— and be able to perform surgeries.

The harsh reality, according to Loyola Marymount's Stephen Ujlaki, Dean of Film and Television, is that the majority of students majoring in film and television will not be having careers in those professions.

The good news is film and TV skills transfer to other jobs in a wide range of marketing, advertising, non-broadcast production, corporate, educational, and social media opportunities. In addition, some jobs only require a 2-year degree, and others are only skills-based. (It's a good habit to look at online production job requirements and pay long before you need a full-time job.)

My point, and one I can't stress enough, is working in production is a roller coaster adventure. One that can pay you well or not at all. Use your creativity to have as little debt as possible (or no debt at all), so you don't get overwhelmed at the start.

It is hard enough to make a living in Los Angeles or New York on a low starting wage. Adding a huge student loan debt really makes for an uphill climb. In many cases, paying your student loans can be like having an extra house or rent payment. And there are many stories of people making the minimum student loan payments, only to see the amount they owe grow or remain virtually the same because of compounded interest. Currently, there are 8 million people with student loans in default.

Do your homework before doing your homework. Be as creative in getting an education (traditional or non-traditional) as you are in your storytelling. Look for grants, scholarships, tapping into the school's endowments, tuition assistance programs through employers, and other ways to keep college costs down. And, of course, there are schools that are relatively affordable. That's especially true of community colleges. And know that getting (and paying for) an education isn't the last obstacle you'll face.

Many starting out in the industry have no other option than to cram with several others into small apartments or houses in order to cover rent. It's not unheard of for people working in production to be living out of their vehicles in Los Angeles. In 2018, the Los Angeles Homeless Services Authority reported that 15,748 Angelenos were living out of cars and vans.

At one point, a produced screenwriter who was one of those living out of his car wrote an article called *From Hollywood to Homeless* where he explained the physical and emotional toll that experience had on him.

If you want a more optimistic homeless-to-hero story, then Tyler Perry is your man. The producer/writer/director/actor spent time living out of his car on his way to building a movie studio in Atlanta and acquiring a net worth estimated over $800 million.

J.K. Rowling is a great example of writer who didn't come from wealth and struggled financially before her success. She was a single mother on welfare benefits when writing her first of many *Harry Potter* novels.

"Rock bottom became the solid foundation on which I rebuilt my life. You might never fail on the scale I did, but some failure in life is inevitable."
—J.K. Rowling (Harvard University Commencement, 2008)

THE 99% FOCUS RULE

"I would say 99% of your effort should go to writing a good script."
—Michael Arndt

If you look at one decade in screenwriter Michael Arndt's career, it's rather amazing. He won an Oscar for *Little Miss Sunshine,* wrote *Toy Story 3* which made over a billion dollars at the box office, and also wrote the script for *Hunger Games: Chasing Fire.* It's valuable, though, to look at the decade *before* he had an agent and *before* he sold a single script to see if there are any clues that prepared him for the success he's enjoyed.

"The question is 'How do you meet an agent?' or get your script to an agent—It's a mystery to me. Everyone sort of is able to find a different path, and usually it just comes to referrals."
—Michael Arndt
2007 talk at Cody's Books in NYC

It's also important to know that Arndt's career path is different than the one that Diablo Cody took in Minneapolis (blogging and non-fiction writing), and it's also different than the one that John Logan took in Chicago (playwriting)— but the one thing that all three have in common is that they focused (99%?) on writing a solid script that made the doors fly open. Cody and Logan also both had various cheerleaders (who happened to be agents) in Hollywood who became aware of their work while the writers still lived in the Midwest.

Writer/director Rian Johnson's advice to people who want to get an agent and work in the industry is to "double down on substance."

It took Steve Martin ten years of learning his comedic routine and four years of honing his comedic talents before he found wild success that eventually led to his career not only in comedy, but also in acting, writing, and music. He has said many times that the career advice he gives is not the advice people want to hear: "Be so good they can't ignore you."

THE 10,000-HOUR RULE

"Researchers have settled on what they believe is the magic number for true expertise: ten thousand hours."
—Malcolm Gladwell

The second chapter of Malcolm Gladwell's book *Outliers* is titled "The 10,000-Hour Rule." Every time you hear about a first-time screenwriter selling a script for six figures, it would be good practice to reread Gladwell's chapter. The chances are high that the screenwriter is one of those "overnight successes" for whom "overnight" actually equaled ten years. Drawing on the work of neurologist Daniel Levitin and cognitive psychologist Anders Ericsson, Gladwell uses the Beatles as an example of the 10,000-hour rule. When the band was playing in their hometown of Liverpool, their stage time was limited to an hour of playing their best songs.

According to John Lennon, that changed when they began playing in small clubs in Germany. "In Hamburg, we had to play for eight hours, so we really had to find a new way of playing."

Before the Beatles exploded in popularity in 1964, they had already performed an estimated 1,200 times. Gladwell writes, "Do you know how extraordinary that is? Most bands today don't perform twelve hundred times in their entire careers."

Many saw Diablo Cody as an overnight success story, but what was overlooked was that she was almost thirty when she sold *Juno*. In interviews, she said that she'd been writing daily since she was a kid. *Daily*. She wrote poetry, short stories, books, journals, blogs, and more. Cody also earned a BA in media studies at the University of Iowa (Although not a part of the Iowa Writers' Workshop, she said that she was drawn to Iowa because of the famed MFA writing program). "Overnight success" Diablo Cody wrote quite a lot before she was discovered.

The same is true for Stephen King, who began submitting stories (and receiving rejection letters) at the age of 12. When King sold his first book at age 25, he'd likely already hit the 10,000-hour mark.

10,000 HOURS VS. 20 HOURS

"In my experience it takes about twenty hours of practice to break through the frustration barrier: to go from knowing absolutely nothing about what you're trying to performing noticeably well."
—Josh Kaufman
The First 20 Hours

"I've never read a screenwriting book. I'm really superstitious about it too. I don't even want to look at them. All I did was I went and bought the shooting script of 'Ghost World' . . . just to see how it should look on the page."
—Diablo Cody

Josh Kaufman considers the 10,000-hour rule further in his book *The First 20 Hours: How to Learn Anything...Fast*. He writes in his opening chapter:

"World class mastery may take ten thousand hours of focused effort, but developing the capacity to perform well enough for your own purposes usually requires far less of an investment."
—Josh Kaufman

Kaufman isn't trying to do any myth busting of the 10,000-hour rule. He just clarifies the conclusion that others discovered. Knowing that something can take a decade on average to master can be overwhelming—a wall too big to attempt climbing.

Kaufman's 20-hour rule helps distinguish notions like "competence," "expertise" and "world-class mastery." If you're just starting out in screenwriting—and especially if you live outside of L.A.—take comfort in knowing that there are working writers and writer's assistants who are not working at their highest level yet. But they are working.

Also keep in mind that even when Diablo Cody wasn't a working screenwriter, and in fact hadn't even tried to write a screenplay yet, her blog written in a Minneapolis suburb captured the attention of producer Mason Novak in Los Angeles. She took a nontraditional path on her way to becoming an Academy Award winning screenwriter.

"Here's my unsolicited advice to any aspiring screenwriters who might be reading this: Don't ever agonize about the hordes of other writers who are ostensibly your competition. No one else is capable of doing what you do."
—Diablo Cody
Juno: The Shooting Script, Introduction

Oscar-winner Chris Terrio (*Argo*) wrote spec scripts for almost nothing, but those led to indie producers paying him $5,000 for a script—or as he says, "on a good day maybe 10,000 bucks. Or just here's lunch if you'll let me be the guy to take your screenplay around, and you're grateful for that."

The bottom line, as screenwriter Bob DeRosa says, is that "There are no shortcuts. There is only hard work. Perseverance. Luck. Craft. Failure. Success. Mistakes. And yes, dreams that come true."

And sometimes dreams don't come true. There are plenty of decent golfers who spent 10,000 hours playing golf but who not only didn't become the next Tiger Woods, but they also didn't even make the PGA Tour. There are no guarantees, even if you hit the 10,000-hour mark.

FAILURE AND REJECTION

"I was so programmed to fail. I had shown no signs of talent as a young man. Do you know what it's like to want to be a writer and get the worst grades in the class? It's terrible."
— Two-time Oscar winning screenwriter William Goldman

If I wanted to scare away timid writers, I would have written about failure and rejection in the first chapter. But I've saved it for now, hoping that you've built up some stamina for the road ahead.

Francis Ford Coppola tells about the time that he got fired after writing a screenplay on General George S. Patton that included what he was told was an "odd" and "strange" opening sequence. But the movie *Patton* not only got made—with the now iconic odd and strange opening sequence —but Coppola won an Oscar for Best Screenplay.

Coppola later said that Oscar saved him from getting fired on the set of *The Godfather* adding, "Often the things you are fired for are often the thing you are celebrated for later in life." Success and rejection are neighbors.

"Here's the secret I have learned in 20 years as a screenwriter. Failure is constant for everyone."
—Screenwriter Susannah Grant (*Erin Brockovich*)

"I have a lot of experience with failure, and I hate it. It's going to happen again, but it's like electroshock therapy. So combined with the pressure that you put on yourself, that's pretty much the jet fuel for writing."
—Aaron Sorkin

"I'm not running to quality. I'm running from failure."
—Alec Berg (*Seinfeld, Silicon Valley, Barry*)

"I remember a five-month period late in 1952 when my diet consisted chiefly of black coffee and fingernails. I'd written six half-hour television plays and each one had been rejected at least five times."
—Rod Serling (*The Twilight Zone* creator)

"To do any kind of creative work well, you have to run at stuff knowing that it's usually going to fail. You have to take that into account and you have to make peace with it."
—Ira Glass, *This American Life* executive producer and host

"When I'm being really honest with myself, the only thing I ever learn from is failure. Because *Breaking Bad* is the rare success I've had in my career."
—Vince Gilligan (Before *Better Call Saul*)

"As you go through the [writing] process, there will be so many people who will tell you that it is impossible and that you can't do it. You'll have your heart-broken so many times, and you just have to sustain yourself with your vision."
—Three-time Emmy winner Diane Frolov
The New Screenwriter Looks at the New Screenwriter, by William Froug

"If you allow yourself to get crippled by the possibility of failure, you're going to rob yourself of a lot of great experiences."
—Edward Burns
Independent Ed

"Take chances, make mistakes. That's how you grow. Pain nourishes your courage. You have to fail in order to practice being brave."
—Mary Tyler Moore

"I've been around a long enough . . . to know that careers are peaks and valleys. And it's just really all about with how much grace and equanimity you can keep walking along in one direction . . . Because for the last two peaks I've experienced there's been five years of valley."
—Writer/Director Frank Darabont (*The Shawshank Redemption*)
Fade In interview with Audrey Kelly

When you start off, you have to deal with the problems of failure. You need to be thick-skinned, to learn that not every project will survive."
—Author and screenwriter Neil Gaiman (*The Sandman, American Gods*)
The University of the Arts Keynote Address, 2012

It's good to know when you face failure and rejection that you are in good company and part of a long literary tradition.

COMMITMENT, PERSISTENCE, AND RESILIENCE

"I would advise anyone who aspires to a writing career, that before developing his talent he would be wise to develop a thick hide."
—Author Harper Lee (*To Kill A Mockingbird*)

Here are some ways that's equipped others to endure failure and rejection.

"I've learned that tenacity is a common part of the personalities of successful writers whom I have met."
—Matthew Weiner, *Mad Men* creator

"I've always felt that if you put me in front of 10 feet of concrete and said, 'Walk through it,' I'd get through it. . . . It's just a question of pushing yourself hard enough through rock. I've never felt like anything could stop me if I really tried."
—Emmy winning screenwriter Craig Mazin (*Chernobyl*)
The Moment with Brian Koppelman podcast

"One characteristic emerged as a significant predictor of success. And it wasn't social intelligence, it wasn't good looks, physical health, and it wasn't IQ—it was grit. Grit is passion and perseverance for very long-term goals."
—Author Angela Lee Duckworth (*Grit*)
Ted Talk

"I'm convinced that about half of what separates the successful entrepreneurs from the non-successful ones is pure perseverance."
—Steve Jobs

"To make a great film, you generally have to make a good one first — and to make the good one, you have to make a not-so-good one even before that. Sure, the exceptions come out of the gate strong, but that is not most of us."
—Producer Ted Hope

"It took years of struggle. Years of not having anything happen, not even getting meetings, not knowing what I was really doing . . . Things have turned a corner. I was really a starving artist for a lot of years. I moved to LA nine years ago, and the first five were really difficult."
—Oscar-nominated screenwriter Luke Davies (*Lion*)

"Nobody achieves anything great by being happy and cozy."
—Mountain climber Alex Honnold (featured in the movie *Solo*)

"There's a secret that real writers know that wannabe writers don't, and the secret is this: It's not the writing part that's hard. What's hard is sitting down to write. What keeps us from sitting down is Resistance."
—Steven Pressfield
The War of Art

WRITING IS WORK

"I began this whole writing enterprise with the idea that you go to work in the morning like a banker, then the work gets done."
—Writer Tobias Wolff (*This Boy's Life, The Night in Question*)

"[Writing] is blood, sweat, and tears, believe me. It is a drag. It is hard work. And it is not one of those kinds of things like people imagine where the muses come and they kiss your brow and there you are kind of the poet in the clouds."
—Writer/director Billy Wilder (*The Apartment*)

While visiting artist Gary Kelley's Iowa studio I learned about Milton Glaser's book *Art is Work*. You don't always hear the words *art* and *work* mentioned at the same time, so here are some quotes to back that up.

"The best advice I ever heard about writing came from Paddy Chayefsky . . . Don't think of it as art, think of it as work. I don't surf the web. I don't gamble online. I just work."
—Screenwriter Billy Ray (*Captain Phillips*)

"I wrote four novels and short stories before I even published anything, and the reason I didn't publish any of those things was because it wasn't any good."
—Harry Crews (*A Feast of Snakes*)

"I wrote screenplays as a way to get into production. I wrote six or seven before I sold one."
—Lawrence Kasdan (*Raiders of the Lost Ark, Star Wars: Episode V*)

"Before [writing] *Buried*, I think I'd written about nine or ten features and two TV specs. Truth be told, it didn't start to click for me until about my seventh feature script."
—Chris Sparling

"Before I got adept at it, I had to write about ten scripts."
—Oscar-winning screenwriter Brian Helgeland (*L.A. Confidential*)

"I wrote 14 scripts before I wrote [*Things to Do in Denver While You're Dead*]—something like that. If I came up with an idea—no matter how uncommercial it was or how stupid it was, it wouldn't matter—I had to get it out."
—Screenwriter Scott Rosenberg (*High Fidelity*)

Mike De Luca: How many screenplays did you write before the first one got produced?
Sheldon Turner: A good 15 probably. You have to be resilient.
The Dialogue: Sheldon Turner Interview (Part 2)

"You'll never be the best looking, you'll never be the tallest, the most talented, most capable, you'll never have the most money—there will always be someone better at whatever you're doing than you are. But you can always be the hardest working person in the room."
—YouTuber and filmmaker Casey Neistat

"Writing is sweat and drudgery most of the time. And you have to love it in order to endure the solitude and the discipline."
—Author Peter Benchley (*Jaws*)

"You have to write every day. It's like lifting weights. It's just the way it is—you get stronger the more you do it, and if you aren't working, you aren't getting stronger. I'm very disciplined about the way I go about [writing]."
—Stephen J. Cannell (creator of 42 primetime TV series)

"We learn to write by writing, not by just facing an empty page and dreaming of the wonderful success we are going to have."
—Novelist P.D. James

"When it comes to screenwriting, it's the writing. You don't hear people who want to play professional tennis ask to be introduced to the head of Wimbledon. No, they're out there hitting a thousand forehands and a thousand backhands. But for some reason, in the case of screenwriting, people don't think that way."
—Oscar-nominated screenwriter Scott Frank (*Out of Sight*)

"Gardens are not made by singing 'Oh, how beautiful,' and sitting in the shade."
—Poet and novelist Rudyard Kipling (*Gunga Din*)

"I always say to people, it is a competition. You know, the hardest working person usually wins. The lazy people don't even get in the door at all. If you're not obsessed, you don't have any shot at all."
—Writer/director Judd Apatow

"I don't know about luck. I've never banked on it, and I'm afraid of people who do. Luck to me is something else: hard work and realizing what's opportunity and what isn't."
—Lucille Ball

Lucille Ball worked her way up from being the "the Queen of B's" for all the B-movies she made to being one of the most recognized actresses in the history of film and television. And a Hollywood pioneer by becoming "the first woman to run a major television studio"—Desilu Productions

WRITING IN SPURTS AND KEEPING THE CANDLE BURNING

It is enormously difficult to get large chunks of writing time if you're working a full-time, non-writing job. But this doesn't mean that you can't chip away at your story in smaller increments. Pulitzer Prize-winning playwright Lanford Wilson said, "I wrote my first play at an advertising agency in Chicago during lunch hours."

"To the young writers, I would merely say try to develop actual work habits, and even though you have a busy life, try to reserve an hour — or more — a day to write. Some very good things have been written on an hour a day."
—Pulitzer Prize-winning novelist John Updike

"When I first started to write novels while running a magazine, I told myself that I would only write for 15 minutes a day. I knew that working for a short amount of time was an achievable goal, and I managed to get 10 books written this way."
—Kate White (former editor of *Cosmopolitan* magazine)

"I used to write on the morning commuter train. It was sometimes no more than a paragraph a day, but it kept the candle burning."
—Author Scott Turow (*Presumed Innocent*)

THE BREAKFAST CLUB FOR WRITERS

Both Ron Bass and John Grisham were working lawyers before they became full time writers. And both had a habit of waking up at 5:00 A.M. to write. I found others who belong to what I call *The Breakfast Club for Writers*.

"I began training for the writing life in 1951, getting up at 5:00 A.M. and writing for two hours before going to work at an ad agency. My one rule; I had to start writing, get into a scene, before I could put on coffee. Two pages a day in the early hours allowed me to turn out five books, all westerns, and over 30 short stories in the next ten years."
—Elmore Leonard *(Three-Ten to Yuma, Get Shorty)*

"[Aaron Guzikowski] finished the screenplay for *Prisoners* while working at an ad agency in New York – getting up at 5 a.m. to write most workdays, penning his thoughts whenever he could at work, then coming home again to write."
—Maria Papadopoulos, *The Enterprise*

WRITE ONE LINE A DAY

"I have a rule: I try to open my script file daily. I say to myself, *I must write at least one line.* It doesn't feel hard or overwhelming. And, strangely, when I do open the file, my brain will often find itself dictating a stew of words or concepts that I had no previous conscious sense would come out of me."
—Producer/writer/director Pen Densham (*Moll Flanders*)
Riding the Alligator

PAGES PER DAY

Every writer is different in how they work, but in *The 101 Habits of Highly Successful Screenwriters* Karl Iglesias quotes three top screenwriters on how they handle the task of getting script pages done every day.

Akiva Goldsman: When I'm laying down the first draft, I try to write 10 pages per day, and then it's a matter of hours like a regular job. I generally don't write at night and on weekends, because the danger of writing is that you could be doing it anytime, so unless you build rules, you're never free of it.

Steven de Souza: I give myself a quota. I tell myself I'll write six pages a day, everyday. Sometimes I slip up and write four or five, but then I catch up the next week, and I do this until I'm done.

Leslie Dixon: I try to assign myself a certain amount of pages, and if I do achieve that quota and it's really quite solid, I will knock off a little early.

It's helpful to remember that if you write 1 to 6 pages per day, you can complete your first draft in just two or three months.

"For me, the goal isn't to write a novel, it is to write five pages a day. They're not perfect, they need frequent revision down the road, but at least they exist."

— Author David Morrell (*First Blood*)
The Successful Novelist audio version

"Write six pages of script a day. Stick to this schedule no matter what. You'll have a finished first draft in roughly twenty days."
—Screenwriter Joe Eszterhas (*Basic Instinct*)
The Devil's Guide to Hollywood

WRITE 2 OR 3 SCRIPTS THIS YEAR

"The smartest things you can do to advance your craft and career are to read scripts, watch movies, be up to date on the current script marketplace/industry, network, and write 2-3 scripts a year."
—Christopher Lockhart

Stacking projects is the term used by some working writers to describe working on multiple projects at the same time. So many things must come together for a film or Tv project to come together that you can't just place your bets on one horse. Even if you're not getting paid to write scripts you can be stacking your own projects.

CLOSING THE GAP

"I don't particularly like [the writing process], but I don't dislike it either. I can tell you that I've come to a somber acceptance that . . . my tastes as a consumer of movies and TV exceeds my talents, so all I can do is try my best to close that gap and to get as best a version of what it is in my head on the page."
—Screenwriter Eric Heisserer (*Arrival*)
Basic Brainheart podcast interview with Hannah Camacho

That is one healthy and humble perspective. It also puts you in competition with yourself. Your better self. You're simply trying to raise your skill set to match the kind of movies and Tv shows you enjoy.

HOW TO WRITE A SCREENPLAY IN ONE DAY

Is it possible to write a screenplay in one day? A feature film screenplay? Even if you've never written one before? Yes, to all of the above. What's the catch? You're not going to write an original screenplay, but one that's already been produced.

Transcribe a film. Write the script based on an existing movie you're watching on your TV, computer, tablet, or phone (If you happen to be a court reporter, that skill should come in handy here).

I first heard this "Transcribe a Film" piece of advice from screenwriter Jim Uhls (*Fight Club*) on a CreativeLive seminar he gave called *The Screenwriters Toolkit.*

"Here's an assignment for you, transcribe a film. Everybody has a way of pausing and rewinding films as they're watching them—this is a big assignment. It's a big job. But it's a very, very valuable thing to do."
—Screenwriter Jim Uhls

Uhls encourages his students to transcribe the whole film. That's great advice. It should instantly go into the screenwriting advice hall of fame. There are many people who for years have been in love with the idea of being a screenwriter—but they've never finished writing even one screenplay. Uhls' advice fixes that in one day. Granted it's not a screenplay that is totally from your own imagination, but it's a start.

Bear in mind that it might *literally* take you all day, as in 24 hours. It's wise to select a movie that has a sub-100-minute running time like *Pieces of April* (80 min.). Personally, I'd avoid *The Godfather* (175 min.) for this exercise.

Using a yellow pad and pen, it took me 20 minutes to write out the opening dialogue-driven scene from *Swingers*. What I wrote lined up within one sentence of the Jon Favreau script. It was a good exercise. If I was typing, it could have been done in about 10 minutes, so I'm guessing it would take anywhere from 6-12 hours to do a whole script.

At the end of the day (or the end of the week if you chunk it out), you'll have a feature script you wrote. Then you can track down the screenplay of movie you transcribed and compare how the screenwriter(s) who got paid to write the screenplay did it.

Then you can begin to analyze how the produced script is different from your own version. But for now you're just going to get it written. No pressure here. You don't have to show this to anyone.

If you've never read a screenplay or taken a screenwriting class, there are just three things you'll want to be aware of as you dive into writing your first screenplay: Slug line, scene description, and dialogue.

1) Slug line/scene headings

This is what's written at the beginning of every scene. Examples:

INT. O'ROURKE'S BAR – DAY
INT. O'ROURKE'S BAR – NIGHT

Does that seem simplistic? Those are slug lines from the Oscar-nominated screenplay *The Verdict* by David Mamet. There are other variations (DUSK, DAWN, AFTERNOON, etc.) but INT or EXT (for interior or exterior) and DAY or NIGHT are commonly used.

2) Scene description/action

Example (again from *The Verdict* screenplay):

Gavin and Laura are in a booth. The remains of a dinner and drinks around them. They are both smoking cigarettes, intent on each other. Both a little drunk.

These four sentences give you a clear idea of the setting.

For the sake of economy, try to limit your descriptions to three sentences or less. If you have to write more, use another paragraph. In writing action movies, you may have a burst of short sentences and paragraphs flowing down the page.

3) Dialogue

Here you're going to just write down the characters' spoken dialogue. Put the character's name in ALL CAPS with the dialogue under it in the center of the page (Screenwriting software makes the formatting a breeze.)

Example from Oscar-winning *Juno* screenplay by Diablo Cody (Major spoiler alert.):

> JUNO
> I'm pregnant.

You can do that, right? There are other technical components of basic screenwriting including parentheticals, transitions, character introductions, capping SOUNDS, camera directions, MORE, CON'T, etc., but unless you already know how to use those, just stick with slug lines, scene description, and dialogue in this exercise.

Here's what those three components look like when put together. This example is from the start of one scene by Damien Chazelle from the Oscar-nominated *Whiplash* script.

INT. DUNELLEN AUDITORIM – GREEN ROOM – DAY

Andrew arrives, panting. Fletcher glares, the band behind him—

> **FLETCHER**
> **Glad you could work us into your schedule, darling.**

> **ANDREW**
> **I'm here. I'm ready to play.**

> **FLECTCHER**
> **Too late. Connolly's playing.**

The goal of this assignment is to demystify the core process as much as possible. If you have screenwriting software like Movie Magic Screenwriter, Final Draft, Highland, or the free Celtx, it simplifies the formatting process. It is possible to write a script in Word or Pages with some formatting knowhow or handwrite scripts as some do.

While doing this, you will be developing muscle memory and building confidence. No analytical or esoteric theories about screenwriting needed.

One of the hardest aspects of learning how to surf is learning how to catch a wave. If the waves are three feet (or bigger) and choppy, it can seem like an impossible task. But if you go out with a surf instructor on a calm 1–2-foot day and have her give you a little push at the right time, all you have to do is watch your balance and stand up. You won't be Kelly Slater, but you'll probably be surfing in an hour or two.

Transcribing a film is like learning how to surf. You just need a little nudge before you head out into the waves by yourself.

This method is in the ballpark of how Oscar-winning screenwriter Quentin Tarantino started his writing career. While taking acting classes, he used to write from memory scenes from movies he'd seen. Along the way, an acting coach realized Tarantino's writing not only deviated some from the actual movies, but was actually better in some cases. The acting coach encouraged Tarantino to continue writing his own scripts.

ANALYTICAL VS. INTUITIVE WRITING

"[S]omebody asked [*Casablanca* screenwriter Julius Epstein] about structure, and an outline and whatever and he said, 'You know, I write page one, if I like it I'll write page two. If I like page two I'll just continue to the end.' But that school of thought seems to be lost a little bit in the current culture of [screenwriting] books and seminars."
—Mike De Luca
The Dialogue Series

The ability successfully transform screenwriting advice into a powerful script can take years. Much growth will be incremental—like moving a grain of sand. But at other times you will have major breakthroughs.

Mike De Luca asked *Fight Club* screenwriter Jim Uhls, "When did you first feel when you had what it takes to be a screenwriter? Did you have a specific moment when you felt the confidence of, *I can do this*? Uhls responded, "It was when the analytical side and the intuitive side merged together, worked together as a creative unit."

Much of what producers, directors, studios, readers, agents, teachers, script consultants, screenwriting books, seminars, podcasts, and others focus on is the analytical side of screenwriting. What works and doesn't work?

Two of the greatest professional basketball players in the history of the NBA, Michael Jordan and Kobe Bryant, were known for their relentless work ethic. A consuming desire to get better. And part of that was analyzing footage of other players and teams looking for weaknesses they could exploit.

As you read biographies of dramatic writers and directors you don't have to get far to see the same consuming passion. Walt Disney had such a desire for perfection he pushed himself so hard that he had a nervous breakdown at age 31. Part of Disney's obsessiveness was trying to make animated characters and animals appear life like. He would have live animals brought to the studio so his artists could analyze how they moved.

Before Moss Hart found success on Broadway, he was attending Broadway plays nightly. He was consistently evaluating what made a play work or not.

Before Tarantino had free access to nightly movies working at a video rental store, he says it was not unheard of for him to see four or five movies in a single day in movie theaters as a youth. I'm sure he was analyzing movies before he was analyzing movies. (Odds are that filmmakers of tomorrow are young people today streaming multiple films in a single day.)

Tarantino said of creating the Mia character (Uma Thurman) in *Pulp Fiction*, "I have no idea where she came from. I have no idea whatsoever." That's intuition. And talent.

"To tell you the truth, I try not to get analytical in the writing process. I really try not to do that. . . . Basically, my writing's like a journey."
—Writer/director Quentin Tarantino (*Django Unchained*)
Creative Screenwriting interview with Erik Bauer

The intuitive side of screenwriting is hard to articulate. The intuitive side isn't as concrete as the analytical side. It could even be called mystical.

Lawrence Kasdan said he didn't know how he came up with Yoda's unique speech pattern ("Much to learn, you still have.") when writing *Star Wars:*

The Empire Strikes Back. That's not that uncommon.

"I don't know that we choose how we write. I think it somehow chooses us. It's very mystical."
—Oscar-winning screenwriter Horton Foote (*Tender Mercies*)

Screenwriter John Milius (*Big Wednesday*) said "All creative work is mystical," and was not in favor of anyone trying to "demystify it."

Oscar-winning cinematographer Janusz Kamiński (*Schindler's List*) was asked the following analytical question: "When you're looking at an image do you go with the philosophy of adding light to get the image or subtracting to take away to get the image?" He responded, "I have no idea . . . I don't know how it happens."

When Mamet was once asked about his creative process he gave this wry response, "You know how Hemingway wrote standing up? Well, I write sitting down."

Aaron Sorkin says the one thing you can't teach about screenwriting is writing dialogue. It's just a gift he has.

Over the years I've spent enough money on Jimmy Buffett concerts, music, and books to help him buy a small island in Margaritaville. When asked on a *60 Minutes* interview about his talents Buffett said, "I'm an adequate musician. I wish I was a better guitar player, and I'm a fair singer. They're not my strongest suits. … I'm a go capture the magic guy."

And he's captured enough magic to have that rare career that's sustained an audience for over five decades, and built an entertainment and lifestyle empire making his personal worth over $500 million. That's a lot of magic.

Maybe Horton, Milius, Kaminski, Mamet, Sorkin, and Buffett are right and it's all just mysterious or just too difficult to explain. Or maybe there's another explanation.

"Artistic creativity—it's magical, but not magic. Meaning it's a product of the brain."
—Surgeon Charles Lamb (who also studies creativity)
TedTalk, *Your brain on improv*

"Years of practice is often mistaken for talent."
—Angela Duckworth
Grit

Referencing the 10,000-hour rule to achieve mastery, David Lee Roth said that legendary guitarist Eddie Van Halen was a 30,000-to-40,000-hour guy. However creativity happens, neurons are fired in the brain, and ideas come out. Some better than others. That's the intuitive side of writing.

The analytical side is the side that informs your screenwriting (or rewriting) by asking things like "Are the stakes high enough?" and "How can I visualize the conflict?" For some writers, just starting the writing process is what leads to creative breakthroughs.

"I can't tell you what's going to happen in the third act, 'cause I ain't there yet. For me, writing is a much more organic process."
—Frank Darabont

"Remember that scripts are not so much written as rewritten and rewritten and rewritten. . . . So plunge ahead regardless. Don't wait to get it right, just get it written."
—Writer/Director Alexander Mackendrick (*Sweet Smell of Success*)
On Film-making edited by Paul Cronin

It is in the writing process that you can arrive at that flow state where some writers say the story writes itself.

FLOW

Psychology professor Mihály Csíkszentmihályi has written extensively about the concept of "getting into the flow." His teachings and writings have influenced a generation of writers, artists, musicians, and athletes.

"Flow is being completely involved in an activity for its own sake. The ego falls away. Time files. Every action, movement, and thought follows inevitably from the previous one, like playing jazz."
—Mihály Csíkszentmihályi

Csíkszentmihályi, in his book *Flow: The Psychology of Optimal Experience*, addresses that state where you perform your best. You're not bored or overwhelmed. You have extreme focus and concentration. Your sense of time is transformed. For the dancer, a few seconds can seem like moments, and for the writer, hours can feel like minutes.

"Once you get into the moment, you know you're there. The crowd gets quiet. Things start moving slowly. You start to see the court very well."
—Basketball great Michael Jordan

To see outward manifestation of a flow state, watch mountain climber Alex Honnold free climb Yosemite's El Capitan in the Oscar-winning documentary *Free Solo*. He has total clarity in the goal he wants to accomplish, and a skill set matched to the challenge.

Getting into a state of flow is more complex than I have time for here, but it seems to start with getting rid of external distractions. Then pushing yourself to the limits in a specific task that you have trained to do.

ADVICE THAT'S 400 YEARS OLD

Lope de Vega was a playwright was born in Madrid, Spain in 1562 and is thought to have written around 1,500 plays.

I was unaware of him until I read *The Tools of Screenwriting* by David Howard and Edward Mabley. The book's introduction by Frank Daniel has sound advice—originally over 400 years old:

"When I have to write a play, I lock up the rules with six keys."
—Lope de Vega
Writing Plays in Our Times (published in 1609)

If you don't lock them up, at least be sure to grip them only loosely.

"I do think it's true that you need to learn all these [story structure] ideas, but be willing to toss them."
—Judd Apatow

"I believe in the three-act structure, I've just never succeeded in doing one. "
— Oscar winning writer/director James Cameron (*Titanic*)

EMBRACE YOUR LIMITATIONS

"Stealing a page from Hitchcock's playbook, I decided on writing a story that takes place entirely in one small location. In my case, this was inside an old, wooden coffin."
—Chris Sparling on writing *Buried*

With just one actor on screen in a single location, *Buried* is almost as sparse as you can get in a narrative film. Sparling said his previously unproduced scripts suffered from "too many locations, and way to many actors."

"You learn from the mistakes you make, you know? You try to, anyway. So with *Buried*, I realized, 'Well, this time, I'm not going to star in it. I just want to direct it. I want to write something. I want to have something produced."
—Chris Sparling
Go Into The Story interview with Scott Myers

He figured he could make a movie for $5,000 without turning his life upside down. He scaled down his concept and came up with "a guy alone in a box for a whole movie." His script gained traction. Shot in Spain with Rodrigo Cortés directing actor Ryan Reynolds, and a $2 million budget, *Buried* was a financial and critical success.

Several years before Ava DuVernay made the Oscar nominated documentary *13th* or directed the $100 million feature *A Wrinkle in Time*, she embraced her limitations by making the short film *Compton in C Minor* on footage shot in just a two-hour window of time in Compton, California.

Filmmaker Edward Burns is a Sundance Grand Jury Prize winner (*The Brothers McMullen*), acted in a film directed by Steven Spielberg (*Saving Private Ryan*), directed Jennifer Aniston (*She's the One*), made a music video with Tom Petty (*Walls*), and wrote the book *Independent Ed*—a solid 25-year run.

When he wasn't securing studio or TV work, Burns embraced his limitations by making several micro-budget films. He shot *Newlyweds* for under $10,000 (not including post-production). He limited the size of his crew to 3-5 people who could wear multiple hats. Set up some deferred payments. He used up and coming actors who did their own wardrobe and makeup. He picked free locations where he didn't have to worry about permits and used little or no lights. He also redefined a schedule by spreading the equivalent 10-12 shooting days over a three-month period. That allowed Burns to do some editing and story problem solving.

BAD IDEAS AND WRITING POORLY

Before Glenn Frey became a rock star, Bob Seger told him that that he wouldn't make it big unless he wrote his own songs. Frey said, what if they're bad? Seger said, "Well, they're going to be bad. But you just keep writing, and keep writing, and eventually you'll write a good song."

Frey figured it out, and with Don Henley wrote the Eagles' classics *Desperado* and *Tequila Sunrise* (incredibly, in the same week) and the lyrics to their #1 hit *Hotel California*.

Here are some quotes that support the view that the road to good writing is paved with writing that's not so good.

"Just write poorly. Continue to write poorly, in public, until you can write better."
—Author and speaker Seth Godin

"The best work that anybody ever writes is the work that is on the verge of embarrassing him, always."
—Arthur Miller

"When you first start writing you're going to suck, and so it's kind of good to keep it to yourself until maybe you don't suck as much."
—David Sedaris

BAD SCRIPT, GOOD PIZZA, GREAT FEEDBACK

"I would have these script readings for *Don't Think Twice* at my house to workshop the film script the way that I workshop my

standup and I would say at the beginning of the reading, 'The script might be bad, but at the end, we're all going to eat pizza.'"
—Writer/Director Mike Birbiglia

In various interviews, Mike Birbiglia explained his writing process from gathering ideas to writing and rewriting his screenplays. When writing, he schedules three hours each morning to write in a coffee shop (but may write for five if the writing is flowing). He encourages writing in a trance, not thinking consciously about what you're putting on the page.

At home he has a corkboard wall full of 3X5-inch notecards containing scene ideas, pieces of dialogue, and what he calls "mind writing quotes" (inspirational sayings by well-known writers).

After he has a satisfactory script, he invites writers and actors he admires over to his "shabby apartment in Brooklyn" for a table read plus feedback. After the table read of the entire script from start to finish, they eat pizza and the fiery discussion begins.

"A lot of people give their thoughts and they really conflict with other people's thoughts. And those people fight with each other, and I listen to that. It's really helpful."
—Mike Birbiglia

HOW MUCH DO SCREENWRITERS MAKE?

"Most screenwriters are unemployed, chronically unemployed."
—Screenwriter Tom Lazarus (*Stigmata*)
Secrets of Film Writing

"It's either very lucrative and exciting, or nothing."
—Screenwriter Anthony Peckham (*Invictus*) on screenwriting

When people think about professional football players' incomes, they tend to focus on the big numbers. Quarterback Brett Favre once had a $20 million dollar one-year contract with the Minnesota Vikings. Payton Manning once had a $99.2 million seven-year contract with the Indianapolis Colts. As of this writing, though, most rookies in the NFL earn under $500,000 per year. Deduct taxes, agent fees, a down payment on a house, and maybe a car or two, and there's not much money left (relatively speaking, of course). Most pro football careers last less than four years (some claim the NFL really stands for "Not for Long"), so you can see why the majority of those who play in the NFL really have under a million dollars to their name when they retire. It's also not hard to understand why so many end up filing for bankruptcy when their short careers are over.

Often when people think of Hollywood writers, they likewise think about the multi-million dollar deals (like Joe Eszterhas banking $3 million in the early '90s for writing *Basic Instinct*). In fact, though, most screenwriters won't make any money at all this year from their writing.

The Atlantic magazine stated a few years ago that the Writers Guild of America registers 50,000 screenplays each year. *Each year.*

According to the Writer's Guide of America-West (WGAW) recent report, 3,775 of its 8,129 union members were unemployed. Depending on different sources, working WGAw members appear to average between $40,000 and $110,000 per year (The key word there is "working"). Considering the cost of living where most writers live (New York and L.A.), this average is far from extravagant.

"Most writers are middle class; 46% did not even work last year. Of those who do work, one quarter make less than $37,700 a year and 50% make less than $105,000 a year. Over a five year period of employment and unemployment, a writer's average income is $62,000 per year."
—2010 Writers Guild of America, West

As a rule-of-thumb, screenplays are 2%-5% of the total budget. While that results in a nice paycheck on a $75 million dollar film, it can also result in a remarkably low amount on a $200,000 non-union indie film.

"When you're not in the [WGA] you're just grateful for anything that'll you give you a month of rent or a couple months of rent. My first couple of jobs were New York independent things . . . of course, there wasn't a lot of money for an untested writer. So if somebody had read a script you'd written on spec then sometimes you'd get paid 5,000 bucks, if you're lucky, on a good day maybe 10,000 bucks."
—Screenwriter Chris Terrio (*Argo*)

Tarantino said that back when he was only making $10,000 a year at his day job "No one was interested in my stuff at all." What jump started his film career was screenwriter and friend Scotty Spiegel (and his writer friends) who threw Tarantino their low-budget overflow re-rewriting gigs.

"So then all of the sudden I was getting paid like $4,000 to do a little dialogue polish on somebody's thing, and I got paid $6,000, and then I got paid $10,000 to do something."
—Quentin Tarantino
The Q&A with Jeff Goldsmith

Of course, what screenwriters make globally will vary greatly. In Nigeria— Nollywood— they are making a lot of movies, but most budgets are sub-$100,000. Some even sub-$10,000. Same for Joe Swanberg's indie films.

And even in Hollywood what screenwriters make will vary. At the top of the Hollywood feature film food chain are working WGA writers who generate writing income several ways. Nailing down those exact numbers is hard, but this is how a few top screenwriters can occasionally make $100,000 or $300,000 a week and millions over the course of the year:

—Writing assignment (developing new script from book, article, or an idea)
—Punch-up a script (take an existing script and add action and make it more dynamic, tweak the dialogue, and/or add humor to make it funnier)
—One to three week polish of a script
—Page one re-write. Take an existing screenplay that has promise, but needs a lot of work, and make it a script worth producing.
—Residuals (DVD/Blu-Ray/digital sales, TV and foreign rights)
—Speaking (college and corporate work)
—Spec work (selling a screenplay without a deal from a producer or studio)
—Story meetings (A gathering of writers to kick around story concepts. Seen by some as a negative direction for the industry, as it's the equivalent of kicking tires.)

On the TV side writers can be paid per script or as a staff writer. The highest paid are the ones who create a hit network show and stay on as producer/writers. If that show stays on the air for five years and goes into syndication, then they can afford to buy a small tropical island. (Largely based on the success of the TV show *Seinfeld* Jerry Seinfeld's net worth hovers around a billion dollars.) A good gig if you can land it, but that doesn't describe most TV writers.

"On balance, television writers today are the highest-paid practitioners of the literary profession in history. But mark the phrase on balance. . . . It's only when you get the top 5 to 10 percent that you find writers and hyphenates who routinely earn six figures a year or more."
— Writer/producer J. Michael Straczynski (*Babylon 5, Changeling*)
The Complete Book of Screenwriting

Straczynski's book was published in 1996 (the current range for a 90-minute or less network story and teleplay start around $30,000). Unfortunately, one of the growing trends today is Netflix and other streaming services that pay writers a flat rate and no residuals.

A friend of mine in L.A. who has written for the networks was once offered a job on a cable TV program that would have paid her just a little more than her unemployment benefits. Everyone isn't getting rich.

"For every writer I know that lives high on the hog I know twenty who buy their bacon at Costco."
—Screenwriter Josh Friedman (*War of the Worlds*)

Even when script assignments are quite lucrative by comparison, they do not always pay as extravagantly as you might expect.

"Let's talk money, because no one ever does. A top tier screenplay deal these days might be for a million dollars or more. Most are far, far less, but let's work with those crazy high numbers, in fact let's say 2 million dollars, though nobody is paying that any more. Wow that's a lot of money. But consider. With a writing partner, that gets cut down to $1,000,000., and after taxes, lawyers, agents, managers, and the WGA, let's hope you get to keep $400,000."
—Screenwriter Terry Rossio (*Shrek, Pirates of the Caribbean*)

Rossio goes on to point out in an interview with John Robert Marlow that it might take six months to work out the contract, and the full deal is contingent on the film going into production. These complications could stretch that $400,000 over a two-, three-, or even five-year period. That's still good money, especially if you have a couple of deals going at the same time. But, as Rossio says, "it's not in the fly-a-Learjet-to-your-own-private-island-in-the-Caribbean category."

The 1991 animated musical version of *Beauty and the Beast* was both a critical and financial success. It was made for $25 million and it pulled in over $400 million at the worldwide box office. It also earned an Oscar nomination for Best Picture. It is listed at number 22 on AFI's Greatest Movie Musicals, and number 7 on AFI's top 10 Animated list.

You'll be surprised at how little the screenwriter made on the screenplay.

"I was paid— I'm going to guess— $35,000 to write the script [for *Beauty and the Beast*]. **Took me four years, as animation does."**
—Screenwriter Linda Woolverton

Because she was writing outside the WGA, there was no "back end" residual money, although she did get a $100,000 bonus after the dust settled. But $135,000 for four years of work (and no benefits) is not the cash bonanza that most people dream about.

Woolverton did say that the opportunity opened doors in her career. And she ended up getting a great return on her time investment on *Beauty and the Beast* when she was hired to write the Broadway musical version, a source of ongoing residual income.

Other opportunities for writers include writing for cable TV and streaming movies. These incomes tend to land in the $30,000-50,000 range with no residual income. On the Done Deal message board writers talk about writing non-union scripts for cable TV movies and making between $15,000 and $30,000 (with no residuals).

So while writers like Aaron Sorkin can make millions from a script, most working screenwriters do not even come close to that number. When starting out, you definitely won't.

Despite the odds, people do find ways to have careers as screenwriters. But if you do have your mind set on a Learjet, then creating an off-the-charts successful TV show like *Seinfeld* is the way to go.

As we head toward the end of this book, I wanted to highlight nine screenwriters and one screenwriting team of two people to show a variety of people and where they came from, and the paths they took, to have careers as working screenwriters.

HOW TO BECOME A SUCCESSUL SCREENWRITER

MICHAEL ARDNT

"I had read enough mediocre scripts and was determined not to inflict another one on the world."
—Michael Arndt

Screenwriter Michael Arndt is a textbook example of slowly building a career. Like Diablo Cody, his first produced screenplay (*Little Miss Sunshine*) not only became a sleeper hit but won an Oscar for Best Original Screenplay. A pretty good start, huh? Except that's not the start.

Rewind a few years and you'll find that he's a New York University film school grad (steeped in the films of Billy Wilder, Preston Sturges, and Woody Allen) who spent 10 years working in the film business as a personal assistant to Matthew Broderick and a script reader.

He quit his job in 1999 and with $25,000 in savings took time to focus on just writing screenplays in his small apartment in Brooklyn. Arndt referred to his unproduced screenplays as "depressing stories where everyone got killed in the end." It wasn't until his seventh script that things clicked. He realized that there's nothing better—when done really well—than a happy ending.

He came up with a happy ending that takes place at a children's beauty pageant, and reverse engineered the story from there. It was a simple story that took place over three days, and where he could develop a family of eccentric characters. The characters were inspired from classic old Hollywood films like *You Can't Take it With You* and *My Man Godfrey*.

He did a detailed step outline with 50 slug lines for 50 scenes, and then added the dialogue that became the screenplay *Little Miss Sunshine*. Before he sent it out to be read, he wrote over 100 drafts of that script. It created buzz as soon as it was sent out, and sold for $150,000. But it would still take five years for the film to get produced and released.

DIABLO CODY

"The fact is, when I wrote *Juno*—and I think this is part of its charm and appeal—I didn't know how to write a movie."
—Diablo Cody

Diablo Cody is that rare screenwriter who has achieved celebrity status. She will tell you that this is not necessarily a good thing, but when she came on the scene in 2007 and 2008 the press took a liking to her.

Her first screenplay *Juno* became a hit movie and a cultural sensation. Produced for under $10 million, it made $231 million globally. It earned Oscar nominations for Best Picture and Cody won the Oscar for her original screenplay.

Cody is a product of 12 years of Catholic education in the Chicago area, and earned a degree in Media Studies from the University of Iowa. She had been writing poetry every day since she was 12 years old, learned to blog (back when it was still necessary to know how to code), and at age 27 had a book published that landed her a guest appearance on the *Late Show with David Letterman*. Those experiences gave her literary chops and pop cultural knowledge that equipped her well for the moment when she turned her attention to writing a screenplay, all while living in the suburbs of Minneapolis.

I was inspired to start my blog *Screenwriting from Iowa . . . and Other Unlikely Places* in 2008, just days after seeing *Juno* and learning of Cody's backstory. I was living in Cedar Falls, Iowa at the time (about an hour north of Iowa City, where Cody went to college), and Cody seemed like the perfect example of an outsider invading Hollywood.

The next month, she collected her Academy Award. Later that year, I was in Minneapolis collecting a regional Emmy for my blog. The day after I won, I drove to the Target in Crystal, Minnesota where Cody wrote much of *Juno*, in the Starbucks located inside.

Adam Vanderlinder was working at Starbucks that day and remembered Cody and pointed out where she used to write—the only spot with an available electric plug. I had the Emmy in my backpack, so I took it out and photographed it while sitting in Cody's writing space.

RYAN COOGLER

Few writer/directors have had the kind of success Ryan Coogler had in his first three films. His debut film, *Fruitvale Station*, premiered at the Sundance Film Festival where it won the Grand Prize and Audience Award. His second film, *Creed*, made over $173 million at the box office and earned an Oscar nomination for Sylvester Stallone. He followed that with *Black Panther,* which jumped into the top 10 grossing movies of all time. On top of its financial success, *Black Panther* earned seven Academy Award nominations, including best picture of the year. Coogler accomplished all of this within ten years of graduating with an MFA from USC's film school.

Surprisingly, Coogler wasn't one of those kids who grew up making short films, dreaming of becoming the next Steven Spielberg. In his freshman year at St. Mary's College of California, he was a football player dreaming of being a doctor.

But after turning in a creative writing assignment, his professor (novelist Rosemary Graham) encouraged him to consider being a writer and "maybe even consider going to Hollywood and writing screenplays." Coogler would later say of that advice, "I thought she was crazy. I didn't even know what a screenplay was."

That day, he bought the *Pulp Fiction* DVD which also included the screenplay for the movie. It was the first screenplay he'd ever read. That night using Word software, he began playing with formatting and typing his first screenplay.

When St. Mary's ended their football program, Coogler transferred to Sacramento State where he majored in Business Administration and took as many film courses as he could. It was during this time that he first learned how to use a camera and editing software. He credits his professor Dr. Roberto Pomo with teaching him how to watch films.

Ten years later, he was at the Academy Awards where *Black Panther* earned seven Oscars nominations, winning three times.

ALEJANDRO G. IÑÁRRITU

Mexico City born Alejandro G. Iñárritu won three Oscars alone for his working on *Birdman* (including co-writing the script*),* and the following year picked up another Oscar for best direction on *The Revenant*. He studied communications at Ibero-American University, a private Catholic school in Mexico City. His career in media began as a radio host before making a transition to working as a TV producer, director, and writer in Mexico.

"I remember, the first time I saw a [Andrei] Tarkovsky film, I was shocked by it. I didn't know what to do. I was fascinated, because suddenly I realized that film could have so many more layers to it than what I had imagined before."
—Alejandro G. Iñárritu

His debut feature film, *Amores Perros*, was shot in Mexico City. It opened at the Cannes Film Festival, and later won an Academy Award for Best Foreign Language Film.

Since then, he has continued to build on what started in radio by working on commercials (BMW, Nike), short films, a branding film for Facebook, cable TV, and features on the highest level. If you want to know what a cross-platform content creator looks like today, study Iñárritu and his work.

SHONDA RHIMES

"I was the kid who got straight A's and was a little too intense in school. Like, I am a perfectionist, and I am going to sit at the front of the class with my hand raised."
—Shonda Rhimes
Fast Company interview

Shonda Rhimes signed a deal with Netflix in 2017 for a salary in the $100 million dollar range, and it signaled to everyone in Hollywood that there was a new way of doing business.

Rhimes grew up in Chicago, attended a Catholic high school, and then studied English and film at Dartmouth College. In college, she wrote and directed student productions, and then went to the USC film school where she studied screenwriting and earned an MFA.

She did an internship with producer Debra Martin Chase while at USC, and then worked various on -production jobs. She did research for a documentary, made a short film, and then co-wrote *Introducing Dorothy Dandridge* starring Halle Berry.

Rhimes wrote the screenplay for *Crossroads* (2012) starring Britney Spears, and co-wrote the screenplay for *The Princess Diaries 2: Royal Engagement* before creating the long-running ABC show *Grey's Anatomy,* which first aired in 2005. As of this writing she has created four TV shows that are currently airing.

CLARE SERA

The problem with looking at people at or near the top of the production mountain is that it can make the gulf between you and them seem unbridgeable. Simply making a living is hard enough.

But not every football player is going to be Tom Brady, not every basketball player Michael Jordan, nor every singer Aretha Franklin. There are, though, many hard-working and talented professionals who found a way to make a decent living as screenwriters.

Screenwriter Clare Sera co-wrote *Smallfoot,* which for one day in 2018 was the top box office film in the United States. The animated film went on to make over $200 million. Sera is yet another example of someone who has had an unusual journey on the road to being a working writer in Hollywood. She was born in Scotland, raised in Canada, and worked as a writer and performer in Florida before moving to Los Angeles.

My path crossed with Sera in Orlando in the 1990s. She studied theater in college in Vancouver, and when Orlando-based improv group SAK Theatre did a tour in Canada one summer, Sera ended up working with them, and joined the group and moved to Florida.

She was able to work alongside a several talented performers at SAK who went on to greater fame in New York and Los Angeles. These included Emmy-winning writer Paula Pell (*Saturday Night Live*), screenwriter Bob DeRosa (*Killers*), Emmy-winning producer/writer Aaron Shure (*Everyone Loves Raymond*), and Emmy-winning performer Wayne Brady (*Whose Line is it Anyway?*). Brady credits Sera and her husband Will for introducing him to improv.

She moved to L.A. in the mid-'90s and joined another improv group, also acting in theater and films before moving into writing. She was mentored by writer/director Karey Kirkpatrick (*James and the Giant Peach*) working as his writer's assistant. She also studied screenwriting in the Act One writing program, and eventually became Kirkpatrick's writing partner.

She's written scripts for every major studio, and also mentors at WriteGirl, which according to its website is "a creative writing and mentoring organization that promotes creativity, critical thinking and leadership to empower teen girls."

In a quirky connection I discovered while working on this book, Clare Sera also worked with Shonda Rhimes on *The Princess Diaries 2*, Shonda as a writer and Clare as an actress. Here's some encouragement she wrote just for this book based on her experiences:

"I have had some success but do not have a shiny career. I got into screenwriting late — I was late thirties, an age where some screenwriters are starting to worry if they haven't "made it" yet. It's a tough business. Nobody aspires to be a working screenwriter whose scripts mostly do not get made. You'll never see that in a class brochure. It's not like being a plumber where you have knowledge and a skill that other folks know they do not have and so you are given respect for that. It's not expected that plumbers are only successful if they are a celebrity plumber with A list toilets on their resume. But, and I don't know if this is true for other laborers, I can't not write movies. It's in my bones and I do feel incredibly fortunate that I make a living doing this, even if so many scripts I write are sold but never made. By the way, it's heartbreaking, every time. But I apparently must keep doing it and I continue to hope that more of my stories will be seen. And I am very grateful it pays my bills and

allows me to be around amazing folk, chasing their own hearts and purpose through storytelling. What advice would I give others? Make peace with the tightrope of art and commerce as soon as possible, because being an artist, pouring your heart out and having folks say no thanks, requires living with a bleeding heart. As soon as you let the callouses grow, you stop being an artist, but if you don't tend yourself, you'll bleed out. I realize now, writing this, that being around folks who live like that is probably an even greater joy for me than getting a movie made."
— Clare Sera

Sera also encourages writers to not limit themselves to writing but to "make three-minute movies, make five-minute movies, make webisodes, because it is a maker culture now. And that's how people get noticed and get movement, with distinct voices and things that are made and not just on the page."

SCOTT BECK AND BRYAN WOODS

"Throughout high school and our college years we just keep making movies and feature films for practically no budget."
—Writer/director Scott Beck (*A Quiet Place*)

Writer/directors Scott Beck and Bryan Woods were in their early thirties when their script *A Quiet Place* became an international sensation. The thriller directed (and co-written) by John Krasinski put a spotlight on Beck and Woods. Despite their young age, they'd been making films together for over 20 years.

They met in middle school in Bettendorf, Iowa when they were 12 years old. They shared a love for movies and began making their own short films, and before graduating from high school they made their first low-budget feature.

They both went to the University of Iowa and majored in communications, while continuing to make their own films. After college they remained in Iowa and formed their own production company, working on their own productions while also building inroads into Hollywood.

Although *A Quiet Place* became the film that brought them national acclaim, they had hedged their bets by writing a number of other screenplays in case Hollywood passed on their unorthodox script. Their original script for *A Quiet Place* was only 67 pages. It included drawings and a map, handwriting, only three words of dialogue, and one entire page that just included one word:

". . . SNAP" in an oversized font. (Inspired by techniques Dan Gilroy used in his *Nightcrawler* screenplay.)

Beck and Woods' scripts are often unconventional by Hollywood's standards. Part of the reason for their bold approach was that even if everyone in Hollywood passed on a script, they knew they could always return home and make their own low-budget version of the film.

"Kind of a lesson we learned growing up in Iowa— we would write things for resources that we had in front of us. Something that could be produced, could be made, and hopefully be an interesting story, too. That's a long way of saying that's somewhat the genesis of *A Quiet Place*. It's like *A Quiet Place* was written for us to shoot back in Iowa for $50,000 if everyone passed on it. It would have been a very, very different version without Emily Blunt and John Krasinski. But it was something we just had a passion for, and we knew worst case scenario that could be plan B."
—Bryan Woods

Plan A with producer Michael Bay and his team worked out quite well. *A Quiet Place* was a hit with fans and critics. Krasinski, Beck, and Woods were nominated for Best Original Screenplay by the Writers Guild of America, and actress Emily Blunt won a Screen Actors Guild award. To get a snapshot of their journey, here's a 2019 tweet from them @beckandwoods:

Sometimes we get asked how to break into the film industry without any connections. Here's how we did it…
Make cute shorts with your action figures that you never show to anyone except your parents
Start casting your friends & family in increasingly ambitious but still unwatchable shorts

Read novels and screenplays for fun, wonder how they were written

Turn every class project into opportunity to film something

Start making no budget features that bore your friends & family, but learn why

Get rejected by every major screenplay competition before graduating high school

Become finalist on Project Greenlight and MTV Best Film on Campus, but lose

Get rejected by every major film festival before graduating college

Develop list of young industry contacts who don't like your work but maybe one day will

Get rejected by every major agency after they tell you they want to sign

Write screenplays no one wants to make or read, learn why

Write screenplays some people want to make or read, but can't

Get frustrated, make one last go-for-broke short film

Show short to shortlist of industry contacts developed after years of networking

Get rejected by many managers but sign with one

If you think all of that sounds like it took a while, you would be correct.

"We probably wrote close to 30 screenplays before we became professional screenwriters. It took a very long time to get there."
—Bryan Woods
SellingYourScreenplay.com podcast interview with Ashley Scott Meyers

LULU WANG

The circuitous route that Lulu Wang took before her film *The Farewell* became an international sensation is an interesting story by itself.

She was born in China and raised in Miami, Florida where she went to an art conservatory high school focusing on piano performance. She didn't have the passion to try and make music her career but was a double major in music and literature at Boston College. And she'd only taken one photography and one filmmaking class before graduating from BC.

She was accepted into law school but opted to move to LA instead.

Through cold calling production companies, her ability to speak Mandarin Chinese came in handy as a translator was needed for the movie *Rush Hour 3*. (Note: Ava DuVerney did PR work on *Rush Hour 3*.)

She read her story *What You Don't Know* for the NPR radio program *This American Life*, which led to her deal to direct the film version—*The Farewell*. The movie debuted at the Sundance Film Festival, was a modest moneymaker at the box office, and a critical success. It also won numerous awards including Best Feature at the Independent Spirit Awards.

FRANCES MARION (1888-1973)

"One could write a history of Hollywood around Frances Marion."
—John Beltone

**"Frances was an original. What she became did not exist in 1913 ....
She had more muscle in Hollywood because she was a gold mine of
ideas—ideas that could become stories that could become scripts
that could become films that could save careers, lives, corporations."**
—Legendary actress Gloria Swanson

Frances Marion was not only the first woman to win an Oscar for Best Original Screenplay (for *The Big House* in 1930), but she was also the first screenwriter to win two Oscars after her script for *The Champ* in 1931.

Marion was born into a wealthy family in 1888, but her mother died when she was young and she was sent to a boarding school that prepared girls to attend colleges on the east coast. She learned to speak several languages, play the piano, and became a gifted artist. Plans to attend college were dashed when the San Francisco earthquake of 1906 wiped out her family's wealth. Six years later, she arrived in Los Angeles at age 24 with the hopes of making a living as an artist. Instead, she became a journalist and a Hollywood legend.

She worked on *The New York Hat* (1912), directed by D.W. Griffith. That began a long relationship working with actress Mary Pickford. She wrote films for the biggest stars in early cinema (Douglas Fairbanks, Greta Garbo, and Jean Harlow). Several of her credits were on short, silent films where writers credited as "scenarists., allowing her to amass over writing credits over her 30 plus year career.

She also made the transition to talking feature films and worked for legendary producers Sam Goldwyn and Irving Thalberg. At one point Marion was the highest-paid screenwriter in Hollywood.

She was under contract with MGM and married to actor Fred Thomson, who at the time of his death in 1928 was billed as "The World's Greatest Western Star." Definitely an early Hollywood power couple.

They built a glamorous home in 1925 known as The Enchanted Hill. It included a large Spanish Hacienda-style house on four acres overlooking Beverly Hills. The home had a barn for horses and living quarters for staff, a guesthouse, an organ, tennis courts, and a hundred-foot swimming pool.

Frances Marion is somewhat forgotten today, but her story is preserved in her autobiography, *Off with Their Heads: A Serio-Comic Tale of Hollywood*. She also wrote one of the first books on screenwriting, *How to Write and Sell Film Stories* (1937).

"It seems almost as if some writers are afraid to hurt their characters, are afraid to make them suffer, or to get them into distressing situations from which they must fight their way out. Yet one of the very first things any fiction writer must learn is that where there is no struggle there is no drama."
—Frances Marion

In a non-Hollywood ending, the home that Marion built was eventually bought by Microsoft co-founder Paul Allen and demolished. When Allen died in 2018, the land was still a vacant lot.

The demolition of that home was another chapter of Hollywood history that disappeared. Perhaps it's a fitting metaphor, as tech groups from Silicon Valley changed the direction of how the Hollywood film industry operates.

HOLLYWOOD VS. SILICON VALLEY

"Silicon Valley has already won. It's just that Hollywood hasn't quite figured out yet."
—Nick Bilton (in a 2017 *Vanity Fair* article)

"You can stop waiting for the future of movies. It's already here. Someday, 1999 will be etched on a microchip as the first real year of 21st-century filmmaking."
—Jeff Gordinier
Entertainment Weekly, "1999: The Year That Changed Movies"

Some movie lovers claim 1999 as the single best year for movies. Here's an impressive shortlist from that year: *The Matrix, American Beauty, The Sixth Sense, Fight Club, The Straight Story, Election, Magnolia,* and *Toy Story 2.*

But 1999 was also when the first noticeable web-centered tremors hit the film industry. Some filmmakers who'd met at the University of Central Florida made a film that had a midnight premiere at the Sundance Film Festival in 1999, and was quickly bought for $1.1 million.

The Blair Witch Project was made on a budget of $60,000 but would go on to make $248 million at the box office. It's still one of the most profitable movies ever (based on initial investment and box office profits). Directors Daniel Myrick and Eduardo Sanchez landed on the cover of *Time* magazine.

Part of the filmmakers' success was due to their pioneering use of consumer digital cameras and internet technology. Because dial-up bandwidth ruled in 1999, websites were still text- and photo-driven. The website for *The Blair Witch Project* (blairwitch.com) created marketing buzz by blurring the lines between fiction and reality. Was the found footage from *The Blair Witch Project* real? Was this a narrative movie, or a documentary? It was the first movie to go viral over the internet.

Of course, other leaps forward had transpired prior to 1999. Other key moments include the use of handheld 16mm cameras in Italian films of the 50s; the invention and expansion of video assist by filmmakers Jerry Lewis and Francis Ford Coppola in the '60s and '70s; George Lucas starting Industrial Light and Magic in 1975; Steve Jobs joining Pixar in 1986; and Pixar's release of *Toy Story* in 1995 as the first computer-animated feature.

But 1999 was unique because that is the year when the film *business* changed into something new. Although the new millennium had started off a little shaky when the dot-com bust began in early 2000, it wasn't long before the film industry and the internet were one.

After that, what you could do with a digital camera exploded. It wasn't just low-budget indie films that were using the technology. Established directors who used prosumer DV cameras (Sony VX1000, Sony PD 150, Canon XL, Panasonic DVX 100 cameras) included:

Michael Figgis, *Timecode* (2000)
Spike Lee, *Bamboozled* (2000)
Steven Soderbergh, *Full Frontal* (2002)
Gary Winick, *Tadpole* (2002; Best Director Award at Sundance)
Peter Hedges, *Pieces of April* (2003)
David Lynch, *Inland Empire* (2004)
Zana Briski, *Born into Brothels* (2004; Best Documentary Academy Award)
Morgan Spurlock, *Supersize Me* (2004; Best Director Award at Sundance)

The Panasonic DVX 100 was the first standard DV camera to shoot in 24p format—mimicking a film look— and became the darling of independent film for a season. Nancy Schreiber shot the film *November* with that camera, and went on to win a cinematography award at the 2004 Sundance Film Festival. That was the first time that award had been granted for digital cinematography.

In larger-budget efforts, directors George Lucas (*Star Wars: Episode 1—The Phantom Menace*), Robert Rodriguez (*Once Upon a Time in Mexico*), and Michael Mann (*Collateral*) shot films digitally with the Sony CineAlta F900.

Russian Ark (2002) showcased how digital cameras with external hard drives attached could shoot continuously for sustained periods. Director of photography and Steadicam operator Tilman Büttner shot the entire 96-minute film in one take.

Digital production, then, was gaining ground on the traditional film industry. Silicon Valley, in the meantime, was still licking its wounds from the dot-com bust, which put almost 50% of the internet companies out of business. But a world of change was coming. But the epicenter was not in Hollywood, but 350 miles to the north. Just south of San Francisco.

Apple (Cupertino) was making early inroads into digital editing with Final Cut Pro. Adobe's Premiere (San Jose) non-linear software eventually became the favorite of filmmaker of David Fincher (*The Social Network*).

Then a wave of change arrived that impacted the film and television industries in ways that rival the impact of talkies in the late twenties, television in the fifties, and cable TV in the eighties.

In 2004 Facebook set up shop in Palo Alto. In 2005 YouTube launched in San Mateo. These companies joined others already in the Silicon Valley: Apple, Adobe, and Google (Mountain Valley). Netflix started in the former gold-mining town of Scott's Valley before moving to Los Gatos.

Netflix started out as a DVD mail order business before adding online streaming to their business model in 2007. I remember watching the documentary *Cocaine Cowboys* online in 2009 and realizing that it was the end of video rental stores as we knew it.

But Netflix wasn't content to just make Blockbuster video stores obsolete. They obtained the rights for *House of Cards* in order to compete against traditional TV and cable shows in producing original content. *House of Cards* began airing in 2013, and director David Fincher won a Primetime Emmy for directing "Chapter 1," the pilot.

In 2017 Netflix won its first Oscar for the short-subject documentary *The White Helmets*. Netflix caused an even bigger stir in 2019 when it did a limited theatrical release of *Roma*, which won three Oscars (Best Cinematography, Best Direction, and Best Foreign Language Film

The changes in the production landscape from *The Blair Witch Project* in 1999 to *Roma* in 2019 were tremendous. Streaming services creating and distributing their own shows (and winning Emmys and Oscars), and utilizing artificial intelligence, data science, and machine learnings creating efficient algorithms are the definition of disruptive technology.

Disruptions also come in many forms as we found out as the coronavirus hit the world in late 2019 and early 2020. Movie theaters shutdown, drive-in theaters (which peaked in polarity in the 1960s) saw a mini-revival, and pop-up drive-in movie theaters emerged at fairgrounds, farms, and on the side of buildings.

And while on quarantine or self-isolation in their homes, more people than ever sought entertainment through streaming services. I used to wonder what the movie going experience would be in ten or twenty years, now I wonder in terms what it will look like next year—or even next month.

EMERGING OPPORTUNITES

Even before the coronavirus began impacting the world in 2019, and movie theaters in the United States closed temporarily in 2020, the theatrical release model was already heading into strange territory.

I don't know what movie theaters are going to look like in 5 or 10 years, but I do believe that emerging opportunities for visual storytellers will continue to grow. And here some quotes that I hope help as you carve out a career of telling stories that are told over 10 hours, 10 minutes, or even 10 seconds:

"There's one thing that keeps coming up to me over and over in my career—this very simple phrase—'The cavalry isn't coming.'"
—Producer/Director/Actor Mark Duplass *(The Puffy Chair)*

"It's a mistake to wait for Hollywood to tell you you have a good idea. If you have a good idea, try to make it on your own as cheaply as possible."
—Producer Jason Blum *(Whiplash, Get Out, Paranormal Activity)*

"You just have to take the plunge and just start shooting something even if it's bad. . . . Pick up a camera. Shoot something."
—James Cameron

"The internet is a miraculous thing. Just share as much as you can, self-publish, blog, podcast, whatever you need to do. Just make sure you are not withholding your gifts from the world. Because you have so many opportunities now. . . . We're in a new frontier."
—Diablo Cody

"I didn't go to film school. Instead, I went to a liberal arts school and self-imposed a curriculum of creating tiny, flawed video sketches, brief meditations on comic conundrums, slapping them on the internet."
—Lena Dunham

"Now young storytellers will come in and say, 'This is my series idea,' 'This is my long form series,' 'This is my episodic series,' 'This is my web series.'"
—Producer Christine Vachon
The Moment with Brian Koppelman podcast

"My token advice [to aspiring filmmakers is] make your own stuff. . . . I'm a real believer in preparation meets opportunity. When this opportunity [to write *Bridesmaids*] came along I really had been at this a long time."
—Annie Mumolo
Script Mag podcast with Jenna Milly

"You know if I'm writing for something that's just on the internet, that we're just performing on something.com— if I'm happy doing it and I can feed my family I'm happy doing that, too."
—Emmy-winning producer Ronald D. Moore (*Battlestar Galactica*)

"What's happening on cable now is more interesting than almost anything happening in features, in terms of performance and narrative. You can explore characters over 10 seasons, something you could never do in features."
—Director and Oscar-winning actress Jodie Foster
Deadline interview with Mike Fleming Jr.

"If I ran a film school, I would require the students to make a feature film for just a thousand dollars. They'd learn tricks that they could apply for the rest of their lives, no matter how poorly the movie turned out."
—Ted Hope
Hope for Film

"[W]ithin five minutes—you can have a blog, a Facebook account, Twitter and be sharing your work. The content creators are the content distributors."
—Photographer and CreativeLive CEO Chase Jarvis

"I got my English degree and I couldn't get into film school, and I just started making my own films on 16mm. And I think that was fortunate for me. I think I was better suited to just start making films and learning from that, than I would have been to learning in a more formal structure."
—Writer/director Christopher Nolan (*Memento, The Dark Knight*)
Vice interview

"Don't try and compete with Hollywood. Take your lack of resources and make it work for you. Look at *Clerks, El Mariachi, Metropolitan,* even *McMullen, Slackers.* All of these films embrace their lack of resources and instead focused on *story or style or characters, and dialogue.*"
—Writer/director Edward Burns (*The Brothers McMullen*)

"When you want to do anything you need to reduce your 'I need list' to very little. Because if you start going, 'Well, I need a crew first. I need a budget. I need a set…'—the longer that list gets, the further away you're going to accomplish that."
—Filmmaker Robert Rodriguez
Spoilers with Kevin Smith interview

Back in the '90s, Rodriguez basically used no true film lights, a non-sync camera, single takes, one ranch, one bar, one pit bull, and one turtle to make his Sundance winning film *El Mariachi.*

These days it's not only common for people to watch movies on their computers, tablets, and phones—but some filmmakers are making movies with their phones.

THINKING DIFERENTLY

"We, the filmmakers, have got to start thinking differently."
—Steven Soderbergh

In 2013, Steven Soderbergh, the Oscar-winning director of *Traffic,* gave a talk that was sort of a State of the Union address on the film industry. He was discouraged and talked about retiring from movies to paint and perhaps direct plays.

He continued to produce and direct some TV shows (*The Knick, Godless, Mosaic*). Then, in 2017, he released his first feature (*Lucky Logan*), and then two more features (*Unsane, High Flying Bird*), that he shot with iPhones using the $19.99 FiLMiC Pro app.

Soderbergh was inspired to shoot with an iPhone after seeing Sean Baker's *Tangerine,* which was also shot with an iPhone.

The entire *High Flying Bird* shoot only lasted 13 days. A first cut of the movie was finished hours after they wrapped production. Soderbergh had a budget ($1.5 million) that could have allowed him to use any number of professional cameras, but he chose the iPhone for aesthetic reasons and because it allowed him to shoot quickly.

Cameras (mobile phones with cameras, mirrorless cameras, and whatever was invented yesterday) will continue to improve and provide people around the world with low-cost, high-quality ways of producing content. New methods of distribution will help those stories get told to a broader audience.

BACK TO THE FUTURE: RADIO DRAMAS (PODCASTS)

"Radio was supposed to die in 1945, when TV came along . . . Now that everybody has a smart phone and everybody's car is going to be connected, it's a brand-new world."
—Alex Blumberg, podcaster and Gimlet Media CEO

In 2012, I was one of the speakers at a workshop for electronic media students at the University of Northern Iowa. I recall one of the other speakers (a traditional broadcast anchorman) telling the students that they would be working in jobs that weren't even invented yet.

When I started my blog in 2008, there were no Uber drivers. And jobs like drone camera operator, mobile app developer, social media influencer, artificial intelligence (AI) engineer, and podcast producer were either non-existent or in their early stages of development.

Rooted in radio history, podcasting merges contemporary audio production and the internet, but it didn't become mainstream until around 2009. It exploded in popularity in 2014 with the *Serial* podcast.

Podcaster Brian Reed said that *Serial* signaled to the podcasting world, "There's a new sheriff in town." *Serial* producers Sarah Koenig and Julie Snyder were the first podcasters to win a Peabody Award. When I started listening to podcasts daily in 2015, *Serial* was the first one I binged on.

The podcast *S-Town*, produced by Reed and Julie Snyder, launched in March 2017 set a record of 16 million downloads in its first week. By the end of the year, it won an Emmy, and the story was optioned to be a movie.

Dirty John, a Wondery true crime podcast created by the *LA Times*, was released in October 2017. By November 2018 the TV series *Dirty John*, starring Connie Britton and Eric Bana, began airing on Netflix and Bravo.

Another key podcast pioneer is *Homecoming*, created by Eli Horowitz and Micah Bloomberg. The podcast became a Netflix production.

"In a very short time Micah has gone from hustling freelance work in a university library to helping run a big budget television show starring Julia Roberts."
—Alex Blumburg
Making a TV Series podcast

"I'm lucky enough to get asked to do all kinds of things. But if I were to be honest, over a 30-year career, I could build a house out of the scripts I *didn't* read."
—Julia Roberts

So how did Roberts end up reading the *Homecoming* script? She didn't. Roberts listened to the series' *podcast* while cleaning her house.

"In essence, we're at the dawn of a new golden age in audio."
—Alex Blumberg

Before Orson Welles made *Citizen Kane*, he entertained (and scared) radio listeners with his *The War of the Worlds* radio broadcast in 1938. And before Lucille Ball created the timeless *I Love Lucy* Tv show, she was popular on the radio show *My Favorite Husband.*

At its peak in the 1940s, radio in its many forms (plays, soap operas, situational comedies, variety hours, sports broadcasts, etc.) were listened to by 82% of Americans according to the C.E. Hopper Company—the major rating system at that time.

Almost 100 years after radio dramas were a popular form of entertainments, it appears we've gone back to the future. *The New York Times* reported recently that half the people in the United States have listened to a podcast.

FROM 8 TO 88

"Location scouting for @thebrooklynnk's directorial debut. A short called Colours. She writes, stars and directs and oh. . . she's 8 years old."
—Sean Baker on Twitter regarding Brooklyn Prince's first film

"Some people glow really early, in their twenties and thirties, then in their fifties they are not doing as much. But I feel that growing up and maturing, constantly maturing—aging is the impolite way of saying it-—I like to think there is an expansion going on philosophically."
—Clint Eastwood
Devil's Guide to Hollywood, written by Joe Eszterhas
(Eastwood was 88 when he directed *Mule*.)

A good deal about movies is characters overcoming obstacles, so it's no surprise to learn of the obstacles that accomplished screenwriters overcame in their lives.

One of the obstacles in David Seidler's life was overcoming stuttering. Another was getting films made. His first script *Tucker: The Man and His Dream* (credited with Arnold Schulman) was directed by Francis Ford Coppola and took ten years to get made. His greatest success, a movie about stuttering and friendship, from idea to screen took 20 years.

When Seidler accepted the Oscar for writing *The King's Speech* he was 73 years old and said, "My father always said to me I would be a late bloomer. I believe that I'm the oldest person to win this particular award. I hope that record is broken quickly and often."

And here's good advice no matter your age:

"People who have a great attitude are the ones that I always end up saying, 'What's your script about?'"
—Shonda Rhimes

SPANNING THE GLOBE

"Do what you can, with what you've got, where you are."
—Squire Bill Widener
(Often wrongly attributed to Theodore Roosevelt)

In 1891, only two years after the Eastman Kodak Company started manufacturing 35mm film with sprockets for still photography cameras, Thomas Edison patented the first motion picture film camera (the Kinetoscope) and the first film viewer (the Kinetoscope).

Like the invention of flight, there is some debate, but 1890 is a great stake in the ground for the birth of cinema. William Dickson led a team of inventors at Edison's lab in West Orange, New Jersey that you can tour today as part of the Thomas Edison National Historical Park.

Projected films and narrative stories were a few years away, and the early films looked more like early YouTube videos than resembling sweeping epics like *Gone with the Wind*, *Lawrence of Arabia*, or *Avatar*.

The first copyrighted U.S. film is known as *Fred Ott's Sneeze* (1894). The entire historic film lasts less than six seconds and contains, well, a single shot of Fred Ott sneezing. Their follow-up film was *The Kiss* (1896). And to come full circle, you can watch those films now on YouTube.

Edison also built the first film studio, The Black Maria, which was a small shed-like building on rails that could be rotated to take advantage of the shifting light of the sun throughout the day. Early subjects were Vaudeville actors, circus performers, and athletes.

Other early films from around the world are *Workers Leaving the Lumière Factory in Lyon* by Louis Lumière (1895) shot in France and featuring workers leaving a factory, and Fructuós Gelabert's *Riña en un Café* (1897) in Spain, and *Arrest of a Pickpocket* (1895) by Brit Acre in the United Kingdom.

Alice Guy-Blaché was a pioneering filmmaker who began developing narrative plots, interracial characters, and special effects in the 1890s.

In the early 20th century films turned a corner in entertaining the public with more complex stories such as Georges Méliès' *A Trip to the Moon* (1902) and Edwin S. Porter's *The Great Train Robbery* (1903). It was becoming a money-making enterprise thanks to Nickelodeon theaters. By 1910 the shift of American filmmaking from the east coast (New York, New Jersey, Florida) to Los Angeles was the birth of Hollywood.

Other countries embraced making movies in its infant stages with some of the most influential being Japan, Russia, Poland, Australia, and Hong Kong. Today more films are made in India than any other country, with Nigeria (often called Nollywood) in second with the number of films being produced.

Three writer/directors from Mexico Alfonso Cuarón (*Roma*), Alejandro G. Iñárritu (*Birdman*), Guillermo del Toro (*The Shape of Water*) have found Oscar-winning success. Polish filmmaker Paweł Pawlikowski (*Ida*) and South Korean writer/director Bong Joon-ho (*Parasite*) are other filmmakers finding international success though telling stories with specificity to their parts of the world.

In North America places like Vancouver, Toronto, Austin, Chicago, and Atlanta continue to build on long traditions of not only making films but turning out filmmakers.

MEANWHILE, BACK ON THE FARM . . .

"All the good ideas I ever had came to me while I was milking a cow."
— Iowa painter Grant Wood (*American Gothic*)

"What can you do when you're absolutely nowhere but feel like you are full of magic and ideas?"
— Mark Duplass

It's fitting to end this book with a story rooted in a land with more cows than people.

242

"We had one foot in Iowa doing industrial videos and one foot in Los Angeles working on graphic design and anything to pay the rent. And in the meantime, writing scripts."
—Scott Beck

Before *A Quiet Place* made Scott Beck and Bryan Woods hot new Hollywood screenwriters, they had connections in L.A. arranged through an attorney friend. Meetings with CAA, ICM, and Gersh coincided with news they were waiting for from Nicholl Fellowship, and the Sundance Screenwriting Lab. With many short films produced and several scripts written but not yet sold, they thought this was their big break.

But they walked away empty-handed. So what did they do? This is how they explained it in an interview with *ScreenCraft*:

SCOTT BECK: We realized that we needed to reassess what we're writing and focus on movies that we were passionate about. So we rolled up our sleeves and wrote a little 15-page short film, which we decided to shoot in Iowa on a very, very, very tiny budget. It eventually played at LA Shorts Film Festival, which is how we were able to get higher-level industry people to see it. And that's what led to us getting our manager.

BRYAN WOODS: Just the act of creating something will always create opportunities for you.

A common question that venture capitalists ask startup companies is, "What's your unfair advantage?" I think the unfair advantage that Scott Beck and Bryan Woods actually had was growing up in Iowa. They had supportive family and friends and, crucially, an active film community to support their creative ventures.

"The best education in film is to make one. I would advise any neophyte director to try to make a film by himself. A three-minute short will teach him a lot."
—Oscar-winning writer/director Stanley Kubrick (*2001: A Space Odyssey*)

If you think Iowa is a long way from Hollywood, consider Uruguay. This is what happened to Uruguayan filmmaker Fede Álvarez after he posted the under-five-minute video *Araque de Panico! (Panic Attack!)* on YouTube.

"I uploaded (*Panic Attack!*) on a Thursday and on Monday my inbox was totally full of e-mails from Hollywood studios. If some director from some country can achieve this just uploading a video to YouTube, it obviously means that anyone could do it."
—Fede Alvarez

Perhaps the most important insight this book can provide is that wherever you live, you can write great screenplays. The trick is to look for and recognize the resources that surround you. Even if you're in a small town no one has heard of—maybe *especially* if you're from such a town—you have stories to tell that no one else can. Look around you at all the resources. Locations. Festivals. Money.

START WHERE YOU ARE, WITH WHAT YOU HAVE

"So many gurus and so few good writers. Where are all these lessons going?"
—Larry Gelbart (*Tootsie*)

For months I struggled on how to end this book and I landed on Hermon, Maine in 1973. There we'll find the perfect grace note that can inspire you wherever you are in the world.

If we could go back in time to that town of less than 2,500 people, we'd see a doublewide trailer. Outside the trailer is a car with transmission problems and inside is a male high school English teacher fried from a week of working with teenagers. His wife works at Dunkin' Donuts and money is so tight they don't have telephone service and can't afford medicine for their sick child. Back in the laundry room he's typing away on an Olivetti typewriter on` top of a child's desk that's balancing on his thighs.

He looks more like the oversized Woody (Will Ferrell) in *Elf* than someone on the verge of becoming one of the most successful writers in history. But that setting is where Stephen King wrote his first two novels and where he was living when the paperback rights for *Carrie* sold for $400,000.

If King's story ended there it would have been a literary success. But he's since written more than 60 novels that have sold more than 350 million copies. And some fine movies made based on his writings include *The Shawshank Redemption, The Shining, Misery,* and *Stand by Me.*

Reading King's book *On Writing* won't guarantee that you will become a best-selling writer, but I think it can make you an incrementally better writer. Today not much stock is put on incremental change, but I think it's greatly undervalued.

There is no question that there is a talent pyramid. But take comfort that every writer at the top of the pyramid today, was at one time not only at the bottom of the pyramid—but once they weren't even a part of the pyramid.

To paraphrase Derek Sivers with a screenwriting context, if more information was the answer we'd all be Oscar and Primetime Emmy Award winning writers. But you have to start somewhere.

King has two pieces of advice that can help you on your journey. The first is to write 1,000 words a day. That's how I started my blog, and by extension that's how this book came to be.

The second lesson he learned the hard way—after bouts with drugs and alcohol, and after getting hit by a van while walking— "don't put your desk in the center of the room." That is… have a life beyond your writing life.

SHALOM

One of the early readers of this book felt like it needed benediction at the end. So following Bruce's lead from *Springsteen on Broadway* where he recited The Lord's Prayer, I've chosen to not reinvent the wheel. Here is a classic centuries old blessing from ancient scripture used in several faith traditions. (One that the family in *A Quiet Place* could have silently prayed in that scene where they joined hands at the dinner table in their time of great distress.)

The LORD bless thee, and keep thee:
The LORD make his face shine upon thee, and be gracious unto thee:
The LORD lift up his countenance upon thee, and give thee peace.
Numbers 6: 24-26

ABOUT THE AUTHOR

Scott W. Smith's blog *Screenwriting from Iowa . . . and Other Unlikely Places* won a regional Emmy in Advanced Media and has received over 1.5 million views. As a producer/director/writer he has worked on hundreds of film, video, and digital productions over the past three decades. Highlights include shooting from a seaplane over the Amazon River, working with Pro Football Hall of Fame members, and recording interviews of Holocaust survivors for Steven Spielberg's project now known as the USC Shoah Foundation. Various productions have allowed him to travel to all 50 states in the U.S. and to five continents. Smith received his B.A. in Cinema and master's degree in Digital Journalism.

CONTACT INFO:
Scott W. Smith
Orlando, Florida
info@scottwsmith.com

BIBLIOGRAPHY

Abel, Jessica, *Out on the Wire*

Akers, William M., *Your Screenplay Sucks!: 100 Ways to Make it Great*

Billingsley, K.L., *The Seductive Image*

Blacker, Irwin R., *The Elements of Screenwriting*

Bordwell, David, *The Way Hollywood Tells It*

Cody, Diablo, *Juno: The Shooting Script*

Cole, Toby, *Playwrights Look at Playwriting: From Ibsen to Ionesco*

Csíkszentmihályi, Mihály, *Flow: The Psychology of Optimal Experience*

DeMarinis, Rick, *The Art & Craft of the Short Story*

Densham, Pen, *Riding the Alligator*

Dmytryk, Edward, *On Screen Writing*

Egri, Lajos, *The Art of Dramatic Writing*

Eldredge, John, *Wild at Heart*

Epstein, Alex, *Crafty Screenwriting*

Epstein, Alex, *Crafty TV Writing*

Eszterhas, Joe, *The Devil's Guide to Hollywood*

Field, Syd, *Screenplay*

Frank, Sandy, *The Inner Game of Screenwriting*

Froug, William, *The Screenwriter Looks at the Screenwriter*

Froug, William, *Screenwriting Tricks of the Trade*

Froug, William, *Zen and the Art of Screenwriting*

Goldmam, William, *Adventures in the Screen Trade*

Hart, Moss, *Act One: An Autobiography*

Houghton, Buck, *What a Producer Does: The Art of Moviemaking*

Howard, David and Mabley, Edward, *The Tools of Screenwriting*

Hunter, Lew, *Lew Hunter's Screenwriting 434*

Kevolin, Richard, *Screenwriting in the Land of Oz*

Krevolin, Richard, *Screenwriting for the Soul*

Iglesias, Karl, *Writing for Emotional Impact*

King, Chandus, *Now Write! Screenwriting*

King, Stephen, *On Writing*

Lavandier, Yves, *Constructing a Story*

Lazarus, Tom, *Secrets of Film Writing*

Lewis, Jerry, *The Total Film-Maker*

Lucey, Paul, *Story Sense*

Lumet, Sidney, *Making Movies*

Mackendrick, Alexander, *On Film-making*

Mamet, David, *Bambi vs. Godzilla*

Mamet, David, *On Directing Film*

Marion, Francis, *How to Write and Sell Film Stories*

McKee, Robert, *Story*

Olson, Randy Houston, *We Have a Narrative*

Pressfield, Steven, *The War of Art*

Raphaelson, Samson, *The Human Nature of Playwriting*

Russin, Robin U. and Downs, William Missouri, *Screenplay: Writing the Picture*

Schrader, Paul, *Transcendental Style in Film*

Seger, Linda, *Making a Good Writer Great*

Snyder, Blake *Save the Cat*

Sorkin, Aaron, *The West Wing Script Book*

Straczynski, J. Michael, *The Complete Book of Screenwriting*

Stevens Jr., George, *Conversations with the Great Moviemakers of Hollywood's Golden Age*

Schwartz, Rick, *What It's Like To Be A: Producer*

Trottier, David, *The Screenwriter's Bible*

Truby, John, *The Anatomy of Story*

Vale. Eugene, *The Technique of Screenplay Writing*

Vogler, Christopher, *The Writer's Journey*

Walker, Michael Chase *Power Screenwriting*

Walter, Richard, *Essentials of Screenwriting*

Wright, Kate, *Screenwriting is Storytelling*

Yorke, John, *Into the Woods: A Five Act Journey Into Story*

Zinsser, William, *On Writing Well*

RESOURCES

BAFTA Screenwriters Lectures
Basic Brainheart website
The Bill Simmons Podcast
Cinephilia & Beyond website
CreativeLive online classes
Creative Screenwriting magazine
The Dialogue Series video interviews
The Director's Cut podcast
DP/30 video interview
Go Into The Story blog, Scott Myers
The Hollywood Reporter
The Inside Pitch, Christopher Lockhart, Facebook group
Let's Schmooze —Doug Eboch on Screenwriting blog
MasterClass online classes
The Moment with Brian Koppelman podcast
MovieMaker magazine
Jim Mercurio's Complete Screenwriting: From A to Z to A-List, DVD
No Film School website
On the Page podcast, Pilar Alessandra
OnWriting, WGA East podcast
Out on the Wire podcast, Jessica Abel
The Q&A with Jeff Goldsmith
The Rewatchables podcast and Facebook group
ScreenCraft website
Script magazine
Scriptnotes podcast, John August and Craig Mazin
Scriptshadow blog, Carson Reeves
TED Talk videos
The Tim Ferriss Show podcast
Wordplay website, Ted Elliot and Terry Rossio
WTF podcast, Marc Maron